SOCIAL MOVEMENTS
PAST AND PRESENT

Irwin T. Sanders, Editor

LET THE PEOPLE DECIDE:

Neighborhood Organizing in America

LET THE PEOPLE DECIDE:
Neighborhood Organizing in America

ROBERT FISHER

● ● ●

Twayne Publishers

LET THE PEOPLE DECIDE:
Neighborhood Organizing in America
SOCIAL MOVEMENTS PAST AND PRESENT

Copyright © 1984 by G. K. Hall & Company
All Rights Reserved
Published by Twayne Publishers
A Division of G. K. Hall & Company
70 Lincoln Street
Boston, Massachusetts 02111

First Printing

Book production by
Marne B. Sultz

Book design by
Barbara Anderson

This book was typeset in
10 point Times Roman with Univers display type
by Compset, Inc. of Beverly, Massachusetts

Printed on permanent/durable acid-free paper
and bound in the United States of America

Library of Congress Cataloging in Publication Data

Fisher, Robert, 1947-
  Let the people decide: neighborhood organizing in America

  (Social movements past and present)
  Bibliography: p. 179
  Includes index.
  1. Radicalism—United States—History. 2. Community
organization—United States—History. 3. Social action—
United States—History. I. Title. II. Series.
HN90.R3F57   1984   361.8   84-4586
ISBN 0-8057-9706-8 (Hardcover)
ISBN 0-8057-9709-2 (Paperback)

To Juliet and Ian

CONTENTS

ABOUT THE AUTHOR

Robert Fisher is associate professor of history at the University of Houston—Downtown and adjunct professor of social work at the Graduate School of Social Work, University of Houston—University Park. He is the author of numerous articles on urban and social history and co-editor with Peter Romanofsky of *Community Organization for Urban Social Change: A Historical Perspective* (Greenwood Press, 1981). Since his days as an undergraduate he has been active in peace movement and community organizing efforts.

INTRODUCTION

If you want knowledge, you must take part in the practice
of changing reality. . . . If you want to know the theory of
revolution, you must take part in revolution. All genuine
knowledge originates in direct experience.

Mao Tse-Tung

The problem with history is that it's written by college
professors about great men. That's not what history is.
History's a hell of a lot of little people getting together and
deciding they want a better life for themselves and their
kids.

Bill Talcott, community organizer

The idea for this book originated in 1973–74 while I was teaching in Boston
and working with a neighborhood organizing effort in Cambridge. In 1973, I
moved to Cambridgeport—a working-class and student populated neighborhood across the river from Boston University, sandwiched between the Massachusetts Institute of Technology and Harvard University—where I quickly
became involved in the founding and development of the Cambridgeport
Homeowners and Tenants Association (CHTA), an Alinsky-style neighborhood organization. This was my first opportunity to assume leadership and
responsibility in a political organizing effort. Like millions of others, I had
been active before in the antiwar movement of the late 1960s, but I was not
really a "movement person" and my participation was limited mostly to political discussions, leafletting, and protest demonstrations. Organizing at the
grassroots level in Cambridgeport in the neighborhood where I lived felt right.
Talking politics with the neighbor next door or the grocer across the street, or

getting a slumlord's vacant building torn down and replaced with a community controlled cooperative garden, grew naturally out of everyday experience with friends and neighbors.

CHTA was founded largely by Steve Meacham, who had the original idea to build an insurgent neighborhood organizing effort around the issue of housing. But unlike the more radical tenant organizations in Cambridge, Meacham sought to unite tenants and resident homeowners in a class-based, not single-interest, organization willing to fight as much for just rents for tenants as tax rebates and a stable neighborhood for resident homeowners. From 1973 to 1976 hundreds of meetings were held in people's homes, churches, and neighborhood cooperatives. We held actions to protest university expansion into, and destruction of, the neighborhood, picketed City Hall to demand improved services, walked in support of strikers in local labor struggles, blocked evictions, and traveled on weekend mornings to the suburban homes of neighborhood slumlords to hand out leaflets informing neighbors of how the man next door exploited poor people.

Unlike new left radicals of the early 1960s, the organizers in CHTA consciously downplayed their radical sentiments and rarely sought to clarify their ideology. The organizers—those neighbors, most often college educated and young, who took a more active role in building the organization—were not leftist "intellectuals." In fact, we consciously sought to get beyond the barriers that radical ideology and rhetoric seemed to foster between activists and workers in the 1960s.

While CHTA won many battles, improved the quality of life in the neighborhood, and raised many people's political consciousness, it ultimately failed to create a working-class neighborhood organization. It remained dominated largely by young, college-educated, white men and women who had been or were still active in the peace and women's movements. The goal of empowering people at the neighborhood level in order to build from the grassroots up a left-oriented, national movement of working people was never approached. Initially most white working-class people in Cambridgeport were suspicious of the politics and motives of CHTA organizers, and the countless hours spent working, playing, and meeting together succeeded in bringing a significant but nevertheless small number of neighborhood natives into the group's leadership. CHTA had even less success with organizing the black residents in the neighborhood, who tended to doubt the primarily white organization's long-term dependability. Nevertheless, CHTA's serious commitment to democracy at all steps of the organizing process continued over time to break down resident suspicions. Despite obvious weaknesses, the organization in 1976 was growing, winning battles, broadening its focus by uniting with other efforts in the neighborhood, and continuing to be self-critical but also moderately self-satisfied. Then the "split" occurred.

The split in CHTA was caused by organizers who were more radical and who pointed out the limits and failures of CHTA's "nonideological" approach. They emphasized that a militant, avowedly socialist ideology—a clearly stated view of how the capitalist system works and why working people needed to join together to oppose it—was lacking. CHTA needed a clear and correct "line" to offer working people; then residents would get involved and devote more time and energy to building a multiracial working-class organization.

A few key leaders agreed almost completely with this criticism. They felt that CHTA needed to come out of the closet and openly advance an anticapitalist ideology. Many of the working-class leaders supported this position as well. And while most participants in the organization agreed to strive toward greater ideological clarity and organize people around a socialist vision, the split occurred because most of the more active members did not share the same socialist analysis and vision. The more individualistic and democratic socialist members emphasized the need to place democracy and democratic process at the center of community organizing; they believed that a socialist analysis would emerge from effective leadership and resident involvement. The more communistic members said that was like the tail wagging the dog and that "letting the people decide" was what CHTA and other "neo-Alinskyite" groups had been doing over the years with only limited success. They emphasized the importance of a clear, socialist ideology in attracting working people and the need for a centralized organizational structure which would provide direction and unity from above without sacrificing democracy at the grassroots. The "individualist" segment believed that the "centralists" had no understanding at all of democratic process, and were fundamentally authoritarian, doctrinaire, and dogmatic. The communists saw their opponents as petit-bourgeois reformers. Everyone was forced to take sides.

This type of split was not novel in the history of the left or neighborhood organizing. As the economic and political conditions of the mid-1970s made effective left organizing increasingly difficult and as many found the "non-ideological" approach to neighborhood organizing of the early 1970s wanting, people seemed to turn on each other and inward to political theory for explanations and solutions.

The split sent people in all directions. Some activists left CHTA, joined more radical organizations, and went to work in factories to do union organizing. Others remained in Cambridgeport and continue today in their struggle to build a cooperative community that supports and empowers neighborhood residents in conflicts with slumlords, university expansion, and so forth. I got another teaching job and, with a good deal of doubt, left Cambridgeport. Organizing with CHTA was one of the most powerful learning experiences of my life. But it left as many questions about political and neighborhood organizing as it had provided answers. Why do grassroots groups succeed or fail? How important is ideology and a long-term vision in the organizing process? How do successful groups balance a commitment to democracy with the need for direction and leadership? What were the advantages and limits of organizing at the neighborhood level? Can groups operating at a community level ever achieve any significant degree of success as social change organizations? How can grassroots groups connect up with national movements or organizations? These questions and many others heightened my interest in studying the history of neighborhood organizing and this book in large measure is the product of my search since leaving CHTA.

One of the central themes of this book, that neighborhood organizing movements must be seen and evaluated within the context of national political and economic developments, grew not only out of my experience with CHTA but also out of changes in the historical discipline. For years people had been taught that the historical arena was limited to politicians in Washington or corporate executives in New York City. This led to a distorted view of how history is made, for it assumed that most people—those of the working class, minorities, women—did not have the power to affect history, that they were not historical actors but only objects of the forces set in motion by "historymakers." Historians were the chief proponents of this elite-serving myth. Courses and books in United States history traditionally limited their scope to the history of white, wealthy men. Even when addressing locally initiated efforts, historians wrote history from a national perspective and from "the top down."

In the 1960s a new group of historians emerged, reflecting both the radical spirit of the decade and different class and ethnic backgrounds from their elders in the profession. They began to study the historical roots of contemporary social problems. They wrote urban, ethnic, family, labor, community, and women's history. They consciously explored history "from the bottom up," and as they did the daily life and human relationships of ordinary people became an increasingly important and valuable part of the historical record.

But the "new social history" had a serious limitation. In the effort to uncover and write a "people's history," social historians rejected traditional approaches and thus tended to ignore political and economic developments at the national level which directly affected the lives of working people. The "turning inward" of members of the profession to locally based issues yielded an understanding of the history of working people and how "ordinary people" play a part in shaping history. But there was an absence of analysis of how the overall system functioned and where working people fit into it.

This limitation began to be corrected in the late 1970s as a better integrated social history emerged. Marxist historians have always written social history within the framework of larger political and economic developments. Increasingly their wider view, if not always their methods and conclusions, came to be adopted generally. "The social interpretation of history," a non-Marxist wrote recently, "places ideas, events, and behavior as well as institutions in a larger context of the overall social system."[1]

What I came to learn from the events and literature of the 1970s was that social developments are part of a total economic and political system—a political economy—in which all strands of life, from the national to local level, intertwine with each other. Most problems that contemporary communities face manifest at the neighborhood level but result from city, state, national, and even international factors. What is most striking, however, is how immune we think we are from the penetrations of the national political economy into our daily lives. We live in local communities, neighborhoods, towns, and cities; we participate in neighborhood organizing efforts on a scale of society where decisions of immediate and direct importance occupy our days. We direct our attention to our jobs, to the price of groceries, cars, and housing, to our health and that of our family. The local area is where we live our lives on a small, intimate, comprehensible scale. And rarely do we know or do anything about decisions made in corporate and governmental centers which will determine our course next year and many years after.

But this is not a one-way street where the national political economy exerts its will over a populace preoccupied with daily living. There is a dialectical relationship between the national and local arenas in which working people and their communities are not only acted upon but also cooperate with, resist, and stimulate national developments. For every national decision to expand the rights of workers in a Wagner Act in the 1930s, or to increase federal social services in a War on Poverty in the 1960s, there were militant local strikes and urban rebellions and protests which demanded and initiated these social changes. For every national decision, from declaring war against the Japanese in 1941 to invading Cambodia in 1970, there were the people who lived their lives at the local level who did or did not consent to fight.

The brief history of neighborhood organizing which follows seeks to contribute to the new social history by viewing the subject within the context of changes and developments at the city and national level, with an eye to the interpenetration between the national political economy and neighborhood-based organizing efforts. Accordingly, this study divides the past century into five periods which correspond with shifts in the national political economy and changes in the dominant form of neighborhood organizing. Each section begins with an overview of the political economy of the era and is followed by case studies of the most prominent or significant neighborhood organizing projects of the time. As sketched in Table 1 and discussed more fully in the Conclusion, the book organizes the history of neighborhood organizing into three dominant and distinct approaches: social work, political activist, and neighborhood maintenance. The goal, then, is to describe and assess the history of the dominant strategies of neighborhood organizing used since the 1880s, and to provide a general introduction, not a comprehensive history, primarily for students and organizers, which does not artificially isolate the subject at the local level.

The need for such a book is evident. Neighborhood organizing is currently experiencing a second heyday. The first period of popularity was the initial decades of the twentieth century, when reformers identified the neighborhood unit as an ideal base for solving the severe problems of the emerging urban-industrial order. The second period of wide interest in neighborhood organizing began in the early 1960s, again in response to an "urban crisis," and interest in neighborhood organizing has continued to grow since. At least three major political parties in the election of 1980—the Democrats, the Republicans, and the Citizens—emphasized the value of neighborhood organizing in their party platforms. Jimmy Carter in a campaign speech in Brooklyn four years earlier said that "if we are to save our cities we must revitalize our neighborhoods first."[2] While his efforts in this direction were minimal, the National Neighborhood Policy Act of 1976 was the first since the Model Cities Act of 1966 to articulate at least some of the needs of neighborhoods, and his Urban Policy of 1978 did note the importance of neighborhood organizing in the city building and revitalization process.

Carter knew what the people in Brooklyn and communities throughout the nation wanted to hear. The list of supporters of the new interest in neighborhoods and neighborhood organization is nearly endless. According to a recent Gallup Poll, 42 percent of the people interviewed belonged or wanted to belong to a neighborhood organization effort, and more than a majority expressed a willingness to take direct action in defense of their neighborhood.[3] Conservative theoreticians proclaim that neighborhood organizing can protect *us* "against the disjointed and threatening world 'out there.'"[4] Leftists active since the 1960s continue to organize tenant and homeowner associations; food, day care, fish, fuel, and bicycle cooperatives; and militant social action organizations to empower neighborhood residents. One recent study sees a "Backyard Revolution" underway in America which has the potential to form a new political movement out of its network of grassroots democratic organizations. Another author proclaims that "Livable Cities" of the 1980s will be dependent on effective neighborhood organizations.[5] It is clear that neighborhoods and neighborhood organizing appeal to a citizenry alienated from its economic and political power centers, and groups spanning the political spectrum from revolutionary to reactionary, from the public and private sector, are seeking to organize, acknowledge, coopt, and profit from this development.

What this contemporary interest in neighborhood organizing lacks is a sense of its past. Neighborhood organizing is not a recent phenomenon; it has a long and instructive history. But few neighborhood organizers or members of neighborhood groups seem to know this. At best they think neighborhood organizing is but twenty years old. Milton Kotler, the current director of the National Association of Neighborhoods and the author of a pioneer book on the subject, *Neighborhood Government,* dramatized the problem when he wrote recently:

> It is time to take stock and consider very seriously why we should support neighborhoods and strong neighborhood organizations. To do this we must remember where the neighborhood movement came from and what happened to create the present situation. The neighborhood movement did not fall from heaven yesterday. *It began in the 1960s.*[6] (italics mine)

This is not to suggest that the history of neighborhood and community organizing has been completely ignored. The work of Frances Fox Piven, Richard Cloward, Harry Boyte, Sara Evans, Lawrence Goodwyn, Mark Naison, Patricia Melvin, Thomas Philpott, Clayborne Carson, Janice Perlman, and Arthur Dunham, to name only a few, has enriched our sense of the history and the process of grassroots community organizing, and this book relies heavily on it. Given this expanding literature and contemporary interest in neighborhood organizing, the time appears right to attempt a synthesis of these materials and to write a history of neighborhood organizing movements.

Before proceeding further, some terms need clarification. "Let the people decide" was a slogan used specifically in new left neighborhood organizing projects of the 1960s, but its ideal of democratic grassroots decision making captures so well the history of neighborhood organizing, its strengths and weaknesses, that it seemed a most suitable general title. Moreover, this work is a *selected* history of neighborhood organizing movements. Many important organizing projects are not included. The intent has been to focus where possible on the most significant organizations and the dominant strategies of neighborhood organizing. Where there already is a large body of literature on

Table 1
History of Neighborhood Organizing: Three Dominant Approaches

	Social Work
Concept of Community	social organism
Problem Condition	social disorganization social conflict
Organized Group	working and lower class
Role of Organizer	professional social worker enabler and advocate coordinator and planner
Role of Neighborhood Residents	partners with professional recipients of benefits
Strategy	consensual gradualist work with power structure
Goals	group formation social integration service delivery
Examples	Social Settlements Community Centers Cincinnati Social Unit Plan Community Chests United Community 　Defense Services Community Action 　Program United Way

Political Activist	*Neighborhood Maintenance*
political unit power base	neighborhood residence
powerlessness exploitation neighborhood destruction	threats to property values or neighborhood homogeneity insufficient services
working and lower class	upper and middle class
political activist mobilizer educator	elected spokesperson civic leader interest-group broker
fellow activists indigenous leaders mass support	dues paying members
conflict mediation challenge power structure	consensual peer pressure political lobbying legal action
obtain, maintain, or restructure power develop alternative institutions	improve property value maintain neighborhood deliver services
Unemployed Councils Tenant organizations Alinsky programs Student Non-Violent Coordinating Committee (SNCC) Students for a Democratic Society (SDS) Association of Community Organizations for Reform Now (ACORN)	Neighborhood Preservation Associations Neighborhood Civic Clubs Property Owners' Associations

an effort, such as the social settlements, the treatment here tends to be more analytical; where little is known, the case studies tend to be more descriptive.

The terms neighborhood and neighborhood organizing also require definition. People can usually identify their neighborhood by name; they can give its boundaries; and they know who belongs and who is a newcomer. But because of intrinsic differences "neighborhoods" are sometimes hard to define. Sociologists Rachelle and Donald Warren, for example, identify six major types of neighborhoods based on the extent that people share a sense of neighborhood consciousness, how often neighbors interact with each other, and what channels exist between the neighborhood and outside groups. Suzanne Keller, another sociologist, offers a comprehensive and a workable definition which better suits my purposes: a neighborhood is a locality with physical boundaries, social networks, concentrated use of area facilities, and special emotional and symbolic connotations for its inhabitants.[7]

This study does not seek to romanticize the value of neighborhoods. The more people turn away from large-scale institutions and corporate and government leaders, the greater the tendency to overstate the virtues of smaller institutions such as the neighborhood unit. But not all neighborhoods are desirable places to live, nor do all residents want to live there. Many people are trapped in neighborhoods by class barriers and racism; others view the neighborhood as only a temporary space, a place to live before moving to a better community.[8]

Neighborhood appears at first to be a conservative concept—a place with boundaries to protect, a space where one can be "safe," a site for raising a family, growing up, and going to school. But this should not imply, as many modern sociologists have been quick to do, that neighborhood organizations are fundamentally committed to maintaining the status quo. Sociologist Emile Durkheim saw neighborhood institutions as progressive "mediating institutions" organized by the powerless which could challenge and limit the power of the state.[9] Neighborhood organizations have as much potential to heighten awareness and promote change as they do to maintain the status quo. It depends, in large measure, on the type of neighborhood, the conditions it faces, its class and racial composition, the motives and politics of the organizers, and the national political-economic situation at the time.

Neighborhoods are territorial spaces whose values, goals, and activities are not inherent but rather mirror the class and racial conflicts of the larger system. Poor people facing problems of unemployment, job discrimination, substandard housing, high crime rates, and only slight hope of improvement stand to gain little, if anything, from using the neighborhood as a vehicle to maintain the status quo. Their class position demands social change, and while they might seek to conserve, restore, and improve aspects of their community, their fundamental goal in neighborhood organizing is to change the conditions which keep them poor and powerless. Likewise, organizations in more affluent neighborhoods most often express the conservative and protective needs of their residents. They oppose commercial development, organize neighborhood police watches, and protect real estate values. The issue is more complex than suggested here. Lower-class and working-class neighborhood organizations also seek to defend their turf and can be as conservative and reactionary as their more affluent counterparts, and neighborhood organizations in more affluent areas often advocate social reform and use their organization to challenge authorities. Nevertheless, class and race factors determine to a large degree the direction and tactics of the neighborhood organizing effort and the extent to which goals can be realized.

In general the term neighborhood organization refers to an institution in which people who identify themselves as part of a neighborhood promote shared interests based primarily on their living or working in the same residential area.[10] The process that they engage in to achieve their objectives is referred to as neighborhood organizing or, covering a somewhat wider area, community organizing or community organization. Neighborhood organizing is often fueled by a conviction that people must take action themselves to realize their aspirations, by an emphasis on organizational autonomy, and by the subordination of all other activity to the priorities of neighborhood issues and concerns. This study focuses on groups that first and foremost identify themselves as neighborhood organizations. Many neighborhood institutions, interest groups, and voluntary associations, such as churches, fraternal associations, and benefit societies, might seem to qualify as neighborhood organizations, but do not fall within these borders. Also not included are the host of racial and ethnic organizations in neighborhoods where residential area was not the primary basis of organization. This comes down to hairsplitting in some cases, as segregation patterns in our cities make it difficult to distinguish an organization based on race or ethnicity as opposed to one based on locality. In some circumstances I have taken the liberty to include organizations which do not fit the mold of a self-defined neighborhood organization in order to describe and assess more fully the variety of neighborhood organizing styles.

The words reactionary, conservative, liberal, and radical, used throughout the study, are relative terms which can hide as much as they explain. Until a more appropriate political vocabulary of neighborhood organizing develops, however, they are the best available. I use them in the following general manner: "reactionary" describes efforts to stop social change and decrease the power of lower-class and minority groups; "conservative" describes attempts to maintain the political and class status quo; "liberal" describes efforts to promote social changes which do not challenge the existing class and economic system; and "radical" describes efforts to advance political, economic, and social democracy which often, though not always, see the capitalist system as the cause of problems.

This book has been a collective effort from the beginning. The craft of researching and writing a book is an individual and often isolating experience, but throughout the project people too numerous to mention assisted the process. Bruce Palmer, Steve Meacham, Harry Boyte, Bayrd Still, Manfred Jonas, and Juliet Clarke read most of the manuscript, and my debt to them is exceeded only by my appreciation of their help. Mark Naison, Patricia Mooney Melvin, Clarke Chambers, Robert Cohen, Morty Simon, Ellen Fleischman, Sara Evans, Bill Cavellini, Barry Kaplan, and Philip Castille read single chapters and their comments were always thoughtful and challenging. Irwin Sanders, the editor of the Twayne series, devoted valuable time, gave continual support to my efforts, and demonstrated a good deal of patience. The same is true of John LaBine, editor at Twayne. I would also like to thank my colleagues at the University of Houston–Downtown, especially Alexander Schilt and Don Elgin for assisting this project with a university-funded leave of absence, and students in my urban history courses who tolerated and supported my interest in neighborhood organizing. Colleagues and friends at the University of Southern Maine, most notably Joel Eastman, who extended university privileges, office space, computer time, and asked for little in return, made my year there a delight. The National Endowment for the Humanities supplied support for research in the social welfare history archives at the University of Minnesota; John Shanahan and the Southwest Civic Club graciously made their records available to me; and Sue Greenspoon's expertise with the word processor and her caring attitude made the final typing and rewriting of this manuscript a relatively painless task. Lastly, my deepest appreciation goes to my family—Leo, Eve, Marcy, Alden, Joan, Juliet, and Ian—who supported this project in countless ways, and Juliet and Ian even had the good sense to desert me for a short time when I needed to finish it.

CHAPTER 1

Social Welfare Neighborhood Organizing, 1886–1929

Industrialization and Liberal Reform

The whole process of modern life, the whole process of modern politics, is a process by which we must exclude misunderstandings, exclude hostilities, exclude deadly rivalries, make men understand other men's interest, bring all men into common counsel, and so discover what is the common interest. That is the problem of modern life which is so specialized that it is almost devitalized, so disconnected that the tides of life will not flow.

Woodrow Wilson, Governor of New Jersey

Woodrow Wilson was an historian, president of Princeton University, governor of New Jersey, and president of the United States. He was never a neighborhood organizer. His sentiment that the conflicts of modern urban/industrial life could be resolved through education and interclass communication was shared, however, by the first generation of neighborhood organizers. In social settlements, community centers, and neighborhood health clinics, in cities throughout the nation, community workers put into practice their plans for "progressive democracy." Their goal, like that of Wilson's, was to resolve the conflicts that had emerged in the prior generation of rapid and often traumatic industrialization, and do so without fundamentally challenging the existing class system.

Life in the United States had changed dramatically in the half century after the Civil War. As Henry Adams put it: "In the essentials of life . . . the boy of 1854 stood nearer the year one than to the year 1900." Adams's view that

1

life had changed more in fifty years than in the 1,850 years before was more accurate for the middle class than for the working class. But the dramatic transformation he spoke of affected all segments of the society.

The cause was the industrial revolution, which began in England in the late eighteenth century, took hold in the textile mills of New England in the late 1820s, but did not become a dominant force in the United States until after the Civil War. The speed and magnitude of the changes during the two generations after the war, however, were awesome. Briefly stated, the following fundamental changes occurred: economic relationships expanded from the personal relations of a village community to the impersonal forces of a national market; goods and methods of production were standardized along with many other aspects of life; people were segregated by occupation and task at work and by class, race, and ethnicity in communities; bureaucratic, institutional forms of control were expanded to socialize the workforce and direct people's public and private lives; and material acquisition was exalted as the primary goal in life. It was almost as if a traditional world had been recast into a modern civilization in one generation. Woodrow Wilson and the activists in the first neighborhood organization movement were part of a liberal reform effort after 1900 that sought solutions to the most obvious problems caused by this rapid economic change.

The astounding growth of cities in the generations after the Civil War attests to their importance as the nuclei of the industrial transformation. Between 1870 and 1920, for example, Boston, Philadelphia, Pittsburgh, and Washington, D.C. more than tripled their populations. New York City and Brooklyn consolidated in 1898 to form a city of some three and a half million people. In the next twenty years an additional two million people stretched the limits of the Empire City. Chicago, a child of the railroads and the industrial revolution, grew from just under 300,000 in 1870 to 2.7 million in 1920. The South was less urbanized and industrialized, but major centers like Atlanta, Birmingham, and Houston grew at similar breakneck rates. Ironically, the creation of a national network of major cities signified not the strengthening but rather the disappearance of the city as an autonomous economic, political, and social unit. As the city became the headquarters of a national economic revolution, local concerns mattered less and less to the corporate leaders who ordered and controlled the direction of industrialization and who focused on national and international, not local, markets.

Nevertheless, the internal structure of cities mirrored the economic transformation of industrialization. Prior to rapid industrialization, cities were relatively small, compact, and well-integrated. With walking being the major means of transportation, the physical distance between the places where people lived, worked, worshipped, shopped, and played was minimized. Neighborhoods distinguished by class, race, or ethnicity appeared as early as the 1820s, but in general the "pedestrian city" was not spatially segregated or fragmented. Between 1870 and 1920, however, cities like Boston grew from a radius of two to ten miles. The pre-industrial walking city was replaced, more or less, by an industrial city that radiated out from a central business district (CBD) in rings of ascending class status, most of which were further segregated by ethnicity or race. This "ring-sector" model of the industrial city is too simplistic to be generalizable to all cities. But the pattern of increasing segregation, fragmentation, and centralized growth occurred in cities as different as Boston, Chicago, and Houston.

The first neighborhood organization movement must be seen as one trend in the national, liberal reform movement called "progressivism." Progressivism grew out of the industrial relations of the years 1870 to 1895, a period characterized by fierce and unbridled competition among capitalists and between capitalists, on the one hand, and workers and farmers, on the other, over who would control and benefit from industrialization. The decade from 1895 to 1905 was a watershed in the transition from the industrial capitalism of 1870–1895 to the finance capitalism and liberal reforms of the generation that followed. Around 1895 bankers like J. P. Morgan of Morgan Guaranty and Trust purchased controlling interest in corporations as diverse as the newly formed U.S. Steel and General Electric from industrial capitalists like Andrew Carnegie and Thomas Edison. Control of key industries began to be consolidated among an elite group of financiers. The period 1895–1905, for example, saw the merger of some 300 separate firms each year into highly centralized and powerful industrial conglomerates.[1]

This economic transformation profoundly affected all relations in the society. Many representatives of small and middle-sized firms in the business world continued to support the logic of "laissez-faire" industrial capitalism. Led by organizations like the National Association of Manufacturers, they supported unbridled competition and the quick dispatch of insurgent worker movements which threatened their ability to compete and grow. But a new strategy among more "progressive" corporate leaders of large corporations like General Electric and International Harvester emerged after 1895 to profit from the changing economic situation. The new economic situation encouraged stability, not competition. This new strategy, since labeled "corporate liberalism," sought, of course, to maximize profits, but it emphasized the shortsightedness of earlier repressive tactics and the need to develop more liberal mechanisms and attitudes which would ameliorate conflict and disorder and promote industrial harmony.[2] Corporate leaders could achieve their objectives better, the corporate liberals argued, by promoting a fundamentally unaltered but peaceful economic, social, and political climate.

As economic power became more centralized, many corporate leaders concluded that the social order too should be stabilized by supporting programs of social concern and social responsibility. At the state and national level government regulations were passed to curb grossly excessive corporate practices, practices which corporate liberals believed bred unnecessary conflict and disorder, and corporate liberals supported ameliorative social and health programs to address, at least superficially, the social by-products of rapid industrialization. In short, corporate liberal leaders of big business and government sought to demonstrate that capitalism worked in the interests of all the people not simply the wealthy, that businessmen were not "Robber Barons," and that politicians were not insensitive to the difficulties of life in the urban/industrial order.

Of course, businessmen and their political voices had always preferred harmony and stability to conflict and disorder. In the past, however, in part because of labor militancy, the cost of stability was too high. With finance capitalism, however, the increased concentration of control in some industries, especially the ability to control prices, coupled with the intervention of the federal government to promote economic stability, made the strategy feasible. The new progressive relations between government, business, and the people did not end industrial conflict and insurgency. But, as an historian of progressive reform succinctly summarized, the nation-wide progressive movement in the years 1900 to 1920 did "achieve order, stability, and control, while preserving the existing class system and distribution of wealth."[3] In these years liberal corporate leaders and public officials replaced repressive measures with reform programs and replaced the Social Darwinist ideology of laissez-faire capitalism, which had dominated the Gilded Age, with a new rhetoric of building a people's democracy through private and public social engineering.

This new political economy was worked out in the decade before World War I by corporate and government officials, sometimes in cooperation with conservative union leaders. It was neither a conspiracy in the sense that it was planned, nor an instantaneous stroke of corporate genius. The initial proponents of social change were workers and their advocates, those at or near the bottom of society, who were benefiting least from industrialization. The corporate liberal vision, which has dominated economic relations in most of the decades since 1900, emerged from liberal experiments initiated by corporate and public officials at the local level to capitalize on the shifting economic situation and to defuse more radical demands for change made by workers, farmers, and even some segments of the middle class. As the strategy proved successful, corporate and government leaders increasingly adopted it.

Liberal reformism became a nationwide political movement in 1900 with the succession of Theodore Roosevelt to the presidency, but it began in the 1880s with reform experiments at the local level. Some of the earliest reform efforts were initiated in cities like New York and Chicago by "communitarian" reformers. Unlike most of their liberal contemporaries in the civic-commercial elite, who emphasized the need for concentrated, centralized, and corporate forms of organization to promote social order, the first social welfare activists sought to address local problems by working at the neighborhood level in face to face relations with the urban working class. These communitarian reformers were among the first to draw attention to the serious poverty, health, housing, recreation, and labor conditions in immigrant and working-class areas of industrial cities. And they were among the first to warn of the need to ameliorate conditions of industrial capitalism lest class warfare result in a cataclysmic revolution. They worked in social settlements, community centers, adult education schools, and neighborhood health clinics located in or near neighborhood slums. These "decentralizers" were ultimately more democratic and open-minded and less tied to corporate economic objectives than liberal counterparts in business and government. But they shared with them the underlying perceptions, ideology, and objectives of the larger reform impulse, and it was not until after 1900 when progressivism took root at the national level that such local neighborhood reform efforts like the settlement movement found prestige and a sound footing.

To be sure, there were many faces and shades of progressivism—from suffragettes and temperance advocates to Woodrow Wilson and the members of the influential National Civic Federation, an association of representatives from the corporate, government, and labor sectors. Of course social reformers did not approach the problems of the era exactly as did their corporate counterparts. But it was ultimately corporate leaders and national political figures, the most conservative elements in the reform movement, who set the tone and parameters of reform activity in the years 1900 to 1920. And it was within the limits of the emerging political economy of corporate liberalism that urban communitarian reformers formalized the first neighborhood organization movement in American history.

The Social Settlement Movement

Like the medieval monasteries, the university settlements, facing the worst results of the industrial revolution, of a new migration, and of the unmanageable growth of cities,

may at first fill a strange variety of functions; but their
deep and abiding use lies in direct effort toward scattering
the social confusion and reestablishing social order.

Robert Woods, settlement worker

The settlement house movement began in the slum neighborhood of the
East End of London, England, when two Oxford University students spent
Christmas eve, 1884, in the half-completed Toynbee Hall. Toynbee Hall was
established primarily to ameliorate the problems of poverty and "bridge the
class gap" between rich and poor. The method was simple if not completely
successful: put college students into working- and lower-class neighborhoods,
have them serve neighborhood resident needs as much as possible, and have
them offer programs which introduced the poor to the student's upper-class
world. Earlier efforts at charity had failed, settlement workers in England believed, because of condescending and hostile attitudes toward the poor. What
was needed was a "new approach to poverty." By working and living directly
in the poverty neighborhood settlement workers hoped to address problems
more sensitively and more effectively than charity workers and, most significantly, they hoped to work with, not for, residents.

Less than two years later, Stanton Coit, a graduate of Amherst with a Ph.D.
from the University of Berlin, spent three months at Toynbee Hall and returned
to the United States in 1886 eager to establish similar "neighborhood guilds"
throughout America. In late summer Coit moved to the Lower East Side of
New York City, an immigrant enclave, where he organized a workingmen's
club which first met in his apartment and then in a small building he purchased. Begun with the support of reformers, labor leaders, and ministers,
Coit named this initial American settlement house Neighborhood Guild. Befit-
ting the optimism of contemporary social activists, Coit declared that within
ten years neighborhood guilds would "be the foundation of a civic renaissance
in America," a civic renaissance based in neighborhoods and committed to
facing the wide range of problems that beset America's immigrant and native
working-class communities.

Of course Coit overestimated the impact of the Guild and neighborhood
self-help programs in general, but the idea did catch on. Independent of his
effort, college women from the upper-class schools of Smith, Wellesley, Vas-
sar, Bryn Mawr, and Radcliffe founded College Settlement in 1898, not far
from Neighborhood Guild. A week later Jane Addams and Ellen Gates Starr,
roommates at Rockford College in Illinois, initiated what became the most
famous settlement, Hull House, in an inner-city, working-class neighborhood

in Chicago, not very far from where Mrs. O'Leary's cow was said to have performed its act of arson almost two decades before.

The settlement workers were in large measure the college-educated daughters and, to a lesser extent, sons of "old wealth," families of "substance" but not great wealth or power. For example, the fathers of Jane Addams and Julia Lathrop, a co-worker at Hull House, were successful lawyers and Republican senators in the Illinois legislature. Many, especially the men, were children of ministers or members themselves of the social reform-minded clergy of the day that developed in response to the gross inequities of industrial capitalism in the Gilded Age. Like Coit, many of these social reformers found their inspiration in trips to Toynbee Hall. But the "alarming" conditions in America's slum neighborhoods provided more than enough nutrients for the settlement movement to spread and grow rapidly. In 1891 there were six settlements in the United States; by 1900 over 100; five years later more than 200; and by 1911 more than 400. As early as 1907, less than a decade after its founding, Hull House had expanded from a single, roomy mansion to thirteen buildings covering more than a large city block.

Settlement workers got involved in neighborhood organizations out of a mixed bag of sympathy, fear, guilt, social concern, and a desire to give purpose to their own lives. The latter was especially true for the women, whose career opportunities were limited to teaching, nursing, library science, and the emerging field of social work, of which settlement work was the most progressive branch. Depending on the individual settlement, settlement workers sought to "uplift" and "Americanize" the immigrant poor, improve health and social conditions, and espouse the virtues of Protestantism, Catholicism, Judaism, or some variant of secular humanism. But all settlements shared an objective: to promote social order by serving as class mediators between the rich and poor, between capitalists and workers. They hoped to inform the upper class about the existence and needs of the "other half" and to instruct the poor that the capitalist class were businessmen and women who, like all people, belonged to "the one great brotherhood of humanity." To be sure, settlement workers had more immediate objectives and each leader had her or his own priorities. But it would be difficult to overemphasize the perception of liberals of this era that society was coming apart at the class and ethnic seams and that anarchy was imminent if "capital" did not mend its ways and if reformers did not go into the slum neighborhoods and ameliorate the "festering conditions" of ghetto life.[4]

To achieve their goals of class cooperation and social harmony, settlement houses offered a wide variety of programs. Some settlements were more vigilant in their commitment to social justice, and their activities reflected it. Others were more conservative, especially the religious-affiliated settlements which were generally more interested in controlling, not advocating for, the poor. Individual differences apart, however, settlements offered classes in English, civics, literature, art, cooking, sewing, dressmaking, and wood and sheet metal working; provided services such as legal aid, employment assistance, laundry facilities, health care, nutritional counseling, day and night nurseries for working mothers, and public baths; and sponsored recreational and athletic programs, neighborhood vegetable gardens, and concerts and theater productions to acquaint neighborhood residents with what they called their "higher life" culture. The more progressive settlements permitted and sometimes encouraged neighborhood groups, labor unions, and even radicals to use the house for discussions on contemporary issues.

Settlement workers chose to organize at the neighborhood level because for them the local community was the appropriate base for reform activity. Robert Woods, the founder of South End House in Boston, described why:

The neighborhood is large enough to include in essence all the problems of the city, the State, and the Nation and in a constantly increasing number of instances in this country it includes all the fundamental international issues. It is large enough to present these problems in a recognizable community form, with some beginnings of social sentiment and social action with regard to them. It is large enough to make some provision for the whole variety of extra-family interests and attachments. . . . On the other hand, it is small enough to be a comprehensible and manageable community unit. It is in fact the only one that is comprehensible and manageable; the true reason why city administration breaks down is that the conception of the city breaks down. The neighborhood is concretely conceivable; the city is not, and will not be except as it is organically integrated through its neighborhoods.[5]

Well-organized neighborhoods, advised by enlightened settlement leaders and furnished with rudimentary social services, would serve as the counterforce to what social reformers saw as the "inchoate anarchy" and greed of nineteenth-century industrial capitalism. But the neighborhood was not to be the culmination of settlement work. Workers disdained excessive localism, especially that practiced by their opposition, the ward politicians. Settlement activity was intended to transcend neighborhood borders. The more progressive settlements, for example, were active at the city, state, and national level lobbying for tenement reform, kindergartens, school nurses, child labor laws, playgrounds, workers' rights, progressive education, and city planning. Settlements were conceived as the locally based "spearheads" of a nationwide liberal reform movement, not simply as neighborhood-based social service centers.[6]

The history of the settlements has been ably detailed elsewhere. What is important to underline here is that their social welfare style of neighborhood organizing did not visibly improve ghetto conditions, increase the power of neighborhood residents, nor alter significantly the elitist practices and biases of traditional organized charities. For example, instead of addressing political and economic problems that undermined ghetto neighborhoods they chose to concern themselves primarily with social issues. In their own neighborhoods, settlements limited their political activity to gathering information on tenement, health, and recreation conditions. When the more adventurous settlements did venture into local electoral battles to take on a ward boss, they almost always lost. They were successful in local politics only in the rare circumstance when the proportion of middle- and upper-class voters in their district outweighed immigrant support for local machine candidates.

Likewise neighborhood residents turned elsewhere—to themselves, their families, their institutions—for economic support. The problems of slum life that neighborhood residents faced were, after all, the result of a lack of economic power to alter their conditions. Working people needed better wages; they needed job security; they needed more control over their economic life so that they too, like the upper and middle classes, could live more comfortably and healthfully; they needed to share more equitably in the profits of industrialization. The settlement's sponsorship of social programs which sought social harmony within a framework of economic inequality reflects the unwillingness of liberal reformers to challenge the economic causes of the poverty that surrounded them. Preferring not to take sides in the class conflict or address the economic roots of problems meant that the settlements served the interests of the class in power by, as Robert Woods said, "scattering the social confusion and reestablishing social order." To have taken the side of workers would have been inconsistent with liberal goals of order and harmony because it would have heightened, not ameliorated, class tensions. Such a position would also have jeopardized settlement funding from philanthropic capitalists. Therefore, settlements focused on social issues, not political or economic ones. Community, not class, was the keyword in the new liberal state.[7]

Where they did address economic problems, as on the tenement issue, settlements pursued a strategy of working with those in power—in government and in the housing industry—rather than working with tenement dwellers. Tenement reform legislation was planned, passed, and, of course, applauded in reform circles without the assistance or participation of those most affected, the neighborhood residents. Settlement reformers failed to address the serious undersupply of decent, affordable, low cost housing. Tenement reformers urged successfully that old tenements be torn down and replaced with parks and playgrounds. Between 1900 and 1917 the city of Chicago alone built ninety new parks and 100 new playgrounds. Code enforcement legislation sponsored by reformers improved housing conditions but also displaced tenants as rents increased to unaffordable levels. Without participation from the poor and without a commitment to serving the needs of the working class, such neighborhood renewal efforts were often antithetical to the needs of working people.[8]

Moreover, the settlements' social welfare style of neighborhood organizing remained elitist, despite the fact that every progressive settlement from Toynbee Hall and Neighborhood Guild to Hull House professed to work with, not for, the people. And without citizen participation, as on the tenement issue, settlement programs were often part of the problem, not the solution, for working class people. John Daniels, the author of a book in 1920 on neighborhood organizing and an advocate of neighborhood democracy, tried to understand the settlements' "top down" approach.

The reasons for proceeding in this way, instead of in a way which actually enlists the neighborhood, are quite understandable. The settlements general motive, to promote the local welfare, is good. The specific object in view, as for instance a playground, is good. The need is believed to be urgent. Therefore the quickest way to obtain the desired object appears to be the best way. To attempt to secure an organized demand on the part of the people of the neighborhood would take a lot of time. Besides, some element in the neighborhood might not agree with the settlement as to the urgency of the need and the best way of meeting it. So, the settlement workers argue, as long as they have the situation in hand and really represent the neighborhood, their best plan is to do the thing themselves, "for" the neighborhood, rather than to take the longer and slower route of having it done "by" the neighborhood.[9]

But this elitist decision-making process derived from more than the magnitude and exigency of the task. The very idea of settlement work to "elevate" the masses to "an appreciation of the higher life" defined the class relationship between "uplifters" and those needing uplifting. When Mary McDowell established the University of Chicago settlement in the Back of the Yards neighborhood no one asked the residents whether they wanted one. Settlement workers in Back of the Yards and elsewhere did not seek to work through existing immigrant neighborhood associations or to organize the existing indigenous leadership. Rather McDowell and other settlement workers moved into a neighborhood, developed a settlement in their own image, furnished it in upper-class style, imposed moral values such as no swearing or drinking wine or beer at the settlement house, and then went out knocking on doors and talking with people in the streets, inviting them to come and take part in settlement activities.[10]

The typical response of most neighborhood residents was to stay away. John Daniels offered why. If community organization is "the local vitalization of democracy, so that the neighborhood truly functions in ways which are 'of' the people, 'by' the people, and 'for' the people," Daniels said, "the reason why most schemes of community organization are not accomplishing much is that they are attempts from without, and usually from above, in which the neighborhood itself has little or no part and to which therefore it fails to make any substantial response."[11] While as early as 1894 Hull House, perhaps the most successful settlement, attracted some 2,000 visitors per week, more than 70,000 people lived in only a six block radius of the settlement. Once settlements were established institutions in the neighborhood most immigrant leaders expressed a good-natured friendliness and willingness to cooperate with them. Community leaders knew that settlements provided valuable social services, especially for women and children. But settlements did not represent the neighborhood or its residents. "They're like the rest," one immigrant community leader noted, "a bunch of people planning for us and deciding what is good for us without consulting us or taking us into their confidence."[12] A black commentator was more harsh, for settlements were even less of a force in nonwhite neighborhoods. "The influence of the settlements in our life is negligible. If they were to disappear overnight, the life, the growth, and development of my people and their assimilation into American life would go on just the same."[13]

Instead of turning to settlements organized and run by outsiders, working-class people relied on themselves, their families, and their own self-help ethnic and religious institutions. Reformers were wrong, not to mention ethnocentric, in assuming that urban slums were "disorganized" and that neighborhood residents needed externally initiated efforts to organize their community. Neither industrialization, immigration, or slum life destroyed people's need for or ability to create supportive community networks. Instead of relying on settlements organized by upper-class outsiders, neighborhood residents preferred to use their own churches, synagogues, mutual benefit associations, and ethnic, labor, and political organizations, not to mention informal networks of support, to advance their collective and personal interests.[14]

Settlement founders and leaders were correct in their assessment about the extent of class and ethnic segregation which divided people in the modern metropolis. Mistrust, antagonism, and chauvinism dominated most interclass relations. Settlement leaders came from the other side of the tracks, a world of privilege, devoid of hard physical work and material discomfort. Their new neighbors in the inner-city slums knew keenly the problems of poverty and industrial labor and viewed "uplifters" with a healthy suspicion. Given this

situation, settlement efforts to legitimize their work and their existence by encouraging resident participation in decision making should have been of paramount importance. This is a first principle of neighborhood organizing. The
absence of such efforts merely underlines the extraordinary extent of class mistrust and ethnic division in the urban metropolis. At Hull House the board of
directors was composed of wealthy residents of Chicago and its suburbs, never
people who lived in the Near West Side neighborhood, except Jane Addams.
When Graham Taylor, the founder of Chicago Commons, relinquished his position as head resident, his daughter Lea succeeded him. Taylor believed that
neighborhood people lacked the necessary skills to be settlement workers because they only understood the working-class world of their community and
were ill-prepared to interpret the slum neighborhood to the upper classes.[15]
The same was true of ethnic-initiated settlements. At the Harlem (New York)
Federation Jewish settlement, founded in 1905 by upper-class German Jews
and East European Jews in order to mold the values of the newly arrived,
proletarian immigrants from Eastern Europe, old guard German Jews permitted no workers and only one member of the Eastern European elite on the
board of directors.[16]

Class elitism, not democratic selection, determined who participated in and
decided on the objectives and programs at Hull House, Chicago Commons,
and the Harlem Federation, three of the more liberal settlements. Most settlements were not as progressive or as sensitive to immigrant and working-class
culture; programs of most Catholic and Protestant settlements, for example,
were often a direct assault on the Old World heritage and self-image of workers. In general, reformers sought an association with the working class in
which they provided the direction and in which fundamental class and power
relationships remained unaltered. It is testament to the hard work and zeal of
these settlement workers and to the severe conditions of neighborhood slum
life that the settlements' services were used even as much as they were.

In sum, there is no question about the sincerity or commitment to social
reform of those who made the settlement their life's work. They lived and
worked in slum areas. They braved small-pox epidemics to inspect tenement
and sweatshop conditions. They faced the frustration of door-to-door neighborhood work in communities where they were clearly outsiders. They even
got shot at when, on the rare occasion, they supported factory workers engaged in labor disputes. Overall, they played a positive role in delivering
needed services, raising public consciousness about slum conditions, and calling for collective action to ameliorate selected problems. What they did not do
is address the causes of these ills. Their vision of *one* community, of *one* democracy consciously avoided the different interests and objectives of the seg-

regated and divided groups in Amerca's cities; they acted as if the assumption of a classless, united society would make it so. They wanted neighborhood residents to have faith that social workers could successfully determine and meet the needs of the poor, and ultimately offered social service solutions to economic and political problems. In response, working-class people took what they needed from the neighborhood services. Neighborhood people knew, though they may not have said it this way, that liberal neighborhood programs primarily served the interests of stability and order by providing only modest reform programs within the framework of deep economic and political inequities. They knew that such social welfare neighborhood organizations served the interest of those in power more than they did the needs of working people.

The Community Center Movement

I am more interested in what you are doing [with social centers] than anything else in the world. You are witnessing the foundations of DEMOCRACY.

Charles Evans Hughes, Governor of New York

By the second decade of the twentieth century, other liberal reformers also interested in neighborhood organizing saw the need for something more effective and widespread than the settlements. Settlements, it was plain, were not fulfilling their stated objective of participatory democracy and, even if they were, 400 settlements were far fewer than Stanton Coit's dream of one in every neighborhood. Moreover, settlements cost money to establish and run, and the interest of corporate benefactors in settlements was seriously limited. In fact, the more officials at the national, state, and local levels supported reform programs to maintain class harmony, the less immediacy there was to fund such private enterprises as social settlements.

In an effort to give their work greater legitimacy, to make it more systematic, more efficient, and more attractive to funding sources, neighborhood workers in the years preceding World War I began to transform their vocation into the profession of "community organization." Professionalization came earlier to most other white-collar occupations; by this time doctors, lawyers, and professors had already raised themselves to the level of "experts." In neighborhood work professionalization began almost imperceptibly before 1914, accelerated during the war, and was formalized in the 1920s when community organization, along with case work and group work, became a subfield of the newly emerged profession of social work. In the process, the focus of neighborhood work shifted from social reform to the coordination of social welfare agencies and activities. This led to programs not only devoid of citizen involvement but also without any interest in democratic participation. In fact, the more community organization emphasized "expertise" the more neighborhood residents were seen as passive "clients" and "recipients" of social services. Nowhere is the effect of professionalization on social welfare neighborhood organizing more vivid than in the early history of the community center movement.

Social reformers active in settlements, recreation, and adult education banded together as early as 1907 to lobby for the use of school buildings after school hours as neighborhood social centers. The effort began in Rochester, New York, where public funding enabled Edward Ward to establish a neighborhood-based civic association in a public school. This was not the first time schools were used after hours as recreation centers. Since the 1890s boards of education in major cities had offered free adult education classes and recreation activities in public schools in the hope of speeding up the process of Americanization. The new social centers were to be different, however, because they were not limited to recreational activities, and, most importantly, because "socialized schools," their organizers argued, could act as magnets attracting citizens whose segregation into class and ethnic groups had obscured their common bonds, loyalties, and responsibilities. Like the social settlements before them, social centers would lend harmony and foster cooperation among the working-class and immigrant elements and at the same time ease some of the difficulty of slum life.

Despite the reluctance of public officials to support a program which might develop into an independent and alternative political machine, the idea of using schools as neighborhood centers caught on as readily in the decade after 1910 as settlements had in the decade before. Schools were used as centers for voting, employment information, recreation, education, health services, and Americanization programs. Attendance at the social center in P.S. 63—the first center in New York City, located on the Lower East Side—was nearly 130,000 in 1911–12, its first year of operation. In 1912 the national campaign platforms of the Democratic, Republican, and Progressive parties all endorsed the social center idea. By 1918–19 community centers—the name changed from social centers around 1915—were operating in 107 cities. Five years later the number of centers more than doubled to 240, and by 1930 New York City alone had almost 500 centers with an annual aggregate attendance of over 4,000,000. By 1930 community centers had clearly met the objective of reformers for widely accessible neighborhood public spaces.

The first centers begun during the heyday of progressivism, between 1907 and 1915, emphasized neighborhood self-help and cooperation. Clinton Childs, the organizer at P.S. 63 saw them as centers of neighborhood democracy:

A community clubhouse and Acropolis in one; this is the Social Center. A Community organized about some center for its own political and social welfare and expression; to peer into its own mind and life, to discover its own social needs and then to meet them, whether they concern the political field, the field of health, of recreation, of education, or of industry; such community organization is necessary if democratic society is to succeed and endure.[17]

The organization of centers nationwide followed a pattern similar to the one at P.S. 63. The People's Institute, a private, multifaceted reform organization working primarily in the neighborhoods of the Lower East Side of Manhattan, sponsored Childs's efforts at P.S. 63. The Institute organized a committee of professional reformers, academics, and businessmen, which identified the neighborhood project area and secured permission from the Board of Education to use the neighborhood school if residents were interested in the idea. Childs, an organizer employed by the Institute, went to live in the immigrant neighborhood, where he identified groups that might support the social center idea and enlisted their help and participation. With the help of local organizations, Childs organized a mass meeting at the school to discuss the projected center. The meeting established a social center committee and formed a neighborhood group, composed primarily of representatives from neighborhood clubs, to govern the center. Childs was elected director of the neighborhood group.

Word spread quickly in the neighborhood that the school was open for after hours use and people responded avidly. The People's Institute and other groups sponsored concerts, weekly civic forums, a child welfare exhibit, and various entertainment activities. An orchestra of some thirty workers and students calling themselves the Beethoven Musical Society, under the direction of a neighborhood resident, gave ten concerts at the center. Political meetings to discuss workers problems and contemporary issues were held and union representatives as well as those from the Progressive, Democratic, and Socialist parties all participated.

Programs varied from center to center and from city to city, reflecting organizers' interests as well as the local political situation. Rochester social centers emphasized civic and political forums. New York City programs ranged from service activities to entertainment and recreational programs, political forums, and club meetings. In general, however, entertainment and recreational programs, not activities focusing on political issues or social change, predominated at most centers. Public officials discouraged political programs. In Rochester, for example, where centers focused on contemporary political concerns, local officials attacked them as "socialistic" and cut off funds.

Ideally, social centers were to be governed "from the bottom up." But from the outset, citizen involvement, as in the social settlements, was limited to membership in clubs and participation in center activities. While club and organization leaders sometimes participated in the initial neighborhood groups, planning and supervision was left primarily to the professional organizers who initiated and directed the centers. The initial ideal of having professionals serve as advisers to neighborhood residents swiftly degenerated into an elitist relationship in which social welfare professionals made all important decisions without the assistance of community people.

As a result, social centers were not much more successful than settlements in transcending the limits of liberal, social welfare neighborhood organizing. Center organizers should have had an easier time of neighborhood organizing than their predecessors. By 1910 residents in many neighborhoods were used to "do gooders" and the more sensitive and progressive social reformers had won some degree of acceptance based on the services they provided. By the second decade of the twentieth century social reform was a permanent feature of the urban landscape and social center activists had a tradition and an historical experience on which to build. The settlement experience should have indicated that institutional longevity could ease tensions with neighborhood people, but not resolve class and ethnic suspicions by itself. The paternalism and elitism of liberal neighborhood organizers on the one hand, and the antagonism and mistrust characteristic of most interclass and interethnic relations on the other, required more than time or good intentions.

Overcoming such barriers was not impossible, but doing so required vastly different organizing objectives and methods than the settlement experience provided. It required meeting the needs of working-class people as they defined those needs. To begin with, people in neighborhood groups at social centers had to be assured that they could run the centers, that the space was *theirs.* Such a people's organization never developed. The public school was not controlled by the residents, nor were the school boards or organizers about to make it so. Organizers improved on settlement practice by asking neighborhood residents what the area needed and what they wanted and by contacting and enlisting the support of community leaders and organizations. But given the class bias of social center organizers and the restraints imposed by using public facilities in cities where local officials feared resident control could lead to independent working-class political organizations, citizen participation in social centers remained largely advisory and token. Without legitimacy as neighborhood organizations run by neighborhood people, organizing practice in the social center movement quickly developed into a professionalized and elite form of neighborhood work characteristic of most social work community organization before and since that time.

Throughout the liberal reform movement of the early twentieth century, there existed a tendency to professionalization, bureaucratization, and centralization. Corporate liberals put this into practice first in their businesses; "good government" advocates of municipal reforms such as the city manager plan followed. In the emerging field of social welfare, community work became increasingly professionalized after 1915, and community centers were no exception. Increasingly center organizers became less concerned with fostering class cooperation and more so with coordinating social welfare programs and developing professional associations which could guide neighborhood efforts "expertly" and systematically. In 1916, for example, they founded a professional organization, the National Community Center Association (NCCA). The NCCA published a weekly newspaper, the *Community Center,* which offered current news on what organizers were doing in their neighborhoods, what methods seemed to work and which did not, and generally how the profession was developing. Professional conferences sponsored by the NCCA enabled community workers to get together, share experiences, and develop a supportive network out of which a better sense of professional identity could arise.

At the local level, many center organizers grew increasingly interested in providing comprehensive planning and professional programs in neighborhoods. In one district in New York City, the Gramercy area, neighborhood workers set up not only a community center but also a Training School for Community Workers and a Community Information Clearing House. The Training Center was the first to offer academic and experiential training to those interested in the new career of community work. The Clearing House was a professionally administered service which provided employment, health, housing, and reform movement information for neighborhood residents. Like the NCCA, these local programs provided identity, instruction, and experience for professional community workers.

Reflecting this new direction, even the rhetoric of citizen participation was rewritten in new professional terms which emphasized the importance of "scientific expertise." When Clinton Childs founded the first social center in New York City in 1911, for example, he saw it as a "community clubhouse and acropolis." John Collier, a leading organizer in New York City who would become the director of the Bureau of Indian Affairs in the 1930s, saw the community center in 1917 as a neighborhood place where "experts" would be based. In his words, "Democracy needs science, and the community movement aims to put science—which means experts—into the people's hands. . . [so that] the laity share the enthusiasm of the expert and the expert becomes in a true local sense the adviser and servant of the citizen."[18]

But that was the ideal, not the practice. Increasingly, the centers belonged to the professionals who ran them, not to the neighborhood residents. Collier's staff were supervisors not advisers. By 1915 in many centers the neighborhood groups which initially consisted of elected representatives from neighborhood organizations were now composed of appointed professionals from local social service organizations and city bureaus. Because of the new emphasis on professional and efficient service delivery, the neighborhood group came to serve not as a vehicle of citizen participation but rather as a coordinating board of service-delivery representatives from hospitals, recreation associations, and the like. Community centers began to look more and more like a neighborhood based, professional social-service bureaucracy rather than a community acropolis.

On the surface, professionalism, in and of itself, does not seem to be a major drawback. Support networks, communication links, training centers, and programs to create a more effective and systematic practice of neighborhood organizing were important and natural developments. But whose interests did the new emphasis on professionalism serve? As historians have shown, the emphasis on "expertise" in most elements of the liberal reform movement made activities significantly undemocratic. The growing professional orientation in the social center and settlement movements reflected liberal reform objectives which degenerated into a preoccupation with competence, peer approval, and the technical aspects of community work. Without a truly democratic theory of citizen involvement and without a history of developing neighborhood-run organizations, professionalism resulted in increasing insulation from the residents. And as professional objectives and concerns became paramount, the initial ideal of neighborhood self-determination became no more than a memory of the social center movement's infancy.

The entry of the United States into World War I sealed this trend. In late 1917 the federal Council of National Defense and local subsidiaries at the state and city levels organized a highly bureaucratic and centralized program to "nationalize neighborhoods" in support of domestic war mobilization efforts. Community center professionals, seeing the program as an endorsement of their neighborhood organizing efforts, wholeheartedly promoted the use of community centers to coordinate grassroots support for programs developed in Washington. In their support of the war "to make the world safe for democracy," center organizers and local social welfare and political leaders transformed community centers into neighborhood-based arms of the state.

Increased supervision and surveillance of activities accompanied wartime bureaucratization. Representatives from the public and private sector were appointed to the neighborhood groups by the city officials and social workers, among others, who sat on local Councils of National Defense. Center programs soon reflected the demands of the war and the new special interest groups represented on their governing boards. Recreation became less important. Forums were watched more closely for subversive activities by community center workers who were under pressure from local authorities. Some programs, for example, were canceled because they were conducted in a foreign language that city officials could not understand and did not trust. Patriotic propaganda dominated civic and social club activity and motion pictures were censored to conform to war objectives. Centers became sites for coordinating Americanization classes, Red Cross relief, Liberty Loan drives, and food austerity programs.

As before, but even more so now, citizen participation was limited to participating in programs sponsored by center professionals. Centers were the sites where residents could enlist to become involved, provide support, and make sacrifices in the war effort. To this end all residents using the centers had to sign a pledge, which read:

I promise to continue within my ability for the period of the war to conserve food as the Food Administration orders, conserve fuel as the Fuel Administration prompts, subscribe to Liberty Loans or buy War Saving's Stamps according to my income, help worthy organizations with books, clothing or funds, give personal labor when time permits.[19]

In a sense, centers prospered during the war years. Activities multiplied, funding increased, and in the end 107 cities in the nation had community centers. The whole "community movement" achieved widespread recognition and prestige during the war. But the bureaucratization, centralization, and professionalization of community work that brought such success also promoted very different values and goals than those first announced by social center organizers a decade earlier. Reform goals of citizen participation, easing class tensions, and providing valuable services devolved under the pressures of war mobilization into outright social control, professional and governmental domination, and repression of dissent. Some neighborhood workers, like John Collier, grew anxious about the increasing centralization and bureaucratization. Most, however, regarded the war-related programs as the conscious application of democratic social engineerng which, if successful, would establish a neighborhood-based, postwar reconstruction program. But all supported the war and the use of centers in war mobilization.

The trend toward professionally controlled and bureaucratic neighborhood work continued in the 1920s. Not only did the 1920s not spawn a postwar reconstruction program as reformers had hoped, it produced a conservative reaction that blamed liberal "do goodism" for getting the United States into the war. During the decade neighborhood service programs devoid of citizen participation and administered by professionals became the accepted norm. Leroy Bowman, a leading theoretician of community organization in the 1920s, went so far as to disparage earlier efforts as "the community religion of a few years ago when the drive was on to go out and get people into community organizations, democratic in the extreme and supposedly dominated by neighborly sentiments."[20] The hard-headed realism of professional community work in the 1920s was supposed to be focused on meeting people's social welfare needs, not the "romantic" ideals of democratic community organizing.

Bowman was wrong on two counts. First, prior community organization had not been democratic. The only thing "extreme" about it was the gap between the stated goal of citizen involvement and the actual practice of elite professional control. Second, programs of the 1920s did not meet neighborhood needs any more than did prewar efforts. Community workers in the 1920s may have spent more time studying and analyzing community problems, whereas their predecessors spoke of the virtues of democracy, but the results of liberal community work in both decades were similar. Recreation programs dominated community centers in the 1920s as they had prior to the founding of the first social centers in 1907. In the 1920s, local officials accepted community centers as part of local government's responsibility and implemented a highly bureaucratic, and centralized, system of well-attended community schools run by school officials and social welfare and recreation professionals.

Although Bowman's remarks reflect social work's break in the 1920s with the ideal of democratic citizen participation, the practice and impact of neighborhood organizing remained fundamentally the same. Community work continued to focus on professional concerns and the efficient delivery of services. Partnership between "experts" and "the people" was no more or less a reality in the 1920s than it had been before. And if the conditions of urban poverty had improved at all, it was not because of the ameliorative recreational services that community center professionals offered as their solution to the conditions of slum life. In neither the social settlements nor the community centers had liberal reformers built neighborhood organizations that were either democratic or effective in combatting the causes of poverty.

The Cincinnati Social Unit Plan

We see democracy not merely as government by the people, or as representative government, but as an organization of US—of ALL of us—through which we ourselves can come together to study for ourselves our common needs; to decide for ourselves which of these needs comes first; to employ the highest technical skill the nation affords in formulating plans for meeting those needs; to study such plans in advance of their operation, and finally to carry out those plans ourselves, not only because we desire them for ourselves but because their nature is such that they cannot be carried out by anyone except ourselves. The aim, the purpose, of such an organization is not the good of some of us to the hurt of the rest, but the good of all of us, as well as of each.

Wilbur Phillips, community organizer

The plan[s] of Mr. and Mrs. Wilbur Phillips for community organization are, I believe, the best signs we have that democracy is yet possible for America.

Mary Follett, settlement worker

The most ambitious, acclaimed, and widely advertised single experiment in neighborhood organizing in the years before the Great Depression was the Cincinnati Social Unit organization. Wilbur and Elsie Phillips were the architects and chief organizers of the "social unit plan," which they tested first in St. Cyril's parish in Milwaukee and then in the Mohawk-Brighton neighborhood of Cincinnati. Like their predecessors in the settlement and social center movements, the Phillipses were dismayed by the increasing segregation of life in urban America. They too initiated neighborhood-based experiments which they hoped would transcend class barriers and get working people to participate in progressive political efforts. They too held great hope in the potential of "experts" to provide solutions to America's problems. The social unit plan hinged on the premise that "experts" should serve the needs of the people and that consumers of social services ought to share joint responsibility with professionals in determining, in a democratic manner, what those local needs were. But unlike settlement and community center leaders who shared a similar vision, Wilbur and Elsie Phillips laid out and implemented an elaborate neighborhood-oriented health care plan that practiced what they preached. In the process, however, their effort to deemphasize the political nature of their neighborhood organizing backfired. To the chagrin of Wilbur and Elsie Phillips, their project in Cincinnati to organize a social unit, address social problems, and forge social harmony soon became embroiled in political conflict that destroyed the organization.

Wilbur Phillips began his social service career in 1906 when, after graduating from Harvard, he went to work for the New York Milk Committee. The New York Association for Improving the Condition of the Poor, a long-standing charity organization, set up the Committee to investigate the quality of milk available in poor neighborhoods and the infant health problems which seemed to result from "impure" milk. There was a heated controversy at the time among health care professionals over whether pasteurized milk and bottle feeding contributed to infant mortality and childhood diseases. The results of the free milk program that Phillips organized in neighborhood milk stations did not resolve this nutritional debate. However, it did demonstrate to Phillips that poverty, not the quality of milk, was the chief cause in poor neighborhoods of the high infant mortality of one out of every six babies.

Phillips' marriage shortly thereafter to Elsie LaGrange Cole helped him decide to leave the Milk Committee. Cole, the Vassar-educated daughter of the superintendent of schools in Albany, New York, was working with women's trade unions and was a member of the Socialist party when she met Phillips. Wilbur joined Elsie in matrimony and Party membership. As members of the more conservative wing in the Party, the Phillipses, like many of their fellow neighborhood workers, thought that class divisions were largely a product of misunderstanding. A capitalist like John D. Rockefeller, whom Wilbur had met once, was for them merely "a thoroughly good man who hasn't the steady stink of poverty under his nose."[21] They believed in the need for a system of production and distribution which was organized, as Phillips put it, for human use, not for profit. For them, the Socialist party articulated best the ideals of brotherhood, human solidarity, and a peaceful transition to a cooperative democracy.

The Phillipses left New York and moved to Milwaukee in 1911 to join the first elected Socialist municipal government. Wilbur convinced the new administration to support an experimental, community-based, democratically organized child welfare program which would put into practice some of his Milk Committee experience. As co-executives of the Child Welfare Commission, a semiprivate organization under the supervision of the city government, the Phillipses set up a child health center in one neighborhood—St. Cyril's Parish. They brought doctors, nurses, and midwives into the center and put them in a working partnership with a committee of neighborhood women who gathered data on infant health problems in the neighborhood and who encouraged other residents to use the new neighborhood health service. Based on the positive results of the project and the supportive response of neighborhood residents, Wilbur and Elsie sought to expand the program throughout the city. Now more than ever before they were convinced that a cooperative commonwealth was possible if residents and experts worked together in a mutually helpful and democratic manner.[22]

But Socialist control of Milwaukee's city government was interrupted by the electoral victory of an antisocialist fusion effort, and the new administration, amid a full-scale attack on socialist programs, phased out the Child Welfare Commission. The Phillipses returned East, temporarily out of work, convinced of the correctness of their approach and scarred by the harsh realities of urban politics. If democracy were to become a reality, they now believed, government had to be restructured along nonpartisan lines from the neighborhood block on up. They called this idea the "social unit plan," and in 1915 they assembled a temporary organizing committee to gather support for their program. At a committee meeting in Washington that year the Phillipses brought together an impressive contingent of progressives. Prominent philanthropists like the Guggenheim and Tiffany families rubbed elbows with socialists Helen Phelps Stokes and John Spargo, industrialists Adolph Lewisohn and William Loeb, Jr., intellectual and political leaders Gifford Pinchot, Felix Frankfurter, and Herbert Croly. These people were among the most influential and acknowledged leaders and supporters of reform prior to the 1930s. The meeting raised $100,000 in support of what was to become in 1916 the National Social Unit Organization (NSUO), and Pinchot, Harriman, and Tiffany, as well as prominent community workers, accepted committee directorships.

The central components of the social unit plan were a Block Council, Citizen's Council, Occupational Council, and General Council. The entire plan rested on the block councils which were composed of block residents; here neighborhood people were to determine their needs and priorities and pass them on to the Citizen's Council for consideration. Each block group elected a block worker, who represented them on the Citizen's Council. Occupational groups of professionals functioned as block groups, each electing a representative to an Occupational Council. The General Council, which served as a governing board, was composed of the members of the Citizen and Occupational councils. In sum, a simple democratic structure, applicable for many types of neighborhood-based programs, would ensure meaningful participation from residents and specialists.

When the Phillipses and the NSUO went looking for a neighborhood in which to base an experimental, child health care center, they chose Cincinnati because social and medical workers there proved to be especially enthusiastic about the social unit plan. Wilbur Phillips spent most of 1917 laying the groundwork for the project. He gave informational lectures throughout Cincinnati and organized support from key professional sectors. In March 1917, some 600 Cincinnatians voted the Cincinnati Social Unit Organization

(CSUO) into existence and established committees to administer the competition between various neighborhoods vying to be the demonstration project
site. The five neighborhoods which emerged as leading contenders, including
the eventual winner, Mohawk-Brighton, came from that section of the "ring/
sector" city that settlement workers called the "Zone of Emergence." The
"zone" was situated just outside the slum core, and its residents were "old
immigrant" Irish or German workers who "had emerged from the slum into
the mainstream of American life."[23] The zone neighborhoods, and especially
Mohawk-Brighton, were more attractive to the Phillipses than the "new immigrant" slum neighborhoods of the inner city because, while the inner city
slums were in greater need of health care services, the "zone" neighborhoods
exhibited more interest and were less difficult to organize.[24]

The social unit structure was quickly set in place. Mohawk-Brighton was
divided into thirty-one blocks, each with approximately 500 people. The
CSUO then contacted known supporters in each block area and asked them to
initiate a block council. Each block council then elected a block worker to
represent and serve them. Voter turnout in the block worker election was 71
percent, far beyond voter participation levels in local elections. All the block
workers were unemployed women, as women tended to be more interested in
and knowledgeable about infant health care. The Phillipses explained the concept of the social unit plan to the block workers and instructed them in the
methods and duties of block organizing. Each worker was paid eight dollars
per week to collect data, develop citizen participation in the block group, dis-
seminate information, and offer services to the block as would a social service
advocate. The Phillipses and a Temporary Organizing Committee also set up
Occupational Groups of doctors, nurses, and social workers, who elected representatives to the Occupational Council. The Physicians Council of twenty
six doctors, for example, elected nine representatives to the Occupational
Council. Teachers, businessmen, and clergymen were also asked to participate
but exhibited little interest. Only six months after establishing the CSUO the
Phillipses had formed the Mohawk-Brighton Social Unit Organization
(MBSUO) with a budget of some $35,000, raised through private contribu-
tions and a $15,000 grant from various Cincinnati social and health
organizations.[25]

The first project, a child health care center, succeeded remarkably. The
nursing staff and block workers made some 5,388 visits to 576 babies, of
whom over two thirds received full medical examinations. This postnatal care
program led the organization into other preventative and prenatal health projects. By 1920, in response to the demand for increased services, the MBSUO
was sponsoring prenatal care, medical examinations for preschool children,

bedside nursing, supervision of local tubercular cases, epidemic disease prevention, and postnatal examinations.[26] In two short years the Cincinnati Social Unit Organization had established one of the most comprehensive, effective, and cooperative public health programs in the nation.

In March 1919, Franklin K. Lane, secretary of the interior in the Democratic Wilson administration, became the honorary national chairman of the National Social Unit Organization, and took the opportunity to announce the organization's plan to set up other demonstration projects around the nation. The social unit plan of Wilbur and Elsie Phillips looked like it was about to achieve widespread success and renown. On that same day in March, however, Mayor John Galvin of the very Republican city of Cincinnati took the opportunity to dampen Lane's optimism by charging the CSUO with being but "one step away from Bolshevism." "It aims at establishing a government within a government," he warned.[27] The Cincinnati baseball team, who would win the World championship that year, were the only Reds Galvin was going to tolerate in his town, especially if they had the potential to build an alternative political force in the city. One year later the CSUO was but a memory. The lessons of its quick demise are instructive.

The Phillipses had defused a similar charge in 1918. Jimmie White, the director of the Department of Public Welfare and the head of Union Bethel Settlement, who had been invited, given his prominent position, to participate in the Social Work Occupational Group, was shocked by the "socialistic ideas" he heard expressed among the social unit leaders, most of whom were politically liberal, not socialist. But Jimmie White was a conservative Cincinnatian and the progressive ideas of the CSUO sounded dangerous to him. White was a close friend of the ultraconservative Charles P. Taft, the multimillionaire owner of the *Times-Star* and the brother of the ex-president of the United States. When White resigned because, he said, the CSUO was really a national political party with socialistic tendencies, Taft made sure that all charges were displayed on the front page of the *Times-Star*. The Phillipses, however, were able in a nation preoccupied with World War I to weather this first storm.

One year later, however, Mayor Galvin's charge occurred amid the "Red Scare," a nationwide purge of radicals orchestrated by the politically opportunist attorney general, A. Mitchell Palmer. The success of the revolutionary Bolshevik faction in the Soviet Union provided the excuse for political repression throughout the United States. Under concerted attack by the elite in Cincinnati, support for the CSUO dwindled fast. The Council of Social Agencies in Cincinnati, a prime funding source controlled by conservative business and political interests, withdrew all financial support, including money already promised. The Council further threatened to cut off funding to any agency that continued to support the social unit. In response, the Phillipses and their liberal supporters organized a plebiscite on the social unit. More than 4,000 out of an estimated 7,000 eligible voters in Mohawk-Brighton declared in favor of the plan; only 120 voted against it. It was an impressive show of support, but the neighborhood referendum was not enough to keep the plan alive.[28] The CSUO closed its doors shortly thereafter, and the social unit idea was defunct nation-wide by mid-1921.

Part of the social unit's problem was the antiradical, antireform, postwar political situation. Neighborhood-based efforts are often affected deeply by national programs over which they have little control, and the "Red Scare" and the "return to normalcy" of the decade after 1919 destroyed many liberal and radical programs. But part of the cause of the CSUO's quick collapse and failure to withstand, even minimally, the attacks of reactionary forces rests with some serious errors in neighborhood organizing practiced by the Phillipses and their progressive cohorts. Some years later Wilbur Phillips summarized the failure of the CSUO as the result of a lack of independent, economic self-support. But this was in reality only part of the problem. Depending on elite support does, most often, doom social change efforts to either a short life or cooption. But the CSUO failed because it never sank political roots in the district of Mohawk-Brighton, roots which would have supported and nourished it in turbulent times.

The social unit plan succeeded largely because of the impressive support of wealthy, prominent, and influential liberal backers at the national level. Securing such support formed an important aspect of the Phillipses' organizing strategy; they put much energy into this activity, and they did it well. They were much less successful, however, getting neighborhood people to participate in the block groups. To its credit, the Mohawk-Brighton experiment attracted and developed indigenous neighborhood leaders; the block workers were active, hard working, and effective intermediaries and advocates. Certainly the social settlements and community centers never approached this level of indigenous leadership in their neighborhood organizing projects. But the block groups rested on these block workers. Most residents saw no need to get involved.

True, the Phillipses and the block workers never had much time to develop indigenous support at the block level and sink the potentially sustaining grassroots. But their style of nonpolitical organizing added to their inability to attract neighborhood people as active participants. The issue of child health care successfully attracted widespread liberal support and convinced the city's elite to permit the demonstration project. But the need for decent health care could have mobilized militant neighborhood support as well. The Phillipses' "post-Milwaukee" brand of politics sought consensus and cooperation with the existing powers, so they never presented health care in the neighborhoods as a political right that neighborhood people might some day have to defend. The Phillipses organized around a conservative strategy. They never emphasized the real need for citizen involvement, never emphasized that without resident participation and a willingness to fight for the program, opponents or liberal benefactors could take away health care services as easily as they had permitted or supported them. Without militant grassroots support, the Social Unit Organization lost battles where its liberal elite support was less powerful than local interests.

The Cincinnati Social Unit experiment reveals that regardless of what some organizers say, neighborhood organizing is a political act with political consequences. Organizing for a more cooperative and more equitable democracy is a highly political act. Mayor Galvin stretched the point when he accused the Phillipses of trying to establish a "government within a government," but he came closer to the truth than Wilbur or Elsie, who thought after Milwaukee that they were "through with politics."[29] The Phillipses saw their community work as being above politics. They saw the social unit as a plan which by its universality would transcend politics and win adherents from all "reasonable" segments of the population. But their lack of a political analysis of the situation they faced and their lack of a good understanding of class and power interests in Cincinnati doomed them and the CSUO to defeat by more powerful and more politically astute opponents.

The Phillipses should have known better. Their experience in Milwaukee demonstrated the fragility of reform programs. Ironically, the Phillipses became more conservative after their experience in Milwaukee, seeking to depoliticize their program and appealing to the lowest common political denominator. But this "pragmatic approach" only helped to get the project started. They were on thin ice from the outset. After all, the Phillipses were outsiders, ex-socialists at the least, with a large following of nationally prominent reformers, who did not necessarily have the same immediate interests as the local Cincinnati elite. Without the potentially militant support of the neighborhood residents in Mohawk-Brighton and without political power at the local level, when suspicion turned to opposition in Cincinnati the Phillipses and the social unit plan had nothing to stand on.

CHAPTER 2

Radical Neighborhood Organizing, 1929–1946

Depression and New Deal

Landlord, landlord,
My roof has sprung a leak.
Don't you 'member I told you about it
Way last week?

Landlord, landlord,
These steps is broken down.
When you come up yourself
It's a wonder you don't fall down.

Ten bucks you say I owe you?
Ten bucks you say is due?
Well, that's ten bucks more'n I'll pay you
Till you fix this house up new.

What? You gonna get eviction orders?
You gonna cut off my heat?
You gonna take my furniture and
Throw it in the street?

Um-huh! You talking high and mighty.
Talk on—till you get through.
You ain't gonna be able to say a word
If I land my fist on you.

Police! Police!
Come and get this man!
He's trying to ruin the government
And overturn the land!

Copper's whistle!
Patrol bell!
Arrest.

Precinct Station.
Iron Cell.
Headlines in Press:

MAN THREATENS LANDLORD

TENANT HELD NO BAIL

JUDGE GIVES NEGRO 90 DAYS IN COUNTY JAIL

Langston Hughes, "Ballad of the Landlord"

The corporate liberal strategy of progressive reform depended on a sound and prosperous economy. Because programs were expensive, they were only instituted when corporate profits were large enough to both satisfy investors and cover the costs of increased wages, improved working conditions, and ameliorative social reform programs. In general the period 1900 to 1929 was one such period of corporate growth and sizable profits. But that era ended with the stock market crash in 1929 and the decade long economic depression the crash initiated. The plans of corporate liberals, not to mention those of working people, were dashed on the rocks of the nationwide depression.

As the depression deepened, frustration with evictions, unemployment, and inadequate relief programs resulted in individual acts of defiance, like the one Langston Hughes described in the poem above. Insurgent groups organized from the neighborhood up to the national level to harness and maximize this energy. Most notably for the history of neighborhood organizing, Communists, Socialists, and independent radicals organized the unemployed in neighborhoods throughout the nation. Tenant unions opposed the unilateral power of landlords. Activist Saul Alinsky began his lifelong work of developing "people's organizations" at the neighborhood level. While such neighborhood organizing projects differed, they all shared the spirit of militancy and radicalism that dominated neighborhood organizing in the years 1929–46.

Cities, the geographic centers of the economic system, were devastated by the depression. Some Southern and Western cities, which were less integrated into and therefore less dependent on the national economy, were not hurt as badly as the Northern industrial centers. Cities devoted more to finance than industrial production tended to fare better. But in general, people could not pay taxes, so many cities simply went bankrupt. State and city officials were helpless. At the neighborhood level, community workers in the settlements, community centers, and the social work profession had few ideas about how to stem the tide. They did, however, turn away from neighborhood organizing as a solution to the economic depression and looked to the national capital for answers. Because, they reasoned, the economy of the nation, not to mention the industrial world, was far more integrated in 1930 than it had been in 1900, a well-coordinated, centralized national plan of action, most likely issued from the White House and similar to domestic efforts during World War I, seemed the only salvation. Decentralized, local responses were viewed by most progressives as an anachronism with little utility in the current national economic crisis.

The White House responded slowly and conservatively. At first President Hoover suggested that the depression was largely a psychological problem. If businessmen would think and act more positively and invest new capital, then prosperity would be "just around the corner." Businessmen, however, foresaw no imminent economic upturn. The demand for products did not exist to warrant chancing capital investments. Better to sit tight. So, as the depression deepened and demand declined further, business laid off more workers and continued to cut their costs. The wealthy could wait until the economy bottomed out or until more favorable incentives for investment appeared. It was the workers who had little to fall back on. In the latter part of his administration Hoover replaced his unsuccessful plan of "think positively" with a strategy of federal intervention best labeled "pump priming from the top." According to this plan, profit incentives to business, initiated by the federal government, would encourage investment and stimulate the economy. Hoover's Reconstruction Finance Corporation (RFC) offered loans to banks and other businesses, and as an afterthought to local government agencies, in the hope of stabilizing these sectors and allowing recovery to filter down through the society. But the program was too hesitant and too limited and had little impact.

When Franklin Delano Roosevelt succeeded Hoover he offered little more than the psychological and trickle down approach of his predecessor. FDR's inaugural message that "we have nothing to fear but fear itself" was no sounder than Hoover's "prosperity is just around the corner." The initial programs of FDR's "New Deal," especially the National Industrial Recovery Act (NIRA), the Agricultural Adjustment Act (AAA), and the first Banking and Securities acts, represented only a more creative form of pump priming from the top. The NIRA, for example, organized committees to maintain wages and employment, but also sought to stimulate investment by waiving all antitrust action against corporations involved in NIRA planning, thereby giving them virtual license to consolidate. The first AAA developed a plan of agricultural subsidies which paid farmers to keep land out of production. The AAA used the power of the federal government to maintain agricultural prices by reducing production at the very time consumers lacked food and could not pay the old, declining prices, let alone the new, subsidized ones. Moreover, most of the AAA money went to large-scale operations, not the tenant farmers and sharecroppers in the South who needed it most. The thinking behind these business-designed plans maintained that if federal programs could stimulate profits and investment (the "supply side" of the cycle) then purchasing power and demand too would be heightened, and a cyclical upturn would be forthcoming.

Roosevelt used this conservative approach without success from 1933 to 1935, a period often referred to as the First New Deal. Business accepted the benefits of the programs, but remained unconvinced that the economy was ripe for investment. In 1935 unemployment and purchasing power were little better than they had been in 1933. During the first New Deal, FDR initiated a number of relief activities, among them the Federal Emergency Relief Administration (FERA), Public Works Administration (PWA), Civilian Conservation Corps (CCC), and Civil Works Administration (CWA), which provided some benefits and jobs. But, in essence, little trickled down to the bottom half of society except continued hard times.

By 1935, however, with a presidential election just around the corner, Roosevelt had more to fear than fear itself. In the early years of his administration, Roosevelt was able to portray himself as the defender of the common man and woman against the interests of big business. "Mr. Roosevelt is the only man we ever had in the White House who would understand that my boss is a sonufabitch," was how one worker put it. And in the beginning of his first term most workers accepted their bad fortune with courage, fortitude, and patience, choosing to stick it out while Mr. Roosevelt did his best to improve the situation. But by 1935 patience was growing thin. The New Deal looked pretty much like the usual practice: government helping business and asking workers to make continued sacrifices. Always the shrewd politician, FDR shifted to a Second New Deal around 1935 which emphasized the "demand side" of the economic ledger. This approach sought to "prime the pump from the bottom" by encouraging employment, thus raising purchasing power and increasing demand. The greater demand for products, the administration figured, ought to stimulate capital investment. Programs like the Works Progress Administration (WPA), Unemployment Insurance, Social Security, Aid to Families with Dependent Children (AFDC), and the National Labor Relations Act ("Wagner Act") gave workers jobs, direct relief benefits, and improved bargaining positions with management. FDR was not a fan of the deficit spending ideas of the English economist John Maynard Keynes. But given the dismal political and economic situation in 1935–36 and the fact that big business had failed to pull into line and support Roosevelt's fiscally conservative program from 1933 to 1935, FDR had few other alternatives if he wanted to ensure his reelection.

The growing discontent and protests of the destitute elderly, workers, farmers, and the unemployed also demanded change. Some five million elderly joined Townshend clubs, a movement begun by Dr. Charles E. Townshend, an elderly physician in California who promoted a plan to secure a federal pension of $200 a month for everyone over sixty. Senator Huey Long of Louisiana mustered a considerable following nationally and launched a powerful attack on the New Deal with his "Share Our Wealth" program. Townshend, Long, and others commanded a considerable number of votes and represented an important electoral threat to FDR and the Democratic party. James Farley, a New Deal tactician, estimated in 1935 that Long alone could receive three or four million votes if he ran on a third party ticket, which could hand the 1936 election to the Republicans. The more Roosevelt saw a rising tide of discontent taking electoral form, the more he moved left to undermine its taking hold.[2]

But it was not only these electoral threats that forced the New Deal into an economic program of deficit spending and social welfare capitalism. Locally based, direct action movements of radicals and workers also pushed Roosevelt and the New Deal further left than they cared to venture. The Unemployed Councils of the Communist Party United States of America (CPUSA), Upton Sinclair's End Poverty in California (EPIC) campaign, Farmer-Labor parties, Socialists, Musteites (the followers of pacifist A. J. Muste), and independent radicals organized mass protests in workplaces and communities which demonstrated the growing militancy and dissatisfaction of working-class people. These activities, unlike those of Huey Long, for example, were viewed less as challenges to Roosevelt's reelection and more as threats to the social order and system of capitalism in general.

But the relationship between local organizing and White House policies was not a one-way street from the local to the national level. FDR's Second New Deal did more than respond to workers' protests; it also encouraged, sometimes unintentionally and reluctantly, future direct actions at the local level. New Deal programs like the Wagner Act, for example, which lent federal support to union organizing efforts, led to the formation, growth, and success of the Congress of Industrial Organizations (CIO). The industrial union movement, in turn, created a mass base for worker-initiated reform throughout the nation, and spawned a political climate that was both conducive to and supportive of left-oriented neighborhood organizing programs. These ranged from unemployed councils to tenant movements and the initial efforts of Saul Alinsky in Chicago. Those begun before 1935 were the direct product of depression-era conditions at the local level. Those begun after 1935 essentially owed their impetus and direction to the CIO organizing campaigns. In sum, the interaction of depression conditions, radical local organizing, federal policies, and a vibrant, national labor movement created a dynamic decade in the history of insurgent neighborhood organizing.

While protest groups developed first and best at the local level where their work was rooted in day-to-day industrial and community struggles, most, like the Socialists and Communists, saw local organizing, whether in the factory or the neighborhood, as essentially the best means for forming a national party or nationwide insurgent movement that could effectively address the failures of a "collapsing capitalist economy." Even Saul Alinsky, who above all thought of neighborhood organizing as a possible end itself, knew that the success of what he called a "people's organization" depended on the coordination of local efforts into a larger, national movement—a community-based, national organization comparable to the CIO. Neighborhood organizing in the thirties was characterized not only by its radicalism but by this dual concern of building an insurgent movement at both the national and local levels.

The Communist Party Organizes the Unemployed

The communists brought misery out of hiding in the worker's neighborhoods. . . . Sometimes I'd hear a communist speaker say something so bitter and extreme, I'd feel embarrassed. Then I'd look around at the unemployed audience—shabby clothes, expressions worried and sour. Faces would start to glow, heads to nod, hands to clap.

Len de Caux, labor activist

The Negro neither fears the communist nor leans over backward in admiration. He (the communist organizer) is just another human being to be judged individually on one

basis—is he fighting for the full and complete equality of
opportunity for black people.

Adam Clayton Powell, Jr., Congressman

FIGHT DON'T STARVE

Communist Party Banner

Almost all Americans in the early years of the depression of the 1930s, and
some for its entire course, experienced economic hardship quietly and relatively alone. Families used up all their savings, borrowed, and pawned their
belongings. They blamed themselves. Some sought solace and direction in
metaphysical solutions like astrology. The responses of others ran the gamut
from depending on established communal networks of assistance to individual
and group looting of grocery stores. As the depression wore on, however,
many workers grew to suspect that their unemployment and poverty were the
result not of a personal failing but rather a collapsed economy, and they began
to think about the need for some fundamental changes in the economic
system.[3]

Radical organizations were quick to promote their vision of a noncapitalist
society and their strategy of how to achieve it. Even before the stock market
crash, for example, Socialists had formulated a national approach to the problems faced by the jobless. But by far the most influential and novel approach
to radical community organizing in the 1930s was that of the Communist Party
of the United States of America (CPUSA). The importance of the Communist
party's neighborhood organizing does not rest on its ability to resolve depression-era problems. At the time other leftist groups, such as the Socialist party,
had organized community efforts of equal magnitude which had more impact
on the passage of remedial New Deal legislation. The CPUSA's contribution
to the history of neighborhood organizing, however, is in its unique approach
and its influence on the radical movements of the 1930s. Most activists now
see the primary goal of neighborhood organizing as awakening people to a
sense of their own power. The Communists saw neighborhood work as a
means of recruiting people into a national organization. Building the national
Party, not neighborhood organizing, they believed, would best advance the
interests of the working class and racial minorities in the United States. To
build a national revolutionary organization they advanced a strategy of "internationalism" in their neighborhood work which, however flawed, was impressive in its class consciousness, range of protest, and breadth of concerns.[4]

On the eve of the depression the Party was limited to some 7,500 members.

The Red Scare of 1919 had decimated their ranks and the political climate of repression in the 1920s continued to keep the Party weak, on the defensive, and underground for much of the decade. Nevertheless, the Party anticipated the "impending collapse of capitalism" and was surprisingly well prepared, certainly more so than any other group, to address the crisis and mobilize their forces around it. The Sixth World Congress of the Communist International (Comintern), the Moscow-based, policy-making body for Communist parties worldwide, predicted in 1928 the imminent economic collapse and ordered Communist parties to initiate more openly revolutionary actions. Concerned about "the Negro Question" the Congress also insisted that the U.S. Party make the organization of blacks a preeminent priority. Accordingly the organizing offensive of the CPUSA to mobilize the unemployed along interracial lines began even before the Great Depression.

Two months before the stock market crash, in August 1929, the Party, now operating above ground, organized a new labor federation, the Trade Union Unity League (TUUL), which sought to build an alternative union to the AFL and to set up councils of the unemployed. Communist party community organizers went into impoverished, working class neighborhoods in the nation's largest cities to build the Unemployed Council movement.[5] Within four months after Black Thursday on Wall Street, the combination of skillful organizing by Communist radicals and the spontaneous dissent growing among the jobless produced an aggressive and vital, Communist-led, community-based movement. As early as February 1930, 2,000 workers in Cleveland and 3,000 in Los Angeles stormed their respective city halls demanding relief benefits. It took police wielding nightsticks and lobbing tear gas cannisters to disperse them. In March, the Party organized an International Unemployment Day, with protests across the country from coast to coast. The marches were orderly and peaceful, except where local officials and police grew anxious and tried to stop them. In New York City, police attacks transformed some 35,000 orderly demonstrators into an angry, fighting mob. Bloodied workers, men and women, tried to flee once it was clear they were unprepared to sustain a police assault. But the police prohibited the retreat, throwing people to the ground and pummeling them. Thirty seven people were arrested and 130 were injured.[6]

As the depression deepened and as authorities grew more alarmed by the insurgent activity of the unemployed, conflict escalated. In October 1930, a CPUSA protest at the national convention of the American Federation of Labor in Boston brought out 200 police, including a special "Flying Squadron" equipped with machine guns, bulletproof vests, and tear gas bombs. Mayhem ensued. The protesters were badly beaten, and Mayor James Michael Curley, the son of Irish immigrants, demanded that the demonstrators, by no means all aliens or Russian, be deported to the Soviet Union. One year later Curley stepped up the repression with arrests for "carrying a placard," "making loud outcries in the park," and public "speaking without a permit."[7] Imprisonment of Communist organizers, attacks on demonstrators, and repressive local ordinances isolated Communists from most of the unemployed who, afraid of the official brutality, stayed clear of radical protest organizations. For some, however, it had the opposite effect. The assaults served to radicalize them and steel their resolve to fight a political system that preached democracy but denied dissent when it challenged the system of capitalism.

The success of the protests rested on the extraordinary commitment and fearless leadership of Communist party organizers. Communist organizers worked hard and seemingly all the time. They organized the unemployed at factory gates, on breadlines, in flop houses, relief centers, and neighborhood street corners. They attended meeting after meeting with workers and Party members. They wrote leaflets and articles, songs and banner slogans. They planned and participated in demonstrations and they led these protests in a most courageous and impressive way. The estimated 4,000 demonstrators arrested in the summer and fall of 1930 while participating in Communist-led actions throughout the nation indicated the intense level of activity generated by a relatively small group of committed, radical organizers.[8]

These initial efforts were impressive for their militancy and for their ability to win concessions from local officials and relief bureaus, but they had a purely ad hoc quality about them. Spontaneity had its virtues; more people could be mobilized for a protest than could be attracted to become members of an ongoing organization. Demonstrations were often exciting and cathartic, while organizations tended to be dull and to require a lot of hard work. Nevertheless, the goal of the CPUSA was not simply to politicize people at demonstrations, or give people a sense of their own power through protest victories. The fundamental goal of the Party was to build an effective Communist organization which could lead a working-class revolution in the United States. The councils were planned to be the mass protest organizations of the Party, designed as "transmission belts" for the recruitment of members into the Party and as community-based organizations which could supplement the Party's union organizing efforts in factories.

When organizing Unemployed Councils the Party would begin by dividing a city or rural area into sections and branches. Organizers who "knew what was going on in the factories and neighborhoods" were assigned by the Party to each section. In places where the Party was already well-established, as in Chicago or New York City, the Party closely supervised the initial organization and direction of the council. In areas somewhat removed from the nation's big cities, organizers had greater freedom but also less Party support. Organizers did not go into a community "cold." They always had "contacts," contacts who might be old Party members or progressive sympathizers active in ethnic and fraternal associations. After agitating, sometimes for weeks, "against capitalism" and talking about the "need for socialism," a local council would be formed. While membership in the council only entailed having to sign up at a council sponsored event and while most members did not attend meetings and could not be counted on to participate in demonstrations, councils usually had an active core among the membership who would attend meetings and conferences and participate regularly in demonstrations. It was from among this core group that Party members would be recruited.

Despite the obvious tension of a reform-oriented, community-based effort seeking primarily to recruit members for a national Communist movement, local councils did become real neighborhood organizations. Local conditions demanded, and Communist organizers recognized, the need for each council to be grounded in the traditions and institutions of the local community. "We made every effort to make the councils part of their neighborhoods," Steve Nelson, a leading Party activist, recalled. "For fund raising we tried to stage events that fit into the cultural life of the community. Most councils relied on bingo, raffles, picnics, and block parties. [In Chicago] since the Catholic church was always sponsoring such affairs, they were part of the natural way of life." In the anthracite region of Pennsylvania council meetings opened with "Hail Marys and Our Fathers." In Harlem, given the local importance of the black church in community activities, it became common practice to begin council meetings with a prayer. Despite their avowed atheism, Party organizers in the United States accepted religious practices and encouraged the participation of progressive religious and community leaders because of their influence in the local community.[9]

Communist organizers also accepted and encouraged local decision making on important organizational issues such as where to picket, what hall to use, who should give the speech at a rally, and when and how to hold an upcoming meeting. These were critical organizing concerns which consumed much of the time and energies of council organizers and members. In this respect, as well as the acceptance by local councils of certain community traditions and institutions, councils were administered from the grassroots far more than would be expected given the autocratic organizing strategy and hostility to local parochialism of the CPUSA.

Like most mass movements of the thirties, and especially those organizing the unemployed, the councils were extremely unstable. Membership in councils was very fluid, for people often left after their particular grievance had been addressed. The Party felt that it was impossible to organize a mass movement of the unemployed without effective party organization, without a core of committed and focused activists to do much of the daily work and to spread the movement. Accordingly, despite the neighborhood character of councils and despite the creative adaptations of Comintern policy, the Party organized, directed, and controlled the local councils. Continuity in the local councils was provided by paid functionaries—local leaders who were given a stipend by the Party for their work and who were most often, but not always, Party members. The bone and sinews—and money—that made the councils work were provided by the Party.[10]

In essence there was never much real autonomy for the local councils. The Party came to neighborhood people with a prearranged ideology, program, and strategy—a "line" they called it—which provided an analysis of current problems and their solutions. They had less interest than later radical organizers in "letting the people decide." The Comintern determined the goals and platform of the Party and, *ipso facto,* the local councils. It was the Comintern that decided, for example, to bring the CPUSA out from underground in the late 1920s, to tackle the issue of organizing the unemployed and racial minorities, and to support a Popular Front strategy in 1935. "Colonization" of white working-class and black communities was fundamental, they reasoned, in order to provide the leadership and direction necessary to build the Party and a revolutionary working-class movement. Most importantly, the councils often developed into highly effectual mass-protest organizations because of the leadership of Party organizers who drew their strength and direction from the Party apparatus.[11]

The Party line to build the Unemployed Council movement developed as early as 1930. The four-pronged "bread and butter" strategy focused on relief, housing, race, and "translocal" issues, the latter being issues outside the community which would concern neighborhood residents. At the outset of the depression people accepted relief reluctantly. But most unemployed workers soon came to see local relief benefits not only as a necessity but as a right. Local welfare offices, however, lacked the funds to furnish all unemployed workers with relief funds, and these bureaus often relied on intimidation or harassment to keep relief requests down. Communist organizers fought for relief funds by representing workers at welfare offices and, if that were not sufficient, staging protests to ensure relief payments. While their goal was to build the Party organization, not simply to win benefits, and while Communists were revolutionaries, not social workers, they nevertheless saw service delivery as one way to win support and members. In Harlem, for example, organizers would take a large group of unemployed to a relief station and demand benefits. If they were refused, they camped in the offices until they received benefits or were removed by the police. The greater the resistance of local officials, the more violent the response of the protesters. Incidents varied from council members breaking down the doors of a Harlem relief bureau and overturning furniture to bloody struggles between police and demonstrators. Communist organizers viewed such protests as one of the best methods for winning benefits and educating participants in the fundamentally repressive nature of the capitalist system.[12]

The second part of the Communists' strategy to build the council movement focused on fighting housing evictions. Tenants often could not pay their rent because they were out of work, but this did not deter many landlords from evicting them. This was an openly callous act and the Party made the most of it. From August to October 1931, 2,185 eviction cases came before the Chicago Renters Court, 38 percent of which involved black families. Communist community organizers accompanied neighborhood people to eviction hearings and staged mass actions to block evictions physically. Not uncommonly members of an Unemployed Council grabbed furniture being brought out the front door during an eviction and took it back into the apartment through the rear entrance. On one occasion in Chicago, for example, several thousand people marched to a house to block an eviction. When the police arrived, the 5,000 people already there refused to disperse. Scuffling broke out, guns blazed, and before it was over police had killed three protesters. By nightfall the Party spread leaflets throughout the neighborhood demanding the death penalty for the murderers. Chicago's elite grew fearful that the city was on the brink of revolution, and made sure that the Renters Court immediately suspended all evictions and the city expanded its relief program. The same kinds of situations led to the same results in other northern industrial centers. By 1931 the Unemployed Councils in Detroit also had stopped practically all evictions.[13]

A third element in the council building strategy was to organize the black community around a platform of interracial cooperation and equality. "Black and White Unite to Fight" was a prominent Communist slogan. As far back as the 1920s, small groups of Communists were working in black neighborhoods, especially in New York and Chicago, sponsoring interracial dances and leading protests against slum housing and high rents. Alone among primarily white political organizations in the thirties, Communists demanded complete unity and complete equality between black and white workers. They addressed the special issue of race, and emphasized that the struggle of white workers could never succeed unless workers of all races were included as equal participants. (It was common practice for industrialists to keep wages down by using black workers as a surplus labor force and as strike breakers.) A Comintern directive on the "race question" in 1930 emphasized that white workers were to "march at the head of the struggle" against Jim Crowism and segregation. This emphasis on black and white unity, one historian writes, "had a catalytic effect on the black community."[14]

No group in the United States had more reason to join a revolutionary organization committed to altering an oppressive system than did the black population. As bad as the depression was for white workers, it devastated the black community. Unemployment figures for workers in some key industries throughout the nation reached 40 percent, but in Harlem, for example, unemployment was 80 percent in 1935. Blacks joined the Unemployed Councils to fight back against unemployment and discrimination and to gain greater control over their communities. Equally important, the councils provided a supportive and racially intregrated political and cultural movement which was an exciting and challenging, if essentially culturally "white" experience. Most of all, blacks joined because the Party and the councils supported their winning relief benefits, stopping evictions, and "taking up black issues," such as antilynching legislation or the Scottsboro case. At a time when little other support existed outside the black community, blacks did not discard allies simply because they were called "reds." No other organization composed primarily of white workers was willing to struggle along side of, on behalf of, and, most importantly, under the leadership of black men and women.

A fourth tactic for organizational building was to address issues which transcended local boundaries but could galvanize and politicize the local community. Community and neighborhood-based organizing was for Communists largely a question of tactics and strategy; it represented no belief in the intrinsic value of the neighborhood unit. Councils were based in neighborhoods hit hardest by the depression, especially black slum areas, because community-based organizing was seen by the Party as the best way of reaching blacks, unemployed housewives, and others who did not work in factories where Party organizing was most active. But limiting campaigns or issues to a neighborhood ran counter to the Party's goal of building an international organization. Organizing that did not transcend local boundaries and make connections with national and international issues the Party considered parochial and potentially reactionary, pitting neighborhood against neighborhood. Three of the most effective organizing issues in Harlem were support of antilynching legislation, defense of the nine Scottsboro boys accused of rape, and opposition to the Italian invasion of Ethiopia. None of these issues affected Harlem residents directly. But community people saw them as important campaigns in the struggle for racial equality, and they held meetings, demonstrations, and direct actions in support of their brethren in the South and in Africa. In one year, for example, Communist organizers held some forty street meetings in Harlem solely on the antilynching issue.

From 1931 through 1935 the Unemployed Councils concentrated on this "bread and butter" strategy of organizing militant protests around neighborhood and translocal issues. Most of the protest was directed at government agencies and officials. In 1935, a switch in Party line issued from Moscow called for a Popular Front in which Communists would ally with all "progressive forces," including New Deal liberals, in the struggle against the rising menace of fascism. Hitler, the Comintern realistically decided, presented a greater threat to the Soviet people and the international socialist movement than the depression-straddled ruling groups in the United States and Western Europe. Comintern required, therefore, that all Communist efforts, no matter where they occurred, be oriented toward building a popular front against fascism. The new line transformed the CPUSA and the councils from opponents into critical supporters of the social welfare programs of FDR and the Second New Deal.

In the spirit of the Popular Front, for example, the CPUSA and the councils joined with Socialist and independent radical efforts in 1935 in a national and unified organization of the unemployed known as the Workers Alliance of America. By the end of 1936 this "national poor people's organization" claimed 1,600 locals and a total membership of 600,000 people distributed among forty-three states. The new organization focused primarily on lobbying for national relief and unemployment insurance benefits in Washington, and accepted the terms of the Popular Front to work with all progressive groups in the New Deal coalition and within the parameters of New Deal liberalism. Calls for reform and opposition to fascism replaced demands for revolution and socialism.

The Popular Front line also sought to respond to organizing problems facing Communist activists. Despite the near complete collapse of the economy in the United States and despite vigorous and militant work by Communists from 1929 to 1935, Party membership and support remained small. Harlem, a key center for Communist community organizing, had only 100 Party members in late 1933. While thousands in Harlem were members of its Unemployed Councils, the national unemployed organization led by the CPUSA could claim no more than 100,000. This was fewer than one percent of the total number of unemployed workers. But the change in line after 1935 made the Party more acceptable. Party leaders deemphasized the need for revolution, developed alliances with local and national progressive organizations, and generally pursued a more "Americanized" organizing strategy. The more they fought for democracy and equality rather than communism, and the more the depression continued unabated, the greater the Party's community support and popularity among workers. The Party in Harlem, for example, grew from 100 in 1933 to 800 members by 1936.[15]

But it was not only the Comintern policy decision and the desire for more influence that caused the Party and its councils to take new directions. The passage of progressive, worker-oriented legislation like the Social Security and Wagner acts in 1935 posed a dilemma for radical community organizers. While the legislation was a victory for grassroots insurgent groups, at the same time it presented the threat of both cooptation and "ultraleft" isolation. The Social Security Act, for example, offered not only benefits but a means of draining radical protest into a bureaucratic relief structure. Welfare bureaus were now more responsive to applicants, setting up relief complaint offices and even establishing procedures that recognized unemployed organizations as the legitimate representatives of relief recipients. According to Herbert Benjamin, a Communist leader of the Unemployed Council movement, "No one could long maintain leadership of the unemployed who would direct the struggle of the unemployed against progressive officials supported by organized labor and progressive forces."[16] Party organizers now emphasized transforming the system not by attacking it from the outside but rather by "boring from within." They hoped that by gaining greater influence in official, labor, and community activities they could continue to make demands on the system and build the Party more effectively.

As late as 1937 the Party remained a militant voice at the neighborhood level for the rights of workers and the unemployed. Its members continued to lead protest activities on rent strikes, campaigns to improve local schools, and efforts to reduce milk and meat prices. They fought back against cutbacks in national social welfare programs, cutbacks which began just a few months after FDR's successful reelection in 1936. In cooperation with the Workers Alliance, in 1937 they helped organize a Hunger March on Washington which received wide support from progressives and radicals. But in general the Party toned down its militancy and began to publicly support liberals as well as liberal programs. Most notably, in 1937 the CPUSA publicly supported Franklin Roosevelt, and the following year the Workers Alliance campaigned actively for New Deal candidates. Not surprisingly, militant community organizing by Communists began to be reduced substantially.[17]

Two elements of the Popular Front strategy especially undermined local community organizing after 1937. First was the emphasis on the fascist threat. For the Party, the international struggle always took precedence over local community concerns, and this was certainly so as the threat of the Axis powers mounted. Second was the Party's increasing emphasis on union organizing. The Party had always judged union organizing to be the most effective means of expanding its influence and the power of working people. With the CIO experiencing extraordinary growth after 1936, partially through the work of Communist organizers, the CPUSA put almost all its energies into factory organizing rather than community work, so that by 1938 the almost singular concern of Party organizers was working with the union. In a few places, such as Harlem, where the "color line" kept most urban blacks out of factory work and labor unions, Communists continued to focus attention on neighborhood-based work. The only way to reach urban blacks was through community organizing. But even in these communities, union efforts, not "black concerns," became paramount. Generally the Party abandoned its vigorous defense of black rights when this defense conflicted with CIO organizing objectives.[18]

By 1938, therefore, Communists increasingly played a conservative role in community struggles. As they sought to appease CIO progressives and to work within the New Deal coalition at the local and national level, their community-based organizing became less successful. Local activists in Harlem began to criticize the Party for sacrificing black and white workers in order to protect its good relationship with liberals like FDR, New York City Mayor Fiorello LaGuardia, and the city's black elite. When members of the black community asked Communists to support a bill in the New York legislature which sought to limit the bargaining rights of unions that discriminated against blacks, the Party refused to do so on the grounds that it was unnecessary. The Party said the unions could police themselves. While this paralleled the position of CIO leaders, it opposed that of black activists and workers. One year later the local Workers Alliance did little in response to cutbacks in the Harlem WPA program. Ultimately, the Party was unwilling to defend the "special needs" of blacks and the relief benefits it and the councils had fought so hard to create. By 1939 the community work of the CPUSA and the unemployed movement had lost not only its support but also much of its credibility.

Although the Party's neighborhood-based efforts were short-lived, they were impressive in many ways. Most visibly, their skillful and courageous use of direct action tactics, most of which were directed at the public sector, helped force those in power to adopt more progressive positions and programs. But the effectiveness of Party organizers stemmed from more than their militancy and courage. Community organizing as practiced by the CPUSA was successful because it emphasized organizational discipline, defined local issues in a national and international context, linked community struggles with those in the workplace, developed alliances between black and white workers, and offered a thorough political analysis of the problems community people faced.

Such accomplishments by radicals had rarely been seen before in this country. In general, militant, disciplined, and ideological Communist organizing gave the people who participated in the Unemployed Councils, and perhaps even people in the neighborhoods who watched from their apartment windows, a confidence in and a sense of their own power to change the political system. It offered a community organizing experience that provided council activists with an important theoretical and practical grassroots political education.

On the other hand, the obvious organizing errors of the national Party deeply affected neighborhood work as well. The Party's political opportunism, its program that reflected the needs of the Soviet Union more than that of American workers, and its autocratic organizational structure which denied the type of criticism necessary to prevent ideological and tactical errors were serious mistakes. The Party's abandonment of support for blacks was a shortsighted and major error. The Party ultimately refused even to support progressive protests against social discrimination, such as that of A. Phillip Randolph's threatened march on Washington in early 1941. The single-minded commitment to the CIO and the Popular Front strategy prevented effective criticism of a New Deal which was intellectually and programatically stagnant after 1937.

More specifically, in its neighborhood organizing work the sources of Communist organizing strength, its internationalism, autocratic discipline and emphasis on the workplace, proved to be weaknesses as well. Their desire to build a mass working-class organization brought the realization that local issues needed a national and even international context. The same goal, however, led to the Party and Comintern's misjudging the value of autonomous, community-based organizing. The Party's goal was to organize a worker's movement in support of socialism, not to build community organizations. Therefore, class-wide concerns always took precedence over local needs in the Communist organizing model. The Party knew that building a socialist movement in the United States was no easy task and that organizing the unemployed was not the way to do it. The unemployed and local communities in general, they felt, were too unstable and too disconnected to form the base of a revolutionary movement.

The Party had always seen neighborhood work as a secondary aspect of the class struggle, subordinate in importance and effectiveness to international concerns and work place organizing. But it overemphasized the distinction between factory and community work. In the early thirties, when union organizing had little promise, the Party put energy into neighborhood organizing. Later, with the emergence of the CIO, the Party not surprisingly focused more and more on union organizing. By 1939, however, when the growing fascist menace abroad demanded the undivided attention of Communists, the Party completely sacrificed its community organizing and with it its unequivocal support of black rights. These were serious errors produced in part by Communist theory and strategy that saw little value to community-based organizing in and of itself.

Neighborhood organizing cannot and need not be the only concern of a national working-class organization. In the case of the CPUSA, organizing workers in factories and addressing international issues complemented and empowered their community organizing efforts. But if local groups belong to a national or international organization, in order to have any chance of success in the long run they must have some degree of independence. Of course, democratic mechanisms must be established whereby communities with competing interests can resolve problems in the interests of both the local and larger group. This type of integrated, federated democratic structure which both respects the integrity of local community organizing *and* provides for coordinated national leadership was not to be found in the theory or structure of the CPUSA. Communists understood that effective Party building developed first and best at the local level, where it was rooted in day to day community and industrial struggles. But their ultimate mistrust of decentralized, neighborhood organizing denied the long-term contribution that such grassroots community organizations could make in sustaining a national organization.

Saul Alinsky and the Back of the Yards Neighborhood Council

If I were asked to choose a single agency which most admirably represented all that our democracy stands for, I would select the Back of the Yards Council. All that you have done for the health, the social welfare, the economic advancement, and the happiness of the people in your community is to me one of the most heartening accomplishments of our time.

Adlai Stevenson, Governor of Illinois

The New Deal did not resolve the economic problems occasioned by the depression. For a time in 1936 the social welfare programs of the Second New Deal stimulated the economy, lowered unemployment, and increased purchasing power. But Roosevelt was essentially conservative in economic matters and preferred not to use deficit spending to maintain the economy. He feared the inflationary effect of federal expenditures which gave people money but did not stimulate investment and production. Accordingly, with the election of 1936 behind him, retrenchment began. Old programs were cut. New programs died on the planning table. Without the stimulus of federal funds, the economy declined again. In 1937 unemployment was almost as high as it had been in 1933. Four years of New Deal had not solved the economic crisis. Only preparation for and participation in World War II would do that.

The New Deal addressed more successfully the political crisis caused by the depression. FDR was unwilling to implement programs to halt the economic slide, but he eagerly promoted efforts which stopped the drift to political disorder and possible revolution. The "achievement" of the New Deal was that despite its failure to halt the depression it did prevent radical changes in the economic and political system. FDR's Second New Deal, for example, consciously stole the thunder of reform from left groups offering an alternative to liberal capitalism. But not without ironic consequences. Radicals, community activists, labor leaders, and workers had fought hard for social security and labor programs in the years before 1935. But they did so in relative isolation. Roosevelt sought to defuse and coopt this nascent movement with the passage of Second New Deal social welfare legislation, and he was able to win workers to the Democratic party in 1936 on a platform that responded to the grassroots demands first raised by radical groups like the Unemployed Councils. But most importantly this legislation and the new climate in Washington also helped initiate a nation-wide progressive social movement. In the years after 1936 workers and organizers forged in the CIO the largest and most militant workers movement the nation had seen since the late nineteenth century.

There is a complementary relationship between social movements and community organizing. Local organizing oriented to social change can exist without a movement, but it will not thrive for very long. When a movement develops, however, community organizations often ride the wave of mass support. In the context of the 1930s, local organizing before 1935 pushed politics in Washington to the left, Second New Deal programs in Washington helped stimulate a national industrial workers movement, and, in turn, the workers movement of the late 1930s and early 1940s spawned and stimulated a host of community organizing projects in working-class neighborhoods. These organizations functioned independently of the labor movement, but took their impetus, militant spirit, and democratic direction from it. The effort of Saul Alinsky in Back of the Yards is the best known and most significant of the CIO "community spin-offs."

Saul Alinsky was not the sort to leave folks impartial. They either loved or hated him. He was abrasive, forceful, witty, antagonistic, irreverent, and not above shocking or lying to people. Some saw him as a menace. Corporations hired detectives to watch him. The Oakland, California, city council banned him. Kansas City police jailed him. The right wing saw him as a Bolshevik agitator, the left as a "system confirming populist." One influential supporter, Charles Silberman, a prominent writer on race relations in the 1960s, saw Alinsky as the hope of democracy. What people were really responding to, however, was less frequently Saul Alinsky the person than the method of community organizing that came to be associated with him. Succinctly stated, if overly simplified, the Alinsky method of community organizing, "Alinskyism," has five essential elements:

(1) *The professional organizer is the catalyst for social change.* Alinsky emphasized the need for well-trained organizers. While Alinsky was seen as an apostle of democratic decision making and indigenous leadership, his method places a premium on the creative organizer "who can do it all." Because community organizing is perceived to be difficult, and because groups face constant pressures and crises that demand critical and correct decisions, Alinskyism stresses that a well-trained professional organizer is the most likely person to make the right choices. Democracy is important; the organizer is even more so.

(2) *The task is to build a democratic community-based organization.* In theory, community-based democracy is the essence of Alinsky organizing. Democracy is defined as the process of self-determination, in which ordinary people make the decisions about things that affect them. For Alinsky, truly democratic organizations can develop only within small spatial units, like a neighborhood, where there are natural bonds of unity and identification. Unlike most other leftist approaches to neighborhood organizing, Alinsky emphasizes gathering the support of traditional community leaders and institutions, people who already have local influence and a wide audience. The organizer is thus regarded as a catalyst, not a leader. Organizers are supposed to work from behind the scenes and work themselves out of a job by training "indigenous leaders" in the skills of community organizing. The people's organization is open to all members of the community—workers, merchants, and union and church leaders—for the broader and more representative the neighborhood coalition, Alinsky believed, the stronger the organization.

(3) *The goal is to win power.* Power is the *sine qua non* of Alinsky organizing. Only by organizing people to struggle for power can democracy be realized; only then can the "have nots" gain control of their communities and their lives. Neighborhood organizations are seen as the interest groups of the powerless and the unorganized. As unions represent factory workers in the labor market, so neighborhood organizations, Alinsky said, represent workers and their families outside the factory. The more power the neighborhood or-

ganization secures, the better it serves the interests of its members. Alinsky emphasized that since people act from self-interest rather than altruism, it is self-interest rather than exalted ideals that should motivate a "people's organization."

(4) *Use any tactics necessary.* This element of the Alinsky method achieved widest acclaim and criticism. He argued that people built organizations and won power by winning victories. He saw the traditional, conservative tactics used by most interest groups as inappropriate for neighborhood organizations of working-class people, who without money or political influence could achieve power only by using all types of creative and militant tactics. Negotiation, arbitration, protests, and demonstrations; boycotts, strikes, and mass meetings; picketing, raising hell, being diplomatic, and being willing to use anything that might work were key elements of Alinskyism. The end justifies the means, Alinsky counseled. Don't let tactics become predictable; don't be afraid to try something outrageous; keep the "enemy" off guard. On one occasion Alinsky advocated tying up all the bathrooms in Chicago's O'Hare airport; the first "shit-in," he called it. The more disturbing the tactic to those in power, the better the results. After all, he argued, working people will not get power, dignity, freedom, or equality as gifts or as acts of charity. They only win them through struggle. The organizer's role is to give people a sense of their potential power and "rub raw their resentments," so that they will be willing to take on those who keep them powerless. "Controversy was the seed of creation," Alinsky liked to say. "Life is conflict and in conflict you are alive." Through struggle people learn.

(5) *A people's organization must be pragmatic and nonideological.* Above all, Alinskyism advises that organizations must be practical if they are to be successful. A program should not be imposed on the neighborhood. All strategies should be considered. Nothing is more successful in organization building than successful actions. Again, the end, not the means, is most important. Alinsky believed that all revolutionary movements are generated from spiritual values and a belief in justice, equality, peace, and brotherhood. But he vehemently opposed "ideological" organizations. In his opinion they were undemocratic because their organizers came with preconceived ideals, goals, and strategies; they did not let neighborhood people make decisions. To let the people decide, Alinsky advocated, no matter what they decide, is the essence of democracy. Imposing a progressive ideology on the neighborhood is counterproductive and unnecessary. Only the progressive ideology that people developed themselves would last. Alinsky believed that democratic processes would yield democratic ideals and goals, and that, most importantly, organizers must have faith in democracy, in people and their traditions.

Alinsky grounded his pragmatism in the promise of pluralism. He believed that the economic and political system could work for working-class people if they could reach the bargaining tables of power. Once they got there, they could make those in power, whether government officials or corporate executives, responsive to their needs. Ideology would only limit the organization's ability to get to the bargaining table. In sum, the central premise of Alinskyism is that skillful, nonideological, democratic organizations willing to use any and all means can ultimately obtain more power and be more effective than ideological radical groups.[19]

The Alinsky method is usually presented, incorrectly, as a timeless approach developed outside of a specific historical context. The reverse is true. The Alinsky method of community organizing grew out of his experiences in Chicago in the 1930s as a professional social worker, his work with the CIO, and his coming of age amid the Communist party's Popular Front organizing campaigns. Alinsky was born in 1909 in Chicago, the son of orthodox, working-class, Jewish parents, and went to public schools and college there. It was at the University of Chicago, where he did undergraduate work in archaeology and graduate work in criminology, that he became interested in social welfare issues. From 1931 to 1940 he was employed as a research sociologist at the Institute for Juvenile Research, an organization that was investigating more effective and more democratic methods of curbing juvenile delinquency in Chicago. From this experience Alinsky came to value community-based organizing, learn the importance of professional organizers, and understand the need for democratic, indigenous participation in community work.

Of equal import was Alinsky's experience with the CIO. The extent of his actual association is unclear, but it seems he was a volunteer CIO organizer for about a year in 1937 and 1938. This experience, brief as it was, impressed him deeply. From his work with the CIO Alinsky learned the importance of struggling for power, of being willing to use a variety of tactics, especially conflict and confrontation, and of needing creative, dynamic, skilled, and committed organizers to mobilize working people. He said he learned that what he wanted to do most was apply the techniques he had "mastered" while working with the CIO to "the worst slums and ghettos, so that the most oppressed and exploited elements in the country could take control of their own communities and their own destinies." The early neighborhood efforts of Alinsky were therefore a kind of "trade union in the social factory"—an instrument at the neighborhood level through which people could bargain, struggle, strike, and advance their interests, just as they did in the CIO.[20]

Significant as well was his coming of political age in the early 1930s amid the radical ferment and growing antifascist movement in Chicago. Alinsky may have played down the role of ideology in the neighborhood organizations he helped develop, but that does not mean that he acted without a world view. All neighborhood organizing is based on certain political, social, and economic assumptions. Otherwise people would not become organizers. In his later years Alinsky saw himself as an "urban populist," but in the 1930s, when he first started out, he saw himself, in typical Popular Front terms, as a "professional antifascist." As a student he spent much of his time involved in Communist party and antifascist related activities, such as stopping evictions, fighting for public housing, and raising money for the International Brigade in the Spanish Civil War and for sharecroppers in the South.

While Alinsky claimed he never joined the Communist party, he seems to have been a "fellow traveler" who borrowed heavily from Party protest tactics and antifascist ideology without direct involvement in the party or acceptance of Comintern line and discipline. His association with the Party taught him that radical organizers, by organizing people for power in grassroots organizations, could counteract the cynicism and despair that led to fascist movements. Ever since the days of the American Revolution, he liked to recall, "radicals" had always served in the forefront of support for democracy and opposition to dictatorship. Moreover, the Popular Front strategy of antifascism brought home to Alinsky the importance of uniting with all potential allies in the community, a sort of neighborhood-based united front. Alinsky never sought to impose or even offer in a systematic way his ideology of antifascism to neighborhood groups. He always objected strongly to Communist autocratic methods. "Pragmatic pluralism" was more in keeping, Alinsky believed, with the process of neighborhood organizing. But his formative experiences with left-wing groups and causes in the 1930s laid the foundation for and fueled his work.

He first put the organizing method into practice in the Back of the Yards neighborhood of Chicago. This was the same neighborhood, thirty blocks south of the Loop and just west of the stockyards from which it got its name, that served as the locale for Upton Sinclair's *The Jungle*. In 1938 there were some 90,000 people living in this four-square-mile community. It was an old, stable, white, ethnic, working-class neighborhood, not uncommon to Chicago or northern industrial cities. Back of the Yards was 95 percent Catholic, mostly second and third generation Poles, Lithuanians, Czechs, and Ukranians. "This was not the slum across the tracks. This was the slum across the tracks from across the tracks," Alinsky said.

It was the nadir of all the slums of America, worse than Harlem is today [1970]. You had this dingy gray mile-by-two-miles of track, south of the big slaughter-houses. Clapboard frame houses, one behind the other. Many of them with outhouses. The neighborhood was practically all Catholic. You never saw so many churches. It made Rome look like a Protestant Gothic town.[21]

Ethnic national rivalry was as much a part of Back of the Yards as were its churches. Irish fought Poles, who fought Lithuanians, who fought Mexicans, all of whom fought blacks. The neighborhood had a militant labor heritage, but ethnic groups were so busy defending their small turfs against invaders they were unable to make gains as a class against the Swift and Armour meat-packing corporations. As the depression deepened, impoverished workers in Back of the Yards increasingly found scapegoats in blacks, Jews, and communists. Like most such neighborhoods in the 1930s, Back of the Yards had more than its share of fascist groups trying to get a following.[22] But for Alinsky and the CIO there was a more serious difficulty than fascist organizing in Back of the Yards, namely, the many priests, and the Catholic church in general, who vehemently opposed the CIO because of its association with "atheistic communists."

Alinsky became involved in the neighborhood through his work with the Chicago Area Project (CAP). The CAP created an experimental program to test whether a democratic, grassroots program to curb juvenile delinquency would be more effective than traditional, authoritarian, and externally imposed approaches. Sponsored by the project, Alinsky was sent into Back of the Yards in 1938 to organize neighborhood youth committees and encourage the kids to develop their own programs. Instead, Alinsky followed his own inclinations and in early 1939 organized a multi-issue neighborhood organization, the Back of the Yards Neighborhood Council, composed primarily of adults. The CIO was trying to form a Packers Union in the slaughterhouses and Alinsky believed that community-wide support in Back of the Yards for this organizing drive was more important than the juvenile delinquency project.[23]

Alinsky envisioned Back of the Yards as a first step in building a chain of progressive "people's organizations" nationwide. These community organizations would be led by neighborhood people, usually church and union leaders, and, Alinsky hoped, dedicated like the radicals in the CIO to an eternal war with the forces of injustice.[24] Alinsky recruited Joseph Meegan, a recreation director in the neighborhood, to help organize the Council. As it turned out, Meegan was a key contact, the indigenous leader Alinsky sought, a man of perpetual energy with a keen sense for the neighborhood and grassroots politics. Meegan and Alinsky set out to build a broad-based coalition in the neighborhood which by its breadth and strength would be a force that officials and corporate leaders in Chicago would have to reckon with.

The first hurdle was getting the priests to unite with radical labor organizers. Alinsky realized that the Catholic church was the most important institution in the community and that no neighborhood-wide organization in Back of the Yards could succeed without it. But the Catholic church possessed a long history of opposing radicals, and Herb March, the president of the packinghouse workers local in the area, was a Communist. Alinsky's forthright, populist style of organizing and his antifascist, noncommunist politics won the support of the liberal, auxiliary bishop of the Catholic Archdiocese of Chicago, Bernard J. Sheil, the founder of the Catholic Youth Organization and a public advocate of the CIO. Sheil proclaimed, for example, that "Catholics could not be in opposition to something that was so obviously for the benefit of all the people."[25]

But most clergymen were not as sympathetic. As Alinsky told the story, he conned other priests who were opposed to the CIO into joining his alliance of church and labor by playing on their pride, asking some if they were *afraid* to join an organization with Herb March in it, and telling others that Herb March "thought the world of them." There is little reason to believe that Alinsky duped the priests. Alinsky often fabricated stories in person and in his writings to make a point—in this instance, that organizers need to be "creative" and pragmatic. Some years later Alinsky described his organizing of the priests in Back of the Yards more realistically.

I'd go in to see this Catholic priest. I'd say, "I heard your sermon denouncing the union, calling it Communist. You know something, Father? Your people nodded and then walked out and joined the union. Know why? They're unemployed, their families are shot to hell and you're not doing a God damn thing about it. You sit on your ass in the sacristy, and you're no longer a shepherd of your flock. Everybody is disregarding you. You want to be a leader? Get back with your people, get out in the streets and fight for the union. The enemy is the meat packer; the enemy is low wages." So he'd do it.[26]

The priests who attended those first meetings of the Council acted out of informed self-interest. Neighborhood instability presented as serious a problem to the church as it did to neighborhood residents. Back of the Yards was in a state of rapid deterioration and neighborhood improvements could only enhance neighborhood stability and strengthen the local churches.

Joseph Meegan organized the first meeting in February 1939. By mid-April, Meegan was acting as temporary chairman of the Back of the Yards Neighborhood Council (BYNC), which included Communists, priests, merchants, and other neighborhood residents. In May the temporary organizing committee drew up a set of by-laws which established a democratic structure with provisions for an executive committee, regular meetings, and an active, participatory membership. Five months after Meegan and Alinsky began their work the BYNC held its first "Community Congress." The date was 14 July 1939, Bastille Day. Alinsky, Meegan, Bishop Sheil, Herb March, local priests, merchants, and 300 to 350 others attended, representing some fifty groups and organizations. "Its sole reason for coming into existence," Alinsky declared, "was to wage war against all evils which cause suffering and unhappiness." Ambiguous rhetoric, to say the least. But people knew what he was talking about. They knew that two days later the CIO packinghouse local was scheduled to go out on strike, and so the Congress passed a resolution in support of the union and its demands.

Alinsky and Meegan had done an impressive job of organizing support for the "neighborhood people's organization" and the United Packinghouse Workers union prior to the community meeting. Once the Congress began, the work was largely completed. In the Alinsky tradition a well-organized meeting should hold few surprises for the organizer. This is not exactly "democratic" but it gave the appearance of being so, and it was effective and efficient. The first Community Congress in Back of the Yards went smoothly as planned. It developed a rudimentary program for the BYNC which emphasized that on issues like labor, health, housing, and juvenile delinquency, the people in the neighborhood, regardless of their national background or political preferences, would unite for common ends. And it beckoned the "beginning of a new solidarity" between unions, churches, and the community.

The motives for this unity were clear to Alinsky. "I'm going around organizing, agitating, making trouble [in the Back of the Yards neighborhood]. At the end of three months, I had the Catholic Church, the CIO and the Communist Party working together. . . . I even got the American Legion involved, because they didn't have a goddam thing to do. They all had one thing in common: misery. Powerlessness."[27] Two days later they had something else in common: a victory. Faced with a united front of labor, community, and church opposition, the packinghouse industry caved in to the demands of the union and the next day raised wages in the stockyards from 39 cents to 55 cents an hour, a 41 percent increase.[28] This was quite a sterling beginning for the Back of the Yards Neighborhood Council. A newly formed community organization allied closely with church and union leaders had strengthened the bargaining position and helped win a major victory for stockyard workers.

Build the organization by winning victories, Alinsky emphasized. From 1939 to the close of World War II this strategy took form in Back of the Yards in an emphasis on service delivery. The Council, under the direction of Joseph

Meegan, set up an infant welfare station in Davis Park Square, where the city employed Meegan as a recreation director. The BYNC held a carnival to raise money, got people jobs in projects of the Works Progress Administration (WPA) and National Youth Administration (NYA), lobbied successfully for hot lunch and milk programs in the public and private schools, set up a floodlit baseball field on land leased from the railroads for one dollar a year, and founded a credit union to provide low-interest loans for neighborhood development projects. The Council also managed to involve teenagers in planning activities in the neighborhood, one of the results of which was a noticeable decline in juvenile delinquency rates.[29]

While service delivery demonstrated that the Council, with the active support of neighborhood people, could win concessions from the city and from business, social change was Alinsky's foremost goal and social action programs his primary interest. In 1944 the BYNC hired a social worker to deal with social work problems in the neighborhood, so that Joseph Meegan could devote more attention to political and social action issues. It was in the Council's social action work that Alinsky cultivated his "conflict" approach to community organizing, which raised strategy and tactics to paramount importance in community organizing, above and beyond questions of ideology, goals, and even democratic structure. Curiously, the use of militant conflict tactics was also what distinguished the Communist party's neighborhood work from most other groups in the 1930s. The "nonideological" Alinsky shrewdly mirrored Communist tactics without adopting communism or Party structure.

The BYNC took on corporations, the Chicago political machine, and even the federal government. In 1941 the Council supported a strike against one of the largest department stores in Chicago. The corporation was trying to break up a warehouse union to which many residents in Back of the Yards belonged. The BYNC set up a soup line to feed picketers, threatened a city-wide boycott of the store, and held a public, mock trial at which the department store owner was portrayed as an un-American fascist who refused to recognize the rights of the workers to form a union. None of these tactics sufficed. The threat of bad publicity, however, finally pushed the business to settle with its workers. The Council drew a simple lesson from this struggle. Conflict tactics, simply threatening confrontation, worked.[30]

In subsequent years the BYNC used conflict tactics to force the Nash-Kelly political machine in Chicago to cooperate with it. In 1943–44 the machine attempted to destroy the Council by firing Meegan from his city recreation job and evicting the Council from its park office. The Council, with CIO and church support, responded with a city-wide campaign to oppose Mayor Kelly's reelection. In a meeting with four Chicago aldermen just before the election, however, the BYNC agreed to stop its campaign. In return it saved Meegan's position and the park office and forced the political machine to recognize and cooperate with it. That same year the Council successfully used conflict tactics in a protest in Washington, D.C. Members went to the capital, inundated congressmen with demands to save a threatened milk and lunch program in the public schools, and came away with the program intact. Confrontation actions like these gave the Council and the Alinsky method the appearance of radicalism, and the reputation for being conflict-oriented and most effective.

The BYNC's accomplishments were impressive. From 1939 through the war and thereafter the Council developed into a powerful neighborhood organization capable of winning victories and demanding concessions from public and private power brokers alike. As early as 1941 Alinsky was able to list seventeen tangible victories won by the Council, among them funding from the city's community chest agency, the Community Fund of Chicago. More importantly, however, the Council's linking of radical union leaders with priests, small businessmen, and neighborhood residents formed a novel and powerful community-based coalition that gave the white, working-class people in Back of the Yards a sense of their ability and power to effect change and restore a sense of dignity and pride in their neighborhood and themselves.

These successes ultimately were overshadowed, however, by the drift of the BYNC to reaction and racism. If judged against Alinsky's own standards, the Council was a success in every aspect but one: it failed to counteract the antidemocratic sympathies in Back of the Yards which had led Alinsky in 1939 to call the neighborhood a "hell hole of hate." While in the early 1950s, more than a dozen years after the Council began, the white ethnic groups in the neighborhood no longer engaged in mortal combat with one another, they had rediscovered an old scapegoat for personal and community problems: blacks. Initially the BYNC attempted to deal positively with the issue of racial conflict. Taking its lead from the CIO experience, the Council sought to manage racial tensions, control rumors, discourage discrimination in neighborhood stores, and encourage priests to oppose racial prejudice in their sermons. But this interest in defusing racism did not last for long. By the early 1950s the Council had developed not into a force for social change but rather into a racist and conservative neighborhood protection organization. To say the least, what happened in Back of the Yards surprised and badly disappointed Alinsky.[31]

The goals of racial equality and democracy were very important to Alinsky. When he was starting out in the Back of the Yards he thought of himself as a professional antifascist fighting the widespread hatreds that existed among working people and eliminating the powerlessness which he felt bred this hatred and potentially fascist orientation. But in Back of the Yards, Alinsky consciously deemphasized ideology, antifascist or otherwise. Process was elevated in importance over goals and the organizing process was guided by pragmatism. The only political education that occurred focused on tactical questions such as how to build the organization or what was winnable.

The approach backfired in Back of the Yards. The BYNC was able to win victories and power. But no one put forth a clear antiracist ideology for members to respond to. Neither the organizers nor the leaders saw the importance of doing political education, especially around issues like racism. Nor did they build concrete coalitions with black organizations, coalitions which could teach through practical experience the folly and destructiveness of racism to all working and middle class people. The Council chose the path of least resistance and ignored all potentially divisive alliances or issues. Conflict between "us" and "them" was encouraged; "in conflict you are alive," Alinsky advocated. But conflict among members of the organization or among residents of the neighborhood over difficult issues like race, Alinsky regarded as destructive. Because the BYNC was community-based, not class-based like the Communist party, community unity and local objectives, not those of the multiracial working class, guided its direction.

Accordingly, Back of the Yards remained a white, ethnic enclave even though the neighborhood was in a direct line of expansion of blacks from Chicago's Near Southside slum, and even though the labor force in the meat packing plants after 1945 was increasingly composed of black workers. The Council was never avowedly racist. "We don't have time for race hatreds," Joe Meegan said. He suggested that blacks did not live in the neighborhood because they had little in common with the white ethnic residents there.[32] But Meegan was avoiding the issue. A study of the neighborhood undertaken in the early 1950s made clear that the churches and most of the leaders in the community opposed racial integration. The BYNC avoided an issue like integration for fear that it would cause dissension among its members and alienate its major supporter, the Catholic church. Alinsky claimed that his organizing method represented the whole neighborhood. But given the emphasis on working with established institutions, finding already established indigenous leaders, and winning immediate victories, the neighborhood elites—priests, small businessmen, and homeowners—became Council leaders and defined the goals and programs of the organization. Over time these elements tended to be the most conservative in the neighborhood.

Ultimately Alinsky's "populist" brand of community organizing in Back of the Yards supported rather than challenged the status quo, and Back of the Yards was not an isolated case. Much of Alinsky-style organizing in the 1960s and thereafter has taken on a parochial and nationalistic cast. This occurs in

part because the organizing method offers no critique of the political and economic system inside or outside the neighborhood, no analysis, other than
"powerlessness," of what causes and perpetuates poverty in the neighborhood, no solution to neighborhood problems beyond "getting power." Alinsky ultimately possessed a strong faith in the ability of liberal capitalism to
resolve these problems. FDR was as much his hero as was John L. Lewis. "I
think he thought the system, properly greased and oiled, worked," one Alinsky organizer put it.[33] Because Alinsky organizing does not question the economic foundation of the existing order or seek to replace the political system
that maintains that order, his approach does not recognize the possibility that
capitalism is not set up to serve the poor and working class, and that it is
ultimately not democratic. The Alinsky approach accepts an interest-group
model of democracy in which organizations compete for resources and pressure the system.

The BYNC did succeed better than most working-class neighborhood organizations because Alinsky was a most effective mobilizer, fund raiser, and
organizer trainer. His shrewd political instincts enabled him to select skillfully
from his experience with professional social work, the CIO, and left-wing organizations to fashion a populist organizing style more militant, democratic,
and effective than the social welfare approach of the settlements but less threatening to established powers than that of the Communist Party. In addition, the
backing of the Catholic church and CIO unions contributed to the BYNC's
limited success as a neighborhood-based interest group. Ultimately the Council grew in power and stature to become a recognized part of the establishment
in Chicago. But while the Council developed into a recognized political unit
in the city, to be acknowledged, offered some benefits, and manipulated, it did
not alter the economic causes that kept the neighborhood blighted, its residents
poor, fundamentally powerless, and unable to compete successfully, as could
people with money and power, in an interest-group style of politics.

The path of the BYNC mirrored in many instances that of the CIO which
had provided the initial stimulus and direction to Alinsky's political work. The
leadership of the CIO pursued a strategy of pragmatism, pluralism, and elitism
which Alinsky followed closely. Use all tactics, especially the threat of direct
action, to force the opposition to the bargaining table. Use Communist tactics
(the CIO even used Communist organizers), but offer no anticapitalist critique
of problems. Downplay ideology. Fight to get into the system. Not surprisingly, the CIO, like the BYNC, moved rightward until by the early 1950s it
was indistinguishable from the conservative, racist, and antiradical AFL.

In order to be effective, community organizing had to be more than the
pragmatic trade union in the social factory that Alinsky envisioned.[34] Alinsky's

method was on the mark in some respects. Working people do need experience with democratic process. They do need power. They do need victories to build strong organizations and give them a sense of their own power. But in poor and working class neighborhoods like Back of the Yards they also need political education. The people in the BYNC needed an analysis which addressed issues of class, race, and democratic values as well as tactics and power. This is not to suggest an analysis that they would swallow without question or thought, but rather one that provided an opportunity for discussion of important issues, a critique to learn from, respond to, struggle with, change, and use. Of course, the downfall of the Back of the Yards Neighborhood Council, like that of the CIO, derived from many factors inside and outside the organization. It did not fail simply because Alinsky chose to pursue an ultimately unsuccessful interest-group, nonideological style of neighborhood organizing. But as events in Back of the Yards were to prove, relying on the skills of an organizer and the influence of traditional community leaders was often not very democratic, and the programs that nonideological, populist-style organizations like the Back of the Yards Neighborhood Council pursued were sometimes not only undemocratic and ineffective in addressing economic problems, they were racist and reactionary as well.

CHAPTER 3

Conservative Neighborhood Organizing, 1946–1960

The Cold War and Antiradical Repression

During those McCarthy days anyone who organized or worked for civil rights was called a Communist. Anyone who talked about police brutality was called a Communist. Everywhere I went to organize they would bluntly ask, "Are you a Communist?" . . . It was fantastic how people were frightened. This was the McCarthy era and they were afraid of their shadows.

Cesar Chavez, organizer

They cry communism but their real fear is democracy.

Henry Wallace, Secretary of Commerce

In the postwar decade neighborhood organizing developed, as before, within a specific historical context that profoundly determined its nature and success. The dialectical relation between developments at the neighborhood level and those in the larger national arena was as evident in the postwar decade as it was in the 1930s. But the highly conservative and vehemently anticommunist political climate in the decade after the war was dramatically different than its prewar predecessor. After the war, radical organizers such as those in the Communist and Socialist parties increasingly found themselves isolated from what seemed like almost all segments of society. As radical organizing weakened under intense pressure, conservative efforts at building support for the

61

Cold War and "protecting" middle and upper-class communities became the dominant forms of neighborhood organizing. Of course, such efforts were not limited to the postwar decade. But the events of these years created an economic and political climate especially conducive to conservative programs and, more importantly, one so hostile to progressive social change as to give the period a decidedly conservative cast.

The fundamental problem that corporate and government leaders faced directly after World War II was how to avoid another depression during peacetime. The United States emerged in 1945 the premier international power. Britain, France, and, most of all, the Soviet Union had experienced vast physical destruction as well as loss of life during the war. The United States, on the other hand, increased its industrial and military might during the war and did not experience any physical destruction to its homeland. But despite this comfortable position as the world's leading power, business and government leaders remained fearful of another depression. After all, in 1945 a wartime economy, stimulated and directed from Washington, was the United States's only tried-and-proved solution to economic depression. At first their worries were allayed, as the vast reservoir of personal savings built up during the war—some $37 billion—fueled the economy from 1945 to 1947. People purchased all the consumer durables they had wanted but were unable to buy during the war. By 1947, however, personal savings were down to $5 billion. The financial fat stored during the war years had been quickly consumed.

To make matters more troublesome, the leaders of the United States did not find themselves undisputed kingpins of the international economy. The victory of World War II had to be shared with our allies, among them the Soviet Union. The Soviet Union could not compete successfully in economic matters with the United States but it did offer an ideological alternative to capitalism that proved attractive to leaders in colonial areas. This meant that after the war U.S. economic expansion abroad—in Africa, Asia, Europe, Latin America, and the Middle East—might not go unchallenged. Without dependable and continuous supplies of raw materials, cheap labor, and new markets for U.S. consumer durables, corporate profits would recede. Amid fear of another depression and the related Soviet challenge, business and government leaders also found themselves in the late 1940s faced with inflation, labor strikes, and protests against racial discrimination, all of which presented additional threats to the internal economic and social order.

The prescription to these ills most corporate leaders favored reflected their preference for a "free market" solution: resolve these problems at home and abroad through peacetime economic growth. This meant out-competing the Soviets abroad and buying social order and economic progress at home with a booming economy rooted in overseas expansion, time-payment purchases of consumer durables, and growth industries such as petrochemicals, electronic technology, and suburban development. But supporters of this corporate liberal vision never got the opportunity to test their plan.

Instead, beginning with the Truman Doctrine in 1947 defense spending served as the cornerstone of U.S. economic growth. The political economy of the emerging Cold War, which emphasized the necessity of containing communism and Soviet imperialism, demanded large allocations for the military and for "foreign aid." With the Cold War serving as its rationale, federal expenditures, especially military allocations, laid a foundation for almost uninterrupted growth from 1947 to 1973 and resolved for some two and a half decades the question of how to prevent another economic collapse. According to one historian,

The military budget . . . became the sponge which absorbed much, if not always all, excess industrial capacity, thereby putting a floor under the capitalist economy. The Pentagon's annual 8 to 10 percent of the GNP provided that critical break-even point of economic stimulus which made much of the rest of the economy viable and far less perturbed by a crisis of demand. . . . As a multiplier in stimulating business it greatly exceeded virtually all others. Until other difficulties arose—as they inevitably would— capitalism could at least resolve the problem of insufficient demand so troublesome during the interwar years.[1]

Of course, "military Keynesianism" was not the only basis of prosperity. New industries, new technologies, suburbanization, the advertising business, the proliferation of automobiles, and highway development, to name a few, also fueled the economy of the fifties and sixties. But allocations to the "military-industrial complex," as Dwight Eisenhower called it, was the rock upon which all else rested. By the time of the Korean War, the Cold War, economic prosperity, and the resolution of domestic problems had become inextricably tied to each other.

Cold War prosperity eliminated many of the domestic problems faced during the depression of the 1930s. Social disorder, mass discontent, rebellion were put to rest in the 1950s by an economic growth rooted in U.S. expansion abroad and military expenditures at home. But this solution raised other problems that had to be resolved if the Cold War society were to function efficiently without disruption and with a minimum of overt coercion. First, how were people to be mobilized to support unpopular foreign interventions, such as that in Korea? Second, given that welfare expenditures had to be cut back or held constant to allow funds to be allocated for defense without taxes skyrocketing, how were segments of the population who did not share in the prosperity to be pacified? Third, how were government and business leaders to overcome the serious shortage of workers and yet keep the lid on labor militancy at a time when demand for labor exceeded supply? Fourth, how could the economy meet the "rising expectations" of affluence now shared by racial minorities as well as those in less industrialized regions of the nation, most notably the South?

To meet these problems called for more than military Keynesianism. Prosperity and a continuous stream of "free world" propaganda was sufficient to ensure the support of most Americans for the Cold War. The promise of economic mobility, as represented in increasing opportunities to move from blue to white collar jobs, to go to college, and to move out of the city into the suburbs, sufficed to keep most people in the nation content and united in support of "us" and opposed to "the Red menace." But not everyone could be counted on to be so agreeable or quiescent. So the velvet glove of prosperity was accompanied by the iron fist of political repression. Anticommunism at home, called "McCarthyism" by those who considered the phenomenon limited to only one man and a few years in the early 1950s, branded all radical critics of the war economy as traitors, liberals as Communist sympathizers, and opposition to the Cold War as skirting treason. This repression, unpopular with many Americans, was intended to mute class and race tensions and prevent any challenges to the political economy of the Cold War by eliminating all leftist and progressive criticism.

Prosperity and repression formed a powerful recipe for halting dissent and few did not fall in behind the cold warriors. The CIO purged its radical affiliates, merged with the conservative AFL in 1955, joined the ranks of cold warriors, and offered up a stable and less militant work force which supported military expenditures and the Cold War. Ex-radicals and liberals joined the crusade against communism, often calling for America to close ranks and fortify the bastions of democracy throughout the world. Most liberals found the tactics of repression upsetting, but remained silent, partially out of fear, and supported the goals and programs of the Cold War. Some activists tried to sidestep the repression. The Community Political Organization (CPO), a left-oriented organization formed in the Chicano community of East Los Angeles in the late 1940s, changed its name in 1947 to Community Service Organization (CSO) so that it would not be confused with the Communist party (CP). David Rosenstein, the president of the National Federation of Settlements, said it even more succinctly in 1953, at the height of the repression: "People in the neighborhoods are afraid to join anything."[2]

In the highly centralized, conservative, Cold War economy there seemed to be little place or encouragement for neighborhood organizing. The roots of the "affluent society" were in economic and military expansion at the national and international level, not in local developments. A contemporary political science text declared in 1953 that "As yet, it is too early to say with assurance that neighborhood groups and practices are disappearing from American cities, but such evidence as we possess indicates that they have been declining and may be expected to diminish further."[3] The burial, however, was premature. Social welfare community workers, for example, believed that community-based, self-help projects remained an important and viable part of American urban life, and they emphasized that community development activities were a far more positive approach to winning the Cold War than were repression and fear. For them, the best way to advance U.S. interests was through community programs at home and abroad, such as the United Community Defense Services and the vast number of community development projects sponsored by the United States and the United Nations throughout the world. These efforts would attest, they felt, to the practice and success of democratic capitalism. Such programs, along with the thousands of neighborhood improvement associations which organized in the nation's new suburbs, best suited the conditions of prosperity and the conservative political climate of the era and became, therefore, the dominant forms of neighborhood organizing in the years 1946 to 1960.

Community Development and the Cold War

Never before on so vast a scale has any nation attempted to build military strength and at the same time expand its consumer goods, and assist in the arming of allies throughout the world. It is a very bold and challenging program . . . [which] calls for a large measure of devotion and unity among our people.

Charles E. Wilson, former head of General Electric,
Director of Defense Mobilization

It is becoming ever more clear that our communities hold in their hands significant power to aid or hinder mankind's struggle for a free world and peace. The unsung job of the community's schools, homes, and factories are the "home work" of American patriots. The call to sane, unflagging, high-visioned community effort is the Call to the Colors.

Harold Buttenheim, Chairman, American
Council for the Community

During the winter of 1950–51 the NBC network broadcast a radio program, "The People Act," every Saturday evening at 7:00 P.M. (EST). Hosted by narrator Ben Grauer and field reporter Elmore McKee, the show's thirteen broadcasts reported "real life stories" of Americans who organized together to solve everyday problems in "typically American communities" like New York City, Baltimore, Toledo, Decatur, Alabama, and Sylvania, Arkansas. These stories told of locally initiated efforts to build a community hospital, ease labor tensions, promote better schools, form a conservation district, clean up a slum area, and enforce local housing codes. Some of these efforts, the program noted, were successful; others were not. But it was the manifestation of the process of democracy, not the results of community action, that most interested Elmore McKee.

The idea for the series took shape, McKee said, in 1947 while working with the American Friends Service Committee in European postwar reconstruction efforts. He was assigned to develop self-help neighborhood centers in the badly damaged areas of Berlin and Frankfurt. Through his work McKee concluded that the roots of fascism rested in the German people's dependence on experts and authority figures, but he wondered whether America was any less authoritarian. How healthy, after all, was direct democracy in the United States amid the anti-Communist atmosphere after the war? Upon his return to the States he toured 15,000 miles and discovered that there were people who were doing things for themselves in hundreds of communities.

These examples of American neighborhood democracy clearly had meaning beyond our borders, McKee noted. The thirteen case studies chosen from his travels for the NBC broadcasts were aired throughout the United States and beamed overseas by Voice of America and the Armed Forces Network to Americans and "friends of democracy" abroad. NBC advertised them as good examples of freedom and cooperation in the United States, "democracy in action." A second series, covering twenty six additional community self-help projects, followed in 1952, supported by a grant from the Ford Foundation and aired this time by CBS. Community organizing had a place in the Cold War, and liberal proponents of democracy like McKee, philanthropic associations like the Ford Foundation, and propaganda outlets like Voice of America appreciated its ideological value.

But McKee was also a sincere advocate of neighborhood organizing and grassroots democracy. A Quaker, he believed that citizen participation in decision making should be the basis of democratic society. He reported in a book, *The People Act,* which chronicled ten case studies from the radio show, that what he had found in the United States was less rosy than the radio programs made it seem. He had found a general lack of faith in people, the same uncertainty about democracy he had encountered in Germany. He had come home to an America involved in a witch-hunt for subversives, hardly the stuff that democracy was made of. The community efforts described in the book and on the radio programs, McKee wrote, were not so much examples of widespread "real democracy" as important bulwarks of a "democracy on trial."[4]

McKee saw America's weakest link as well as the hope for a "free world" in the practice of democracy at the grassroots level. For him as well as other liberal proponents of decentralization, community development projects at home and abroad could strengthen democracy, and in turn strengthen efforts of the United States in the Cold War. A group called the American Council for the Community (ACC), composed of distinguished liberals such as John Dewey, Stuart Chase, and Frank P. Graham, organized a North American Conference on the Community in the spring of 1950 because, they said, "the North American democracies have the vital job of demonstrating the workability of responsible freedom in the modern world. . . . The heart of the job lies in the local community units. These are the masonry blocks with which free nations and a peaceful world are built." One year later the ACC proclaimed that all communities in America needed to be strengthened and integrated "to meet any eventuality—whether it be cold war, hot war, or no war."[5]

The practice of community organizing in the postwar era was deeply affected by the economic policies and political climate of the Cold War. Most of the community work of radicals either came to a halt or took a more conservative approach. For Saul Alinsky, the anticommunism of the early 1950s made a wasteland of his community organizing. People were afraid to stick their necks out and get involved. Radical activity atrophied. Social welfare community work, on the other hand, adjusted itself to the new political realities and enlisted in the crusade against communism. Not all liberal community workers joined the cause, of course, but for those who did, the goals, programs, clients, sites of projects, and available funding for neighborhood work were determined by Cold War objectives.

Of course, the major community development projects of this period sponsored by the United States took place in Third World nations, not within our borders. Community development abroad was not simply a process to create conditions of economic and social progress for the whole community and with its active participation, as the United Nations defined it in 1955. It was also intended to "prevent the spread of Communism" and "to build customers for an ever expanding [U.S.] economy," as Phillip Ryan of the National Social

Welfare Assembly frankly noted.[6] The subject of community organizing projects abroad is fascinating and instructive, but one, unfortunately, beyond the bounds of this study.

The primary community organization project within the boundaries of the United States in the decade after World War II began with discussions in the fall of 1950 to establish the United Community Defense Services (UCDS). UCDS was the joint effort of the National Social Welfare Assembly (the leading professional council of social work agencies) and the Community Chests and Councils of America (the leading funding source for voluntary social welfare activities). These two agencies brought together fifteen social welfare organizations to organize communities "destabilized" by military-related projects.[7] The United Community Defense Service was one element of the United Defense Fund (UDF), a social welfare program subsidized by local Community Chests to address the "emergency" defense situation in Korea and Southeast Asia. Most UDF funds during the heyday of the organization from 1950 to 1955 went to its best known program, the United Servicemen's Organization (USO).

UCDS was charged with easing social problems that accompanied defense mobilization in "critical defense areas." Most of these communities were located outside of large cities. The 227 critical defense areas cited by the federal government in 1951 included 740 separate communities and towns, 86 percent of which had populations of under 25,000 before "defense impact." After "defense impact" more than twenty million people lived in these areas, more than one sixth of the nation's population. Critical defense areas housed armed forces bases, defense-related production plants, and hydrogen bomb development projects. Many critical defense area communities were located in the West and the South, reflecting the flow of defense contracts and corporate capital after the war to more rural areas with lower labor costs, lower taxes, fewer unions, and congressmen with seniority in Washington.

Not all critical defense areas were "destabilized" by the installation of a new defense industry or army base. UCDS estimated that one quarter were "overwhelmed" and one third needed outside assistance. At the Savannah River site, on the border of South Carolina and Georgia, the H-bomb project there urbanized and industrialized this rural area with "a force almost comparable to the bomb itself," reported the president of the UCDS:

Everyone living on the plant site—a tract of land 20 miles long and 15 miles wide—was forced to move out. Even the dead could not rest in peace. 100 cemeteries were to be moved outside the restricted area. People began flooding in, until perhaps 300,000 new people were added. The population of Augusta [Georgia] doubled. Some of the small South Carolina towns increased as much as ten times. . . . Something close to chaos resulted.[8]

Insufficient housing was the major problem in most defense areas. Police protection, health care, hospitals, schools, sewage disposal, and water supply were also usually insufficient or nonexistent. The demand for services grew with the population. In China Lake, California, the site of a newly developed Naval Ordnance testing station, population boomed from 100 in 1944 to over 20,000 people ten years later. But inadequate services were not the only problem. Prostitution, gambling, night clubs, and transient trailer camps sprang up on the strips leading to and from the army bases and plants in defense areas. And racial discrimination and conflict made conditions more difficult in critical defense communities in the South. In Savannah River, housing for blacks in nearby Augusta had been severely overcrowded before the advent of the atomic energy project. To make matters worse, two housing developments built with government funds and intended for blacks were taken over by Du Pont and rented instead to their white employees. At the AEC site in Paducah, Kentucky, guards denied access to the premises to black applicants for jobs. In Savannah River, Du Pont did not hire black workers until pressure from the National Urban League and a need for workers forced them to do so.[9]

Few community residents—black or white—opposed the defense projects. Local officials, landowners, and businessmen stood to make a good deal of money from the boom; workers stood to improve their standard of living and secure stable, permanent employment. Many local residents, however, were bitter about the extent and intensity of the transformation to their area and the concomitant social problems that the community was left to handle. A community worker described the situation in Paducah, Kentucky:

The people are resentful. They feel they did not want the H-bomb installation but that it was put there by the Federal Government and so it should take the responsibility for military problems relating to it such as housing, etc. There is a lot of bitter feeling in the community and marked cleavage between the former leaders and the new labor leaders. Finally there is much resentment toward outsiders coming into the community and telling them what to do.[10]

In the military spirit of the day, the United Community Defense Services labeled its efforts to resolve social problems in critical defense areas "Operation Community Organization: National." Time and time again, UCDS leaders declared that community organizing was critical to the defense of the United States, that community organizers could be used as domestic "troubleshooters" and could assist in the Cold War struggle against communism. This interest in international issues was relatively novel for community workers. But their goals and methods were traditional.

UCDS organizers usually went into a community alone and uninvited. They visited the local chamber of commerce or welfare office, familiarizing themselves with local problems and resources. After this initial "reconnaisance" and after reporting back to UCDS central headquarters in New York City, organizers tried to gather support for social welfare projects. Projects ranged from establishing health investigations, day camps, and immunization clinics to developing permanent social welfare institutions and planning councils. The type of project usually depended on which member group in UCDS sent in a community worker. The American Social Hygiene Association organizer usually addressed problems of prostitution and gambling. Community workers from the National Recreation Association focused on recreational programming. All organizers in UCDS, however, emphasized the importance of getting the backing of influential leaders in the business, political, and social life of the community.

Securing the support of local elites was especially important because UCDS was largely ignored by federal and corporate funding sources. This was not because UCDS was out of step with the Cold War politics of the era. In their appeals for support, UCDS always underscored the role that professional community work played in supporting the Cold War. In 1954 and 1955 UCDS hired Elizabeth Wickenden, a leader in the field of social work and a consultant with contacts in Washington, to draft funding proposals. Her analysis, overwhelmingly approved by UCDS leaders, emphasized the symbiotic nature between social welfare expenditures and national security. In a democracy, she stated, voters and their elected representatives determine national policy. Military defense protected these common policies and our common institutions. The report continued:

Once a democratic nation commits itself to the need for an expanded program of military defense such a program must be considered to exist for the benefit of all its people. No sharp distinctions can properly be made in this situation between considerations affecting people's "welfare" and those affecting their "defense," for defense has become an accepted safeguard to their welfare.[11]

What was good for the military, the government, and defense-related industries not only was good for the people but reflected their democratic will.

The role of social welfare community organizers, accordingly, was to "lubricate" the total social machine. In this connection social welfare programs would take the place of repression. "Facilitating social services substitutes in a democracy for the terror and compulsion used by totalitarian nations in forcing their citizens to adapt to defense objectives," Wickenden wrote. People in a democracy had to be willing to sacrifice immediate benefits, including their own freedom of action, she said, in the service of the national interest.[12] In a class-stratified society, where some made immense profits and others struggled to make monthly payments, it was the role of government and community work to equalize the burden as much as possible and to convince people of the need to sacrifice for national objectives. Community workers in UCDS, like their social welfare predecessors, fundamentally accepted the existing system and sought, within the limits of that system, to ameliorate social inequalities in support of the objectives of those in power.

But the 1950s differed from the early twentieth century. Arguments like Wickenden's on the critical importance of social welfare fell on ears more attuned to other concerns. Unlike the atomic energy sites developed during World War II, where the federal government constructed and operated whole defense communities, Atomic Energy Commission sites and critical defense areas in the 1950s received little, if any, federal support. The Federal Security Agency, which supervised the defense community mobilization, received about $4 million annually during the height of the Korean War. Most of these funds went to finance water and sewer projects, and Congress made sure to legislate that none of it could be used for health, day care, recreation, or other social welfare services.

Corporate support for social projects was little better, and then only because they could not afford to be as aloof as the federal government. In Savannah River, Du Pont sent representatives to community meetings, built approximately 7,500 barracks, bought two housing projects for white personnel, and hired a recreational worker for programs in the trailer courts. They also paid higher wages than local businesses. From their point of view that was a sufficient contribution to the community. The policy of Du Pont, one field worker reported, was "to avoid entanglements that would result in their operating any type of community project or pertaining thereto."[13] A similar pattern was evident in other critical defense communities. In Arkadelphia, Arkansas, a center of bauxite production, the element critical to the production of aluminum, Reynolds Aluminum said they were only interested in the social welfare programs of UCDS "in the event problems develop."[14] The contribution of government and corporate sources to local community welfare programs was marginal at best because it did not have to be otherwise.

In places and times of economic crisis or social turmoil professional social welfare community workers find support for their efforts. This was true in the period 1900–1920 and the 1930s, and would again be so in the 1960s. But it was not the case in the 1950s. The fifties were prosperous. A large percentage of the population improved their socioeconomic position. But prosperity alone does not explain the period's conservatism and lack of concern for social welfare programs. The decades before World War I and the 1960s were periods of prosperity which nonetheless evidenced much interest in social reform programs as a means of addressing problems of social disorder and insurgency. The fifties, however, had a more effective means of maintaining social control and unity. Massive doses of propaganda promoting united opposition to communism were reinforced by a campaign of national and local repression.

The combined effect of prosperity, propaganda, and repression was profound. No one in the nation remained unaffected, certainly not community workers. In critical defense communities organized labor strongly supported the Cold War consensus. At the same time, loyalty oaths and tight security measures made dissent treasonous. In many of these communities, and especially in the South, something akin to a police state existed for blacks and radicals. Even liberal critics kept quiet. There was little threat of insurgency or opposition. In such places and periods of history, social welfare community workers are isolated and ignored. They are left to perform minimal tasks in an unsympathetic, unsupportive environment. They are simply not needed to ameliorate social problems or maintain social order.

Such was the situation facing community workers in the early 1950s. Member organizations and organizers for UCDS openly supported Cold War objectives, nevertheless, because they believed in them and because support for the Cold War was the best method to secure at least minimal funds to keep social welfare programs alive. But community workers would have to wait until the 1960s for large-scale funding. Then, when the federal government was faced with urban rebellions throughout the nation, a new set of political leaders began to realize again the function liberal community work could play in the political economy.

Neighborhood Improvement Associations, 1880–1948

Mr. Speaker, there must have been a celebration in Moscow last night; for the Communists won their greatest victory in the Supreme Court of the United States on yesterday when that once august body proceeded to destroy the value of property owned by tens of thousands of loyal Americans in every state in the Union by their anti-covenants decision [*Shelley* v. *Kraemer*].

John Rankin, Representative from
Mississippi, 4 May 1948

The most prominent form of neighborhood organizing in the 1950s were the neighborhood improvement associations that proliferated throughout the nation, most notably in new, affluent suburban areas. No matter what their title—civic clubs, homeowners or property owners associations, or neighborhood protection organizations—all shared common objectives, organizing styles, and structures. The improvement approach to neighborhood organizing is distinct from the two more widely known methods discussed this far, the liberal social welfare and radical activist approaches. In improvement associations the goal is twofold: enhancement and protection. Enhancement includes efforts to secure public services, promote uniform and homogenous development, control taxes, provide neighborhood-based self-help programs or services, and, in general, oversee the development of the community. Most importantly, however, the association serves to protect property values and community homogeneity by opposing commercial development and excluding members of lower classes and racial minorities.

Moreover, neighborhood improvement associations do not, as a rule, use protest or confrontation tactics to advance their objectives. On an intraneighborhood issue they generally rely on peer pressure. In relations with other neighborhoods or city officials, the leaders of improvement associations work quietly and cooperatively behind the scenes as interest-group "brokers" for their neighborhood. While membership is quite high, in many communities running as much as 100 percent, membership activity is usually quite low. At such times when a neighborhood is "threatened," people will come to meetings and get involved in the association. Generally, however, a handful of lawyers, businessmen, realtors, developers, or politicians living in the neighborhood organize the association and play the leading and only active roles. There usually are no paid staff and no external professional organizers. The organization funds itself privately through fees and colllections within the neighborhood, and rarely does affiliation or activity extend beyond neighborhood or city limits.

Neighborhood improvement associations are not usually considered by either social scientists or activists as part of the history of community organizing. Their constituency is very different from the social welfare and radical activist styles of neighborhood organizing. Until most recently, neighborhood improvement associations were generally not found in working-class and minority neighborhoods. Moreover, in the improvement association approach to neighborhood organizing, organizers are usually indigenous leaders, whereas in social welfare and radical activist approaches the distinction between organizers and leaders is critical. Most significantly, the improvement association is fundamentally conservative; usually it can be found resisting, rather than joining, progressive social change efforts. This conservative form of community organizing, however, predates the other approaches to neighborhood organizing, and, according to one historian, is more common, lasts longer, and can exhibit more pressure in political politics than organizing efforts in working-class and slum neighborhoods. This is to be expected, given the fact that people in these neighborhoods are more affluent and generally more able to join formal organizations than are people in slum communities.[15]

Like most forms of neighborhood organizing, this type has changed little since its inception. The first neighborhood improvement associations developed along with the first suburban neighborhoods in the 1880s. As the industrial city grew and as trolley lines made it possible for the more affluent to live further from the central business district, "streetcar suburbs" developed in cities as diverse as Boston, Chicago, and Houston. Often these new communities were part of the city proper, or in the process of being annexed. They were not autonomous localities, nor did they want to be. The costs of lighting, drainage, schools, and police and fire protection were too much even for upper-class communities. It was cheapest and most expedient to secure these amenities by remaining part of the city and using political influence to get the city to provide them.

In the generation after 1880 neighborhood improvement associations, especially those in more affluent communities, organized successfully to bring pressure on city officials to provide basic urban services to their neighborhoods. Baltimore, for example, had more than thirty neighborhood associations within the city and its suburbs by 1900. The Federated Improvement Association, an organization of neighborhood improvement associations in Cincinnati, included thirty six neighborhood affiliates and 8,000 members in 1913.[16] A path-breaking sociological study of neighborhood and local life in Columbus, Ohio, in the early twentieth century captured in its description of neighborhood organization in an affluent suburb there the essence of these early improvement associations.

It was promoted by a number of the most enterprising citizens of the community including one of the city's most prominent councilmen. No local organization of the city has been more active in the promotion of local interests, or has achieved more for the territory served than the Hilltop Improvement Association. Its field of activities included negotiations with the city council for the procuring of local satisfactions, such as a recreation building, street-car accommodations, city deliveries, etc. It has also stimulated local pride in the care of property and in the repulsion of undesirable commercial encroachments, and at the same time has done much to engender a feeling of neighborliness and sociability among the people."[17]

Likewise, neighborhood improvement associations sprouted throughout Chicago's suburbs. The Woodlawn Improvement Association organized in the affluent Woodlawn neighborhood in 1882 to keep the sidewalks in this large and then sparsely settled district free of snow. In 1903 the Neighborhood Center Committee of the Woman's Club of Chicago organized a Neighborhood Improvement League of Cook County, with some thirty participating neighborhood organizations. By 1909 there were fifty-five member associations in the League. Almost all of them represented newly developed suburban communities. They focused on securing public services from the city or providing their own basic necessities. The Fine Arts Society of Oak Park, initially the Oak Park Improvement Association, expanded its art criticism to "conducting spring cleaning campaigns, making public inspection of the entire village, and photographing all property not cleaned up, for publication."[18]

Certainly not all neighborhood associations were based in peripheral communities as affluent as the Hilltop in Columbus or those noted in Chicago. Nor were all as successful. As with most transactions in interest group politics, the extent to which neighborhood improvement associations secured public services or supplied their own neighborhood needs was directly proportional to the economic and political power held by individual members of the association. What makes people with less power less effective in city politics also explains why inner-city and working-class neighborhood organizations were less effective as neighborhood interest groups. Because the people moving to the urban periphery in the years before World War I were from the more affluent and influential segments of the urban population, their neighborhood associations commanded a disproportionate amount of political and economic resources for improvement efforts.

The initial concerns of the first improvement associations were community enhancement and development, although in the South neighborhood protection practices accompanied enhancement from the outset. William Wilson, the developer of the Woodland Heights neighborhood in Houston, advertised in 1909 that the neighborhood deed included "protective restrictions" which preserved "the original beauty of the property," banned commercial development, forbade the sale of liquor in the subdivision, and detailed architectural restrictions for new homes and home improvements. "You are also protected from colored neighbors, as the lots are sold to white people only," Wilson assured.[19] While deed restrictions were common in suburban neighborhoods throughout the nation at this time, race and ethnic restriction clauses appeared more prominently in the South where a legalized and official system of segregation was thoroughly enforced.

The black population was relatively small in most Northern cities prior to 1914, and the system of *de facto* segregation by class and race served to keep blacks and most working-class people out of the developing suburban fringes. But the color line was no more permeable in the North than in the South. In 1897 the Woodlawn Improvement Association in Chicago threatened to "make war" on a hotel on the outskirts of the neighborhood that was renting rooms to black customers. Five years later a similar confrontation ensued with a hotel owner who sought to convert suites into apartments for blacks. The Association stopped him as well, and by 1910 it had effectively removed any black presence in the neighborhood.[20]

Around the time of World War I improvement associations in outer city neighborhoods in the North began to shift their focus from neighborhood enhancement to neighborhood protection, from securing services to excluding lower classes and racial minorities, especially blacks. They now consciously resisted social change, advocated racial segregation, attacked "block busters," and even allied with right-wing organizations like the Ku Klux Klan. In 1919 in cities across the nation racial tension heightened as white ethnic neighborhood organizations, in alliance with city officials and realtors, sought to prevent blacks from moving into their neighborhoods.

Neighborhoods like Woodlawn in Chicago, once the preserves of the affluent, were now inhabited by first and second generation immigrants who had managed to climb a notch up the economic ladder. Segregationist hiring and residential practices continued to keep the black population poor and ghettoized. Until World War I they posed no "threat" to the homogeneity of the once upper-class, now middle-class, outer-city neighborhoods. From 1915 to 1920, however, in cities like Chicago, the black population more than doubled as black laborers came North to fill industrial jobs created by the war. As housing deteriorated in the black ghetto under the massive population pressure and as competition for housing grew increasingly keen, the small, black middle class sought to move out. Before the war this would not have been a problem. It was common in Northern cities for a few blacks to move into a neighborhood and slowly but steadily for the whites to "relinquish" it, just as the upper class had relinquished it before to the white, ethnic middle class. As long as available new housing and space existed, class and racial conflict was generally avoided. But by 1917 there was little available housing, and tensions began to mount.

Resistance to neighborhood change and integration took many forms. Racial zoning had been declared illegal in 1917 when the Supreme Court in *Buchanan* v. *Worley* deemed unconstitutional a Louisville racial zoning ordinance that restricted areas in the city to whites and other areas to blacks. In the absence of outright judicial support, however, improvement associations in many cities formed a "united front" to keep their neighborhoods "white." In Hyde Park–Kenwood in Chicago the association used newspaper publicity, blacklisted realtors, held mass rallies, boycotted merchants, and intimidated black residents. When that failed to stop black immigration, vigilante groups armed with pipes, bricks, bats, and bombs stormed the house of black "invaders." From 1917 to 1921 fifty-eight homes recently purchased by black families were bombed in Chicago, about one every twenty five days. In the spring of 1919 two bombs went off each month. Efforts like these at "neighborhood protection" led to race riots in Chicago, St. Louis, and New York.[21]

Bombings and tension continued in "disputed" neighborhoods of America's large, Northern cities in the first years of the 1920s, but began to die down with the housing boom that began in 1922. The process of segregated neighborhood succession continued steadily, if slowly, in most Northern cities from 1922 to 1926 as white, ethnic, middle-class neighborhoods bordering black ghettoes became middle-class black communities. For the duration of the housing boom, improvement associations did little to stop the pattern of residential racial change. When the boom ended around 1926, however, white homeowners and realtors sought a new device to protect their investments. Unable to secure legislation to create and zone exclusive racial areas, neighborhood improvement associations, supported by realtor associations like the National Association of Real Estate Boards (NAREB), drafted "restrictive covenants" primarily to exclude racial minorities. In 1924 NAREB gave state commissions the right to revoke the license of any realtor who introduced blacks into white neighborhoods against the wishes of that community. This policy was implemented prior to 1924 by local realty boards.

In 1926 the U.S. Supreme Court lent its weight to the issue, upholding the validity and enforceability of restrictive covenants. Covenants proliferated throughout Northern cities. By 1930 more than 175 property owners' associations in Chicago had enforceable racial covenants and three fourths of all residential property in the city was bound by such restrictions. None of this property could be sold or rented to blacks.[22]

The history of neighborhood improvement associations in Chicago was repeated throughout the nation. Associations focused on community enhancement projects, especially when the neighborhood was first developing. Community development improved property values and the quality of community life. People were willing to move on to "better" neighborhoods, however, as long as housing was available and affordable. Commitment to "the neighborhood" was as transient as the urban population of the early twentieth century. In times of housing shortage or recession, however, when people did not have the money to move, white neighborhood improvement associations bordering black or lower-class ghettos took on a decidedly segregationist and militant stance.

The Cold War had a profound impact on neighborhood improvement organizations. United States competition with the Soviet Union abroad demanded something be done at home about institutionalized racist practices. American political and business leaders found it difficult to present themselves as leaders of the "free world" in Asia, Africa, and South America, while the nation perpetuated a humiliating and exploitative system of legalized racial segregation within its own borders. As President Truman put it in 1946:

Our position in the post-war world is so vital to the future that our smallest actions have far-reaching effects. . . . We cannot escape the fact that our civil rights record has been an issue in world politics. The world's press and radio are full of it. . . . Those with competing philosophies have stressed—and are shamelessly distorting—our shortcomings. . . . They have tried to prove our democracy an empty fraud, and our nation a consistent oppressor of underprivileged people. This may seem ludicrous to Americans, but it is sufficiently important to worry our friends. The United States is not so strong, the final triumph of the democratic ideal is not so inevitable that we can ignore what the world thinks of us or our record.[23]

The National Association for the Advancement of Colored People (NAACP) was quick to capitalize on this new "liberalism" in Washington. While its opposition to restrictive covenants had begun in 1925, in twenty years of nearly constant litigation the NAACP had made little headway in securing a clear-cut decision against them. The situation, however, seemed more promising in 1945. In addition to Cold War pressures, masses of black people had migrated from Southern rural areas to Northern industrial centers during the war, found jobs, tasted a better life, and were willing to go to the polls or even protest to defend it.

In the wake of these developments, property associations organized to resist social change. In Washington, D.C., the Federation of Citizens Associations, formed to prevent residential integration, had sixty nine neighborhood affiliates by 1944. Neighborhood improvement associations won lower court cases supporting racial covenants in Los Angeles, Chicago, Columbus, New York City, Detroit, and Washington, D.C. They lost only one local case, in St. Louis, in the Marcus Avenue Improvement Association area, and since it was lost on a minor technicality, they appealed it and had the case reversed by the Missouri Supreme Court in *Shelley* v. *Kraemer.* The Marcus Avenue Improvement Association (MAIA), like most neighborhood associations, had a good deal of strength in local courts where they could marshal the force of local public opinion. They packed the courts with association members, got prominent businessmen and realtors to testify about the harmful effects of residential racial change, and were thus able to win their day at the state level.

But when the case got to the U.S. Supreme Court, the local neighborhood improvement association had no national organization, no allies powerful enough to counteract the liberalizing pressures of the Cold War. The Court declared racial restrictive covenants unenforceable. J. D. Shelley, the plaintiff in the case, and his family were allowed to remain at 4600 Labadie Avenue, on the fringe of the Marcus Avenue neighborhood. Within a short time the segregationist MAIA had folded, most white residents had fled from the neighborhood, and it became a black middle- and working-class community.[24]

Of course, the history of improvement associations prior to 1948 varied widely, depending on the unique historical situation and local conditions of each neighborhood. Improvement associations appeared in lower-class as well as upper-class, black as well as white, inner-city as well as suburban neighborhoods, in metropolitan environs as different as New York, St. Louis, Atlanta, and Los Angeles. Nevertheless, certain general patterns of development are discernible. Most started out the same, designed to coordinate and lobby for local services. To the extent that neighborhood racial and class homogeneity was threatened, however, to the extent that the neighborhood bordered lower-class and minority communities, improvement associations took on a decidedly protectionist and reactionary caste. Those improvement associations that were not threatened by social change—either because their class background and the spatial structure of the metropolis isolated them from poor and minority people or because the social control mechanisms of the city, especially in the South, prevented integration—focused fundamentally on neighborhood conservation and enhancement. Without social change pressures, neighborhood organizations in these communities emphasized securing such amenities as new schools, playgrounds, and swimming pools in order to enhance the quality of life in their neighborhoods as well as increase property values. The nature of any given neighborhood organization was thus directly related not only to national developments, such as the "Shelley" decision, which transformed entire neighborhoods and local associations in less than a decade, but to the specific class, racial, and spatial relationships of each city and neighborhood. As we will see in the following discussion of neighborhood improvement associations in the 1950s, this was certainly as true after 1948 as it was before.

Neighborhood Improvement Associations after 1948: Houston Civic Clubs

We must all be on the lookout for [deed restriction] violations, report them, and stand ready to help the Restrictions Committee protest them.

Southwest Civic Club (Houston)

While all neighborhood improvement associations concern themselves with the dual goals of enhancement and protection, the history of associations prior to 1948 indicates that some were far more protective and defensive than others. After 1948, however, the large majority of neighborhood improvement associations were organized in suburban areas geographically distanced from the neighborhoods of the central city, and thus these associations appear more akin in style and focus to the first generation of improvement associations, founded in affluent, elite neighborhoods on the urban periphery, which sought enhancement more than protection.

The massive suburban development boom of the postwar years, which spatially transformed the modern metropolis, was stimulated and engineered by the federal government. As military spending fueled the development of "critical defense areas" in the South and West, so federal expenditures opened rural areas on the urban periphery to suburbanization. Low interest, insured loans from the Federal Housing Authority (FHA) made it possible for the white middle class to leave their outer-city neighborhoods and move to newly developed suburban communities. Within a few years after the federal government in 1948, by court decision, had made it more difficult to restrict blacks from neighborhoods, it passed FHA legislation which encouraged white residents to "flee" outer-city neighborhoods and leave them to newer residents. The rub for minorities and the working class was this: the FHA program tacitly declared inner- and outer-city neighborhoods ineligible for low-interest loans, thereby condemning almost all interior neighborhoods in the metropolis to a slow but steady decline. Over the course of the following generation, the central city and its immediate neighborhoods were either abandoned or destroyed by neglect.

Similarly, the Federal Highway Act of 1956 constructed thousands of miles of inter- and intraurban roads which built a transnational network of turnpikes and parkways. People now could move to the suburbs if they wanted to, if they had enough money, and if they owned a car. Corporations and factories also moved to the new urban periphery, following and leading workers out of the central city. Thousands of new autonomous suburban towns emerged and with them a new metropolitan form. Whereas the industrial metropolis represented a growth in city size from a radius of two to ten miles, the new urban sprawl of the "multinucleic" metropolis encompassed a radius in each direction of twenty five miles or more. Low density, single family housing, purely residential areas, automobiles and freeways characterized the new metropolis. No longer were people dependent on the central business district, the downtown area, for employment or shopping. The new multicentered metropolis had employment and shopping opportunities scattered about in "industrial parks" and "shopping malls," all within driving distance from the new residential suburbs.

In most metropolitan areas the new suburban developments were autonomous entities, self-governing and independent of the central city. In many of the "sunbelt" cities, like Los Angeles and Houston, which first experienced large-scale urban growth after 1945, the newly formed suburban areas were annexed as part of the central city. But whether they were legally independent of the central city or not, the new suburban residents tended to join together to create a sense of community and order out of their subdivisions of houses, streets, sidewalks, and trees. One of the more prominent forms of organization was the neighborhood improvement association. These associations, like their counterparts in developing suburbs in the early twentieth century, focused primarily on securing and providing services, community development activities. After all, the suburban boom of the 1950s had eased competition for space in the multinucleic metropolis. There was little need in the fifties for neighborhood improvement associations in new suburban areas to adopt a protectionist cast.

Excellent examples of postwar community organizing are the neighborhood civic clubs—numbering more than 600 in 1980—which abound in the city of Houston. Such widespread neighborhood organizing in Houston comes as a surprise to most. Houston seems to be little more than a massive urban sprawl, connected solely by freeways and a boom-town atmosphere. Moreover, it has a well-deserved reputation as a highly conservative city, not the sort where one expects cooperative efforts like neighborhood organizing to abound. In 1947, for example, John Gunther in his *Inside America* said that "with the possible exception of Tulsa, Oklahoma," Houston was "the most reactionary community in the United States."[25] Curiously, while no single image suffices for the Bayou City, the blend of extraordinary growth since the early 1940s and a "laissez-faire" political environment has combined to forge a mass of conservative, neighborhood associations throughout the city which are almost identical to associations in suburban areas throughout the nation.

In Houston, deed restrictions and civic clubs are said to take the place of zoning. Land use has been determined by private interests and the profit motive ever since the Allen brothers, two New York City entrepreneurs, first began to market Houston in 1836. This is not to suggest, however, that the city has no form of land use management other than the speculations of land developers and businessmen. In residential neighborhoods, once the land is developed, land use is determined, rather explicitly, by deed restrictions. Drawn up initially by the developer, such deeds include land-use controls, architectural restrictions, and, until recently, racial covenants. Under this type of land-use management, individual homeowners are ultimately responsible for enforcing restrictions. They are the ones who have to take a "violator" to court to prevent a chicken farm or a Colonel Sanders from moving in next door.

In order to facilitate the enforcement of deed restrictions and remove the burden of enforcement from individual residents, many neighborhoods organized local civic clubs.[26] While Houston's neighborhood civic clubs, all situated in neighborhoods within the city limits, perform a rather unique land-use control function, their history, especially since World War II, is very similar to that of most neighborhood improvement associations in affluent suburbs which have zoning. These suburban communities, like most of their counterparts in Houston, are situated away from lower-class and minority neighborhoods and therefore their associations do not have to deal with pressures of class or racial transformation. Instead they tend to focus primarily on neighborhood enhancement rather than protection.

Deed restrictions came into use in Houston in the 1890s with the development of residential subdivisions. Prior to the first subdivisions in Houston and other cities, land was purchased in small parcels, usually by individual homeowners. The initial, inner-city, six "wards" in Houston were settled in this manner without deed restrictions. After 1890 large parcels of land were developed on Houston's periphery and these subdivisions were regulated by deed restrictions. In 1909, a brochure for Woodland Heights, one of the first outer-city neighborhoods in Houston, advertised its deed restrictions as one of the virtues of purchasing land there: "In order to keep Woodland Heights the strictly high grade residence section it is, and to guard against all undesirable features, we have placed certain restrictions on this property as to the character of the improvements and the nature of the use which are embodied in all our deeds, and are binding not only upon the purchasers, but upon their heirs and assigns."[27]

Civic clubs were quickly organized in these new "streetcar suburbs." Their *raison d'etre* was restriction enforcement, but they also functioned as traditional improvement associations, supplying necessary services and lobbying City Hall for street repairs, park development, and schools, just like associations in the North. As development boomed on Houston's periphery, some three miles from downtown in the 1920s, so did neighborhood civic clubs, as each new subdivision came complete with a set of enforceable deed restrictions. But Houston civic clubs in the 1920s did not pursue restrictions with the reactionary zeal of their outer-city counterparts in Chicago or St. Louis. Deed restrictions were seen primarily as a means of protecting property values and preserving neighborhood homogeneity, not as a method primarily intended to exclude blacks, for white homeowners in this bastion of racial segregation were less threatened by neighborhood racial transformation than were their Northern counterparts.

Deed restrictions in Houston in the 1920s included racial clauses limiting ownership and tenancy to "Caucasians and whites only." But competition for housing between blacks and whites was slight and well controlled. With some 138,000 people, the city had a relatively small population. The number of blacks in the city was sizable, around 34,000 people, but the percentage of blacks, 24 percent, was not expanding. Most important, this was the South before the Civil Rights movement of the 1960s. Segregation was the law of the land. The entire system—institutions, power brokers, police, and day-to-day relationships—enforced Jim Crow. Two separate societies existed, one black, the other white. Blacks were concentrated in three older areas of the city and moving into a white area was suicidal, if not impossible. People "knew their place." Before 1948 residential racial transformation was not a "problem" for Houston's neighborhood civic clubs.

Civic clubs in Houston achieved their heyday in the decades after World War II. So did the city. From 1940 to 1960 Houston's population increased from about 400,000 to nearly 600,000. Suburban construction boomed as well. Federal highway development made the outlying areas more accessible, and federal housing loans put the purchase of a single-family home within the reach of the middle class. Developers rushed to meet the demand.

The Braeswood area, located in the southwest sector of the city, was one of the more popular new subdivisions for upper-middle-class whites. Less expensive middle-class housing could be found in other parts of town, but the Braeswood area offered ranch homes with central air conditioning and central heat, three bedrooms, modern kitchens, and two bathrooms for around $20,000. In many ways the subdivision was undistinguished: small plots of land, gridiron street pattern, few trees, only a few house models from which to choose. But it was pleasant enough, accessible to downtown, and on the "right" side—the west side—of the city. The Braeswood development opened in 1951 and by the end of the year there were 6,000 people living there.[28]

The Southwest Civic Club (SWCC) was organized in the Braeswood area on 13 February 1951, and held its first meeting one month later. Eighty-eight residents attended. The goals of the organization were clear: enhance and pro-

tect the neighborhood and enforce deed restrictions. Like earlier neighborhood
improvement associations, initial activity focused on securing neighborhood
physical necessities. Houston prided itself on limiting the role of government
in the affairs of "private" citizens. This meant that taxes were low and public
services were few. Neighborhood residents were expected to furnish their own
needs. Accordingly, civic clubs coordinated neighborhood support and financ-
ing for services the city would not supply, like mosquito fogging or street
lighting.

But the SWCC did lobby City Hall, often with success, for improved services. Residents paid sizable property taxes compared to other neighborhoods
in the city and they expected something in return. A meeting on flood control
in November 1951 brought out some 200 neighborhood residents. They resolved not to support county officials who were seeking two new tax measures
unless promised road and ditch repairs were completed. The county government responded slowly, but eventually met the neighborhood's wishes. Over
the next few years the SWCC effectively lobbied for traffic signs and lights,
improved water pressure, road paving and repairs, a new library, park, and
elementary school, and a fire station. To accomplish their objectives, the club
might hold mass meetings or sponsor letter writing campaigns to pressure City
Hall and county officers. But most often club successes resulted from personal
contacts between club leaders and city officials and prominent businessmen.
SWCC leaders over the years included state representatives, realtors, lawyers,
and urban planners, each with some contacts and varying degrees of influence
in the city and county. In neighborhoods like Braeswood, the prestige and
contacts of individual members, enhanced by the backing of a civic association, enabled the organization to be heard and win services.

From its inception deed restriction enforcement was a central activity of the
SWCC. The process of private deed enforcement maintained neighborhood
homogeneity effectively, but not without serious drawbacks. The first steps in
restriction enforcement were informal: a resident would complain to the civic
club, the club president would write a letter or pay an informal visit to the
"violator." Most often people were simply unaware they had broken the deed.
In one case a young boy was raising two lambs in his backyard for a Future
Farmers of America project. The deed prohibited the keeping of livestock in
the neighborhood. The resident reluctantly complied. Sometimes more formal
action, like the threat of a civil lawsuit, was required, and it was here that a
fundamental problem faced neighborhood civic clubs. Court cases were few
and far between because defendants realized the potential expense and the
court's support of deed restriction enforcement. On one occasion the SWCC
secured a "permanent injunction" against a chiropractor from practicing in his

home. On another, they took a motel operator to court, forcing his business out of the area. But court expenses were high for the club as well as the defendant. One violation pursued all the way through the courts could wipe out the club's entire restriction fund, and more. Only the wealthiest civic clubs, like the River Oaks Property Owners Association, could finance frequent court battles. Deed restriction enforcement was potentially an expensive means of protecting property values.

It was also divisive. Neighbors had to keep watch on, oppose, and threaten each other with court suits. It was easy to oppose a filling station trying to move in the neighborhood. But what about telling neighbors that they could not extend their carport to the lot line or convert their garage into an apartment for the family of their son or daughter. Given the problems of constant enforcement, potential expense, and intraneighborhood tension, neighborhoods with active civic clubs, surprisingly, also ardently supported zoning proposals in 1948 and 1962. Civic clubs preferred to make enforcement of deed restrictions a public rather than a private function, one supported by tax monies and administered by local officials.

While the SWCC, like all civic clubs in Houston, established a democratic structure for resident participation, the affairs of the club were handled by a half-dozen men, usually businessmen or professionals. Membership was not opened to women until 1956, and then only to women who were "resident owners of real property." The club had four elected administrative officers, ten "area directors," and "block captains." Meetings were run democratically, in that all members could vote, but generally resident participation and interest was slight. The early years of the SWCC were the peak time of resident activism. The neighborhood was young, people were just getting to know each other, and basic amenities still needed to be secured. The residents wanted a community organization. In 1955 85 percent of the residents paid $6.75 per year to join the club: $1 for membership, $1.25 for the restriction enforcement fund, and $4.50 for mosquito fogging. Meetings that addressed an "emergency issue," like flood control, could bring out 200 residents. But even in the heyday of the SWCC most monthly meetings were poorly attended. "Everybody is willing to do everything they are asked to do, but [they] don't attend the meeting," lamented an officer in 1955. Often no more than ten or twenty people came. Block captains and a regular newsletter kept neighbors informed of club activities and this sufficed for most. Elections for club officers were rarely contested. Residents willingly accepted the suggestions of the ad hoc nominating committee, which was appointed by the board of directors. Members were grateful that someone with leadership skills and, quite often, political or business influence, was willing to assume the burden.

Over the years the organization became even less participatory and less democratic. In 1956 the number of annual general meetings were reduced from twelve to five. The board of directors continued, however, to meet monthly and direct the affairs of the club. In 1958 membership hit a low point of only 43½ percent of neighborhood residents. The reasons were obvious. The Braeswood area was becoming more stable and most initial services and amenities had been provided. Many people, moreover, were not pleased with the club's mosquito spraying service and chose to do without the fogging. Perhaps most important, neighbors did not feel threatened. The board of directors proclaimed the need to "Sell the Civic Club" in the neighborhood, but to little avail. In 1963 membership was up slightly to 48 percent, but remained a far cry from dues payments in the initial years. This pattern of elite leadership and declining resident interest seems nearly universal in Houston civic clubs. The SWCC, like other neighborhood civic clubs, was, after all, fundamentally a neighborhood-based interest group, and interest groups, especially those in affluent communities like Braeswood, do not require democratic or active citizen participation.

Despite their overt political function as neighborhood interest groups—as coordinators and lobbyists for neighborhood services and protectors of property values—civic clubs picture themselves as nonpolitical. While they do not directly support candidates for public office, the most effective civic clubs, like the Southwest Civic Club, serve a parapolitical function by influencing local officials and power brokers on behalf of the neighborhood and by serving as informal conduits of information about the needs and developments in the community.[29] The SWCC never shied away from addressing political issues. Over the years it invited speakers and sponsored programs that reflected the conservative politics of club leaders. Speakers warned club members of the hazards of federal deficit spending and taxing powers. The club coordinated civil defense progams at the neighborhood level. It showed films like *The Land of the Free* and *Communism on the Map*, the latter advertised in press releases throughout the city as "a fully documented film on how the communists are spreading their doctrine throughout the world." These activities were not seen as political because residents supported them. Issues which might cause dissent within the civic club, like partisan politics, were off limits. But political activity was acceptable when it preserved, or at least did not disrupt, neighborhood homogeneity.

The fundamental issue facing most outer-city neighborhood improvement associations in the 1950s was racial integration. In response to black activism and the pressures of the Cold War, segregationists organized in the North and the South in both neighborhood-based and broader organizations like the Citizen Councils to resist residential and school integration. In Houston, civic clubs located in neighborhoods contiguous to the black ghettos on the east side of town actively resisted integration. For example, Riverside—called by some "the Jewish River Oaks"—situated east of Braeswood along Braes Bayou, was a select white neighborhood in the 1940s. With the "Shelley" decision in 1948, white residents in Riverside grew alarmed about the expanding black ghetto to their north. In 1952 they formed the Greater Riverside Property Owners Association (GRPOA) to prevent integration. They told white residents to sit tight, not sell, remain in the neighborhood, and they tried to raise money to buy property for sale and to "buy out" blacks who had already moved into Riverside Terrace.[30] Signs declaring "This house is not for sale" were frequently seen posted on porches. Bombs exploded at the house of the first black family who moved into Riverside in 1953. But none of this was very effective. Once the pattern of residential change was apparent, white homeowners sold quickly, even at lower prices, and realtors were eager to help them do so. The white residents of Riverside moved to newly developed subdivisions in the southwest of the city, like Braeswood, which provided good housing and appreciable distance from the black ghetto.

Because Houston was growing at a breakneck pace after World War II, competition for living space was minimal, limited only to those areas, like Riverside, that bordered the black ghettos of the city. Residents in neighborhoods like Braeswood shared similar segregationist sentiments with their white counterparts in Riverside. As late as 1970 only thirteen of the neighborhood's 8,654 residents were black. But residents in Braeswood, like most suburban residents in the 1950s living five to ten miles from the central city and the black ghetto, were not as threatened or effected by integration pressures as in neighborhoods that bordered the black ghetto in both Southern and Northern cities. Nevertheless, organizations formed even in southwest Houston to address this issue and protect property values.

In the 1950s an umbrella organization of local civic clubs in southwest Houston, the Allied Civic Clubs (ACC), formed to deal with district-wide issues which went beyond subdivision boundaries. Among other activities the ACC organized workshops on community leadership training and restriction violations, supported a drive toward district representation on the city council, and became a strong advocate of zoning. The ACC also helped coordinate opposition to residential desegregation in southwest Houston. ACC leaders recognized that the "Shelley" decision made it difficult to prevent a black family from moving into a white neighborhood. Indeed, "there is no reason now to believe that this is possible," they lamented. But ACC could stop wholesale neighborhood transformation and panic selling; ACC leaders called this objective "neighborhood stabilization."

Where integration threatened to destabilize a neighborhood, the ACC advised its constituents to remain calm. "Emotional panic of white neighbors solves nothing and is, indeed, self-defeating. The way of neighborhood stabilization is much better." Be alert to potential problem houses, such as a G.I. financed home which did not sell quickly. If a black moves into the neighborhood, call a meeting quickly with residents of the immediate area. Urge them to sit tight. Beware of "unethical" realtors who "stir up race prejudices." If "wildcat realtors" are put out of business, then "every all-white area in Houston that wishes to remain all-white will have a much better chance." The ACC further requested residents to report wildcatters to the Houston Board of Realtors, the Better Business Bureau, and the ACC, so that such realtors could be singled out and ostracized. The advice was clear: "neighborhood stabilization" was the best way to protect property values.[31]

The SWCC, a member organization in the ACC, followed the recommendations. As late as 1970, when a black family moved into the neighborhood the civic club president quickly wrote a letter to residents in the immediate area, advising them that "a frantic rush to get out will devalue our properties and deteriorate our neighborhood." The letter identified the realtor who sold the property, and went on to praise the quality of the two Negro families who currently resided in the community: one a doctor, the other an attorney, both "educated and cultured." "Sit tight and face this situation with realism, courage, and goodwill. . . . The value of your property and the future of your neighborhood depend entirely on what you people do."[32]

In summary, the strategy of neighborhood stabilization sufficed to "protect" Houston's more affluent white neighborhoods. Most blacks could not afford to move there and for those who could a few other areas of the city were opening up which were equally attractive and more hospitable to middle-income black families. Neighborhood improvement associations in the North before and after World War II tried the "sit-tight, do not panic" strategy, but with little success in white communities contiguous to the expanding black ghetto. Similarly in Houston, where white neighborhoods bordered the black ghettos, as in the Riverside area, neighborhood stabilization was equally ineffective. Throughout the nation where pressures by blacks for more and better housing were great, violent conflict ensued, bombs exploded, whites resisted militantly, and then, ultimately, moved out.

This was not the case in the Braeswood area, nor in other affluent suburban neighborhoods, North and South, which were more removed from lower class and minority, inner-city areas by geographic distance and class barriers. In Houston the largest concentration of blacks remained on the east side of town, away from suburbs in the west like Braeswood. Protecting the neighborhood from racial change was less important to the SWCC than were the routine tasks of service acquisition and maintenance. Throughout its history the SWCC concerned itself with enforcing deed restrictions, keeping out commercial development, and doing mosquito fogging. The extraordinary distances separating races and classes in the new multinucleic cities in the South and the metropolitan areas in the North clearly enabled affluent residents to segregate themselves more successfully and easily than before. Prior to the fifties such separation had been a "luxury" shared only by residents in the most affluent suburbs. But with the federal government subsidizing through highway and housing programs the mass suburbanization of metropolitan centers, upper-middle and middle-class suburban developments, whether within or outside the city limits, were removed and isolated from the central city as never before. In turn, improvement associations in these neighborhoods took on the role of maintenance and service lobbying efforts, rather than the combative and defensive style of associations in white neighborhoods that bordered the black ghetto.

CHAPTER 4

The Neighborhood Organizing "Revolution" of the 1960s

Poverty and Race in the "Affluent" Society

I, for one, believe that if you give people a thorough understanding of what it is that confronts them, and the basic causes that produce it, they'll create their own program; and when the people create a program, you get action. When their "leaders" create programs you get no action.

Malcolm X, organizer

As preceding chapters have demonstrated, the stop-gap solutions and tenuous class and race relations of one decade often became the central problem and basis for change in the next. And each new situation seemed to breed new forms of neighborhood organization activity. For example, in the postwar decade military Keynesianism did not resolve the fundamental inequity and instability of the economic system. Large numbers of people, especially nonwhites, did not share in the fruits of United States expansion abroad. Repression served as only a short-term political solution to the threat of dissent and rebellion, and as repression lessened in the late fifties disaffected groups organized to protest their condition and to win power. If conservative neighborhood organizing was the dominant style of the fifties, then radical organizing efforts responding to the contradictions of life in the "affluent society" characterized the succeeding decade. The shift in organizing styles and goals was similar to that which occurred from the twenties to the thirties.

The most innovative efforts in neighborhood organizing in the early part of the 1960s were the quasi-anarchist experiments initiated by the Student Non-

violent Coordinating Committee (SNCC) and Students for a Democratic Society (SDS).[1] Each emphasized the value of radical, community-based organizing and each focused its attention on developing new forms of grassroots
political action based on the concept of participatory democracy. These groups
were important innovators in a new style of community organizing, but only
one of many types of grassroots efforts during the decade. These early projects
of SNCC and SDS were followed by a most dramatic, violent, and unorganized community response to the inequities of the "affluent society," the inner-city ghetto rebellions of the years 1964 through 1968. As in the "progressive era" and the thirties, the federal government responded to this disorder
with programs designed to undercut radical activity and palliate conditions. Its
Community Action Program (CAP) launched the largest, most systematic
neighborhood organizing project ever tried. The various "war on poverty"
programs of the decade successfully defused social disorder and coopted a
good deal of political militancy. But the events of the decade, especially the
urban rebellions and the rise of revolutionary leaders like Malcolm X, pushed
many radicals further left rather than into the "establishment." Calls for participatory democracy of the early sixties were often replaced after mid-decade
by avowedly socialist, anticapitalist critiques and programs for revolutions.
The decade's political and economic concerns, the early programs of SNCC
and SDS, and the "Great Society" projects are the subjects of this chapter.

In the fifties and sixties, conservatives, liberals, and radicals shared a pre-
vailing opinion that military expenditures and wars helped ensure prosperity in
capitalist nations.[2] The signs of material wealth that adorned the "affluent society" reinforced the perception. By 1971 GNP exceeded a trillion dollars,
whereas twenty years earlier it was one fourth that. Almost everyone owned a
refrigerator, a television, and a vacuum cleaner. More than a third of the population had an air conditioner, a freezer, a color television, and more than one
car. Large numbers of Americans were able, either through increased real
wages, installment buying, or both, to improve their economic standard of
living. Thrilled by this success, apostles of the Cold War economy proclaimed
the beginnings of a new economic era. Business leaders had made similar
pronouncements in the 1920s, but this time, postwar boosters declared, it was
true. America, they said, was in the process of building a "people's capitalism," characterized by ever-rising real incomes, the abolition of poverty, and
the rapid spread of stock ownership among masses of Americans. Prosperity
for all, spread more equally throughout the population, was the promise. It
turned out not to be the reality.

Real income and wages (adjusted for inflation) did rise from the late forties
until 1973. For some twenty five years the fruits of America's international

economic empire, federal deficit spending, and new technologies promoted the longest sustained period of economic growth in our history. Average unemployment in the fifties was very low and the recessions that occurred were relatively minor. But a greater degree of economic democracy did not accompany this prosperity. The class-based prosperity of the "affluent society" did little to resolve income inequities and stock ownership did not increase enough to warrant claims of a "people's capitalism." As conservative a source as *Business Week* noted in 1972 that wealth concentration had changed little in the United States from 1929 through the 1960s: "If anything, it increased slightly."[3]

Social theorists began to warn of impending class and race conflict if the glaring inequities of postwar prosperity were not addressed. In 1958, in his facetiously titled book, *The Affluent Society,* liberal economist John Kenneth Galbraith questioned the vacuous quality of life created by America's single-minded penchant to produce, purchase, and consume new products. He warned that amid America's material affluence there was a large population living in poverty that would one day revolt and cause costly social disorder. Michael Harrington's *The Other America: Poverty in the United States,* published in 1962, was an even stronger statement. According to prosperity's evangels, Harrington wrote, providing basic human needs, such as food, shelter, and clothing, was no longer a problem; the central concern now was how to live happily amid all this luxury. But this vision of a luxurious, affluent society was class-limited and distorted; poverty was widespread in America. Harrington estimated that some forty to fifty million people were trapped in a "cycle of poverty." Poverty was a rural as well as inner-city, Southern as well as Northern problem. It hit the aged, female-headed households, and the young the hardest. Suburbanization had simply made it "invisible" to those who did not want to see it, Harrington added, by heightening class segregation in the postwar metropolis.[4]

While nearly 80 percent of those below the federal government poverty line of $3,000 in 1960 were white, the 22 percent who were Afro-American represented nearly half of the entire black population in America. But poverty in the 1960s came to be seen as a "black problem" not simply because of its extraordinary concentration among Afro-Americans. That had always been the case. What was different in the early 1960s was the intensity of opposition by blacks to this economic oppression.

The rising threat of black, urban disorder resulted in part from demographic shifts underway since the turn of the century. As late as 1910, 90 percent of blacks lived in the South and 75 percent lived in rural areas. After 1910, partially in response to the lure of industrial jobs created by World War I, black farmers began to leave the rural South. They headed first to Southern and then Northern urban areas. This trend accelerated during and after World War II as 1.5 million black agricultural workers left the South in the 1940s. In the next decade another 1.5 million departed, so that by the mid-1960s 75 percent of the black population in the United States lived in cities and more than 50 percent lived outside of the South. This extraordinary population shift equaled the massive migration during the late nineteenth and early twentieth centuries of Southern and Eastern Europeans to the United States and rural native whites to the cities.

The mass migration of blacks, especially after World War II, was more a result of "push" rather than "pull" factors. The modernization of Southern agriculture after the war reversed a period of economic decline in agriculture begun after World War I. In no more than two decades, large-scale, highly mechanized, industrialized farming replaced small, labor-intensive operations in the South. Between 1940 and 1960 half the farms in the South disappeared, while the average farm size nearly doubled. Ten years later the average farm size had doubled again. Mechanization, new technologies, new crops, and federal policies dramatically lessened the need for tenant labor in the South. Between 1950 and 1965, a presidential Advisory Commission on Rural Poverty reported, new methods and machines increased farm output in the U.S. by 45 percent— and reduced farm employment by the same percentage. Agricultural workers were literally thrown off the land. Some white tenant farmers found jobs in the newly developing industrial mills in Southern cities, but black agricultural workers continued to find themselves barred for the most part from such employment. In response, over three million blacks left the rural South and headed north to cities such as New York, Chicago, Newark, St. Louis, Detroit, and Cleveland.[5]

In the course of a generation from 1940 to 1970 a black rural peasantry was transformed into an unskilled urban proletariat. The number of black residents in New York City tripled in thirty years, from 458,444 to 1,668,115, increasing from 6.1 to 21.2 percent of the city's population. In Chicago the jump was even more dramatic, 277,731 and 8.2 percent in 1940 to 1,102,620 and 32.7 percent in 1970. In 1940 Newark was a city of primarily first- and second-generation Eastern European immigrants, with only ten percent of the population Afro-American. By 1970, reflecting both black in-migration and white out-migration, Newark was one of the growing number of Northern cities with a majority of black residents.[6]

In many ways the economic position of the new black migrants was little better than it had been in the rural South before the war. Socially, culturally, and politically Northern cities were more open. But ghetto and slum living, job ceilings, color lines in all areas of life, and powerlessness repeated in Northern cities the same severe economic hardships and impoverished circumstances, in new and unfamiliar communities, that black workers had experienced in the South for generations. The median income of black workers was half that of their white counterparts. Unemployment figures for blacks were startling. In Watts, the Harlem of Los Angeles, just before the first riot in 1964 up to one third of all black residents were unemployed. Black teenage unemployment nationally was 22 percent, low in comparison to 1970 figures but more than double that of white youth. Four million blacks subsisted on welfare programs in 1966, and this was only a portion of those who needed or qualified for assistance. A 1967 Department of Labor study noted that more than 20 percent of black ghetto residents who were *working full-time* had earnings below the government poverty line of $3,000. In total, 37 percent of ghetto families reported incomes below that figure.[7]

To make matters worse, at the very moment that masses of unskilled, uneducated, poor black farmers were moving to cities up North, businesses and white property owners—the basis of the urban tax structure—were leaving the city for the suburban hinterland. At the very moment that more funds were needed for public services to train recent black migrants and at the very moment that masses of unskilled laborers arrived looking for work, much of which required higher skill levels than ever before, the sources of jobs and the tax base to support public services were leaving the city. Worsening poverty, declining urban educational programs, deteriorating housing, increasing crime and drug use, booming welfare rolls, and spiraling infant mortality and disease rates combined to create an urban crisis and fan the flames of discontent.

The decade of the sixties was thus something very different for the inner-city, minority poor than the society of abundance and prosperity pictured by most recorded observers of the American scene at the end of the 1950s. The fruits of empire and Cold War politics aided many corporations, stockholders, and those segments of the middle class who were able to secure the skills and perform the tasks demanded by the private and public sectors. But for farmers and minority and ethnic workers outside the mainstream, the sixties offered a challenge of a very different sort. In reponse to the gap between the theory and reality of the "affluent society," in response to the discrepancy between the idea of a society of abundance and the reality of systematic poverty and powerlessness experienced by millions of citizens, people did not sit idly or passively by. An important and influential minority of poor people and activists joined neighborhood and national organizations, participated in demonstrations, teach-ins, and civil disobedience actions, carried signs and threw molotov cocktails, and demanded "Freedom Now" and "Power to the People."

Like the 1930s, the 1960s was a decade of important radical ferment and social change. It is certainly too soon for historians to evaluate the period effectively and probably too late to capture its boundless spirit, vitality, and hope. Such limits aside, the decade is a critical one in a history of neighborhood organizing because of the quantity, variety, and impact of its neighborhood organizing projects.

New Left Organizing Projects: SNCC and SDS, 1961–1965

[The civil rights movement] was an experience that totally changed the lives of people who participated in it. . . . I had grown up in a society where there were very clear lines. The older I got, the more I found what those lines were. The Civil Rights Movement gave me the power to challenge any line that limits me. . . . [It] said that if something puts you down, you have to fight against it.

Bernice Reagon, SNCC organizer

[We need] a politics of responsible insurgence rooted in community after community, speaking in comprehensive terms to the felt needs of their locales, offering specific alternatives to specific problems of inequality, industrial stagnation, inadequate schools, civil defense, and so on. . . . We have no more difficult and more necessary task today than a race to create genuinely independent political constituencies who will not be satisfied with the New Frontier.

Tom Hayden, SDS organizer

In the history of neighborhood organization, the 1960s will be remembered as a decade of mass insurgence, radical politics, and youthful experimentation, as a time when the notion of democracy was reinvigorated with participatory content. The most innovative efforts were the student-initiated projects of the Student Nonviolent Coordinating Committee (SNCC, pronounced "snick") and Students for a Democratic Society (SDS). In Southern rural and urban areas and in Northern urban ghettos these student activists, black and white, experimented with what it meant to develop democratic grassroots organizations. From 1962 to 1965 SNCC's community organizing work in the rural and urban South focused on registering voters and protesting segregation in public accommodations. From 1963 to 1965 SDS, through its Economic Research and Education Project (ERAP), focused on community organizing primarily in poor neighborhoods of large, Northern cities. Independently, they forged two autonomous but interrelated groups of radical activists—a "new left"—the likes of which had not been seen since the Cold War began.

The radical ferment of the 1960s grew out of the Civil Rights movement. The mass struggle for black equality in the second half of the twentieth century began during and just after World War II as it became clear to increasingly militant black leaders that the battle for democracy must be fought at home as well as abroad. Following 1945 the Cold War increased pressure for racial equality. As President Truman put the liberal viewpoint: the "top dog" in a "world which is over half colored ought to clean his own house."[8] And with good reason. State Department officials estimated that approximately 50 percent of Soviet propaganda against the United States focused on the race issue. With Truman's order to desegregate the armed forces in 1948 and with the Supreme Court's *Brown* v. *Board of Education of Topeka, Kansas,* decision in 1954 to desegregate public schools in the South, the federal government lent support to the cause of racial integration. Given the rising militancy and activism of black leaders, these actions helped spawn an insurgent, mass movement for racial equality throughout the South.

Beginning with the Montgomery bus boycott in 1957, led by Rosa Parks and Martin Luther King, Jr., middle-class black leaders, with support from affluent, liberal whites, initiated a mass movement of nonviolent, direct action protest against the most obvious forms of racial discrimination in the South. They operated in organizations like the Southern Christian Leadership Conference (SCLC), the Congress for Racial Equality (CORE), and the National Association for the Advancement of Colored People (NAACP). But they sought to build a *movement* of moral outrage and civil disobedience, not a powerful civil rights organization. As such the movement took its character and leadership not from a specific organization, but rather from a shared vision of "beloved community" and a strategy of "passive resistance." Martin Luther King, Jr., best articulated the conception of a true democracy, but neither he nor SCLC developed organizational forms that could sustain the concept in practice. Instead they followed a strategy of elite-led, nonviolent direct actions designed to expose the viciousness of racism and win the minds, if not the hearts, of those in power. The movement, however, became more participatory and turned to greater militancy in 1960 when black students engaged in ad hoc sit-in protests at segregated lunch counters and joined "freedom rides" which challenged segregation in public transportation.

SNCC began in October 1960, on the heels of the student sit-in activities. Initially it was seen as the organized but independent student arm of the Southwide civil rights movement. One year later, it was a good deal more than that, a group of full-time organizers working to stimulate protest and launch social change efforts throughout the Deep South. More specifically, SNCC organized voter registration drives and protests in communities where black people had not voted or collectively challenged racism since the days of Reconstruction and Populism. Here were the cream of black and white youth, most of them college educated, 180 strong at their peak in the winter of 1965, organizing challenges to segregation in the den of the lion.

Despite important and fundamental differences, the early programs of SDS in Northern urban neighborhoods mirrored, as much as differing conditions would allow, the origins, objectives, and style of SNCC projects in the South. SDS began in the spring of 1960, in the midst of the first sit-in demonstrations. But in its first few years the new, campus-based, highly intellectual organization was unsure of its role or its constituency. In 1963 SDS turned for direction to what was then the only compelling activist model, SNCC's community organizing work. In that summer the newly created Economic Research and Action Project received from the United Auto Workers a grant of $5,000 to "emphasize economic issues on campuses and communities." Influential SDS leaders like Tom Hayden and Rennie Davis pointed to the slum neighborhood, not the workplace, as the best site for radical organizing. By the summer of 1964 SDS had raised $20,000 and began ten ERAP community organizing projects with approximately 100 student volunteers. The ERAP projects occupied SDS's attention for two years, through 1965. At its height the project involved some 200 organizers in ten cities. The organizers were often the brightest, most intellectual, upper- and upper-middle class students at the most prestigious and academically demanding universities. As in SNCC many of the white, Northern-born members were "red-diaper babies," the children of communists and socialists, and the Southern white students were often the children of liberal ministers. And as in SNCC, organizing for SDS was more than a difficult and exhilarating experience. For most it became a way of living, seeing, and behaving.[9]

Both organizations identified themselves as "nonideological." This was not surprising for SNCC, which was rooted in the moral crusade of the Civil Rights movement. It was, however, more significant for SDS, since SDS was founded as the student branch of the "old left," the democratic socialist League for Industrial Democracy (LID). The world view and tactics of new left organizations, however, jibed with little of the LID's socialist critique. It was not as though the student activists were more "radical." The Port Huron Statement, written in 1962 and perhaps the best expression of early SDS thinking, was not a revolutionary document. It included little explicit criticism of capitalism, class domination, or imperialism. But it was quite clear in its rejection of old left thinking. In 1964 Rennie Davis articulated the thoughts of many SDS organizers when he stated:

We know of no satisfactory blueprint for full employment, shared abundance, equality and democracy. We have only limited ideas about the sources of power or the strategy of change which will carry us into a new society. We have found little information on organizing in the 1930s that has proved relevant to our operations. . . .[10]

Bruce Payne, a SNCC activist, echoed the point:

SNCC people generally refer to themselves and their organizations as "non-ideological." By this they mean that they do not have any *total* view of political and social life that enables them to offer a blueprint for the kind of society they would like to see in the future. They also mean they are not committed to the views of any existing political organization—that they are not Marxists, Socialists, or Democrats. The absence of a full-scale program has as its concomitant an emphasis on immediate action.[11]

Nevertheless, both organizations shared definite ideas about the future of society and "the movement." They advocated in their words and behavior a moral revolt and nonconformity to "the system," which they said restricted self-expression and self-realization. They rejected the liberal faith in modest reforms and anticommunism. Accordingly, earlier left strategies of building coalitions with liberal and mainstream labor organizations were replaced with an emphasis on direct action and the formation of locally autonomous, insurgent, community organizations. Moreover, SDS and SNCC, the former more explicitly, rejected all centralized, bureaucratic, hierarchical forms as practiced in both democratic socialism and corporate capitalism.

This critique led SDS away from the old left's concern with organization and power, but they did not replace it with an alternative formal theory of society, history, and radical change. Instead they substituted an all-embracing political credo which emphasized democratic action and relationships, processes, and values. "Participatory democracy," they called it. "Let the people decide." In SNCC and SDS participatory democracy became an ideology of both goals and methods, a vague vision of how to get people together, act together, and win power together.[12] This perspective was fundamentally anarchistic, not socialistic. New left activists in SNCC and SDS wanted to create a spontaneous, decentralized, antiauthoritarian movement that would stand in marked contrast and as an alternative to the dominant system of bureaucratic structures, representative government, and leadership by professionals. The current system perpetuated elite control over the poor and powerless, they said, and offered people little opportunity to participate in public decisions.

Because of this, most people felt totally ill-equipped to do so and therefore left politics in the hands of the elite.

The outlines of the new left vision were drawn by the conditions of Cold War America. Kenneth Keniston, the psychologist, described this historical response well:

The fear of the abuse of power, or irrational authority, and of dominating leadership is in many respects a legitimate reaction to a world in which power, authority, and leadership are used cruelly rather than benignly. The various positions, styles, and forms that cluster around the concept of participatory democracy are an important attempt, no matter how incomplete and experimental, to devise new forms of organization and action that will humanize the organized and vitalize the actors.[13]

A unique organizing style resulted. Simply put, the new left approach to community organizing included these common ingredients:

(1) *Be a catalyst, not a leader.* Given that uneducated, poor people can represent their own interests effectively, the organizer ought to be a catalyst for social change, not a community leader. The organizer should give community people skills and confidence and, as Alinsky had suggested in Back of the Yards, work her or his way out of a job.

(2) *Let the people decide.* Jimmy Garrett, a SNCC activist in Mississippi, described the organizer SNCC sought. The organizer "got the people together and said, 'You decide, you make decisions about your life. You decide about voting. You decide about demonstrating. Just as you are. You don't have to be articulate or politically developed. You know your conditions better than I, better than any one.' " An ERAP staffer in Cleveland put it this way: "We just talked with the women. They decided they wanted to do something. We said we'd help them do whatever they wanted."[14]

(3) *Develop loose organizational structures.* This would encourage maximum, meaningful participation by community people. They practiced consensus decision making. They rotated meeting leaders. Tasks were assigned on a voluntary, ad hoc basis. SDS and SNCC organizers believed a loose structure enabled people with no prior political experience to speak and act without being embarrassed about the opinions they expressed and without being dependent on "higher-ups." In the Newark ERAP project, for example, the program committee was composed of "representatives from all the blocks, the staff, and *anyone who could attend the meeting,* one man [*sic*], one vote." The committee would meet weekly and make all policy decisions, decide its own organizational forms, and be chaired by an elected president rotated once a month.[15]

(4) *Establish places in the community free of external restraints.* In ERAP the "community union" (the local office site) belonged to the neighborhood people. It was, one organizer said, probably the only "institution in the world where a destitute alcoholic can stand up and give a lecture, occasionally brilliant but usually incoherent, on political strategy and be listened to with complete respect."[16] You could find activity at community unions which ranged from leaflet preparation to sleeping and carousing. Keys to the centers were often distributed liberally to neighborhood people. Because SNCC generally was better grounded in the local culture, its community shelters ranged from churches to community centers and the SNCC office. They used any site where people could meet and talk comfortably and in safety.

(5) *Develop indigenous leaders.* The organizer was to "use his [*sic*] dynamism to project other people—tell them they can lead—ask people questions rather than give them answers."[17] SNCC, for example, rejected the traditional organizing style of SCLC and CORE in which elected or appointed leaders from outside the local community directed activities. These same leaders, SNCC was quick to note, left as swiftly as they came, leaving community people leaderless and vulnerable. SNCC and SDS emphasized that leadership had to be developed among the people so that *they* could advance and protect themselves.

(6) *Create supportive personal relationships.* Organizers had to be willing to remain in rural communities and urban neighborhoods and build strong personal relationships with local people. Trust and confidence between organizers and community people were the building blocks of grassroots organizing. From the standpoint of outsiders without a specific program which could attract people, the best way to get people interested was through developing personal as well as political ties. Supportive, nonmanipulative, noncompetitive relations between organizers and community people would prefigure future ways of relating in the new, truly democratic society.

If those six tenets were the organizing theory of the new left, a position paper written by SNCC staffer Charles McLaurin, who grew up in Jackson, Mississippi, outlined the organizing process. First, become part of the community. Find a family to stay with, preferably a well-known family in the community. "It may just happen that you are not able to find a place for weeks; but do not give up." Make contacts. Talk with people about the community; they are the ones from whom you will get a real community education. Canvas the whole community one afternoon. Talk with them, laugh and joke with them. "Do most anything that gets some attention on you." Find out what bugs people. Take down names and addresses of people who you talk with, especially those who seemed like potential leaders. These will be key contacts later. Identify a core group of talkers and interested people. Set up a meeting, in a church or empty building, perhaps even in the home of the family where you live. Plan some action at the first meeting. "You put suggestions before the group. Let them talk over the suggestions, about paved streets, stop signs, street lights, or recreational facilities, and how the vote can get these and more." It might take ten or more of these meetings. Let the group elect a chair and appoint committees. Stop by the homes of core group members, talk with them regularly. Visits show that you are interested in the community and people's family and personal life, not only in political meetings. Developing a feeling of being close together will help overcome the fear that people have about getting involved. "Suspicion comes from mistrust. So many have led us wrong, that it is hard to trust people we don't know. You must be friendly, reliable, and most of all trustworthy. With this, suspicion will disappear. When the people trust you and trust your judgment, suspicion will be a thing of the past."[18]

At its best the development of leadership was a two-way street in which the poor provided courageous models of insurgency for the students in SNCC and SDS. For example, McLaurin recalled one day in Indianola, Mississippi, when he took three elderly black women to register to vote at the court house.

As I opened the [car] door to get out I got a feeling in my stomach that made me feel weak. . . . At this point I was no longer in command, the three old ladies were leading me, I was following them. They got out of the car and went up the walk to the courthouse as if this was the long walk that leads to the Golden Gate of Heaven, their heads held high. I watched from a short distance behind them; the pride with which they walked. The strong convictions that they held. I watched as they walked up the steps into the building. I stepped outside the door and waited, thinking how it was that these ladies who have been victimized by white faces all their lives would suddenly walk up to the man and say, *I want to vote.* This did something to me. It told me [that] . . . the people are the true leaders. We need only to move them; to show them. Then watch and learn.[19]

A vivid example of the actual process of community organizing in SDS was the ERAP project in Chicago. While conditions in Chicago differed from other ERAP communities, the organizing process there demonstrates nicely how SDSers sought to put their theory of participatory democracy into practice. SDS sent Joe Chabot, a student at the University of Michigan, to Chicago in September 1963 to organize primarily white unemployed workers. He attended dozens of meetings over the course of several months, observing the activities of established neighborhood organizations like settlements and churches and educating himself about local conditions and politics. Chabot made little headway initially. He attributed this to the lack of "readiness" of white unemployed youth to join political organizations. A break came when he was able to form an alliance with the Packinghouse Workers Union (UPW), the same left-oriented union that Alinsky allied with in Back of the Yards. The UPW wanted someone with resources and energy to do organizing among the unemployed, and Chabot was eager to do so. Because SDS based its ERAP organizing on the theory, advanced by a number of economists in the early 1960s, that the postwar boom was about to end and because SDS thought a vast constituency of discontented, potentially radical unemployed would result from the impending economic crisis, Chabot, with the assistance of some UPW staff and an organizer from the American Friends Service Committee, assembled a core group to plan how to organize the unemployed.

This core group labeled their operation JOIN—the Committee for Jobs and Income Now. They established offices on both the South Side and North Side. Each morning Chabot and others would hand out leaflets at the unemployment office, talk with people at the JOIN offices, answer the phone, hold meetings, serve coffee to folks who dropped by. By the sixth week of operation, 400 to 500 men had come to the North Side JOIN office and participated in discussion with ERAP staffers. Thursday evenings ERAP staffers held organizing meetings for those members of the unemployed who seemed most interested in getting further involved in JOIN's work. Anywhere from five to thirty people attended these organizing sessions. More than a dozen workers were attending meetings regularly in the first few months after the office opened.

For the experienced and skillful activist, organizing can be difficult and exhausting work, and it was even more so for ERAP organizers. Often fresh from college, with little or no organizing experience, they went to live in what were for most of them foreign colonies of poverty. They received no salary and lived on a subsistence allowance that kept them fed primarily on powdered milk and peanut butter and jelly sandwiches. Unlike settlement workers who sought to create upper-class islands, like Hull House, in inner-city slums, ERAP organizers sought to become part of slum life.

Hours upon hours were spent leafletting unemployment offices, talking with people, attending meetings, addressing the most rudimentary concerns and political positions, and often with few results to show for it. Rennie Davis, active in the JOIN project in Chicago, described the process well:

> Probably all of the ERAP community workers have developed a deeper sense of the extreme slowness of building a permanent community organization on a program of fundamental change. . . . An organizer can spend two or more hours with a single

individual. Through hundreds of conversations, slowly, clusters of unemployed contacts are made and identified on city maps. One person in a large unemployment area is approached about having a meeting; he agrees, but has not the time to contact neighbors. So the JOIN worker calls every unemployed by phone or sees them in person. Thirty people are contacted; eight turn out. One is a racist, but his arguments get put down by the group. One (maybe) is willing to work and has some sense of what needs to be done. The others go round and round on their personal troubles. The process is slow. . . .[20]

The JOIN strategy was most successful in Chicago, where ERAP focused on organizing unemployed Appalachian whites, but it was seriously limited even there by the fact that the impending economic crisis and high rates of joblessness never materialized. In other project sites the JOIN strategy to organize around the issue of unemployment failed miserably. What worked better in projects in black neighborhoods in Newark, Cleveland, and elsewhere was a new strategy oriented to other community issues and sarcastically called GROIN (Garbage Removal or Income Now). ERAPers found it more effective and easier to organize black women around issues like welfare, day care, schools, recreation, and rat elimination than to organize black men around unemployment problems. Women staffers in ERAP, however, were the only ones who felt comfortable organizing around GROIN issues such as food stamps or welfare benefits. Women organizers in both SNCC and SDS had always done some of the best organizing, while men always remained center stage and dominated the organizations. With the GROIN strategy, however, women organizers rose to the forefront in a number of projects. In Cleveland, where women assumed leadership, ERAP organized welfare mothers around social service issues. In Chester, Pennsylvania, a black community two miles from Swarthmore College, the GROIN strategy resulted in a public school boycott. Subsequent demonstrations there led to the arrest of 200 community people and fifty Swarthmore students and the formation of an executive committee of fifteen Chester adults. This committee proceeded to write a thirty seven demand platform which called for fair and full employment, new schools and housing, adequate health care, and police reforms.[21]

Such short-term successes aside, by almost every measure the ERAP program was a failure. Few of the projects were able to sink effective roots. Few were able to get many people, other than ERAP staffers, to meetings. Political education was minimal. ERAP organizers learned quickly that the impoverished recent migrants to urban America with whom they were working were not easily moved to mass collective action by outsiders who were young, white, and from affluent backgrounds. ERAP's stated goal of building "an interracial movement of the poor" remained a distant dream. Only a few of the projects, most notably in Chicago and Newark, even lasted beyond 1965.[22]

In some respect, working in SNCC was even more difficult. Organizing blacks in the Deep South meant risking your life. Reactionary elements there were well-organized and had a long history of violence against black people and white "agitators." If you were black, from the South, and in SNCC, a visit to your home town could mean jeopardizing not only your life but that of your family as well. Nevertheless, SNCC staffers had organizing advantages over their counterparts in ERAP. Southern black communities were knit more tightly by generations of experience and struggle than were Northern black slums, and SNCC grew out of a civil rights movement that was widely accepted and very popular in black communities in the South. Moreover, the issue of voter registration provided a focus and a measure of success for SNCC that the ERAP projects never achieved. At the least, SNCC's work in voter registration and desegregation actions hastened the pace of civil rights reform in what seemed in the early 1960s to be an almost impenetrable system of segregation. But as a recent biographer of SNCC put it, the organization's major achievement was its "unparallelled success in breaking through the socialized inhibitions of blacks in the rural South by undermining the legitimacy of existing white dominated institutions."[23]

As the federal government took up the mantle of desegregation during 1964–65, however, new left organizers, and especially those in SNCC, found themselves in a quandary. What strategy should a radical organization follow now that the federal government had become a champion of civil rights reform. While SDS gave up on community organizing, returned to college campuses, and began to organize students in 1965 around the antiwar issue, SNCC in that same year began to splinter into supporters, on one side, of a loosely structured participatory democracy and, on the other, of a tightly organized socialist revolution. By 1966 SNCC was advocating revolutionary black nationalism, and its style of organizing, best exemplified in later groups like the Black Panther Party, changed accordingly. But neither SDS nor SNCC had the historical impact each had hoped for.

Three factors most undermined their work in the period up to 1965. First, and perhaps the most serious problem facing the ERAP and SNCC projects, was the decimated state of the left in the early 1960s. This situation placed enormous burdens on the student left and deprived them of a national organization which could lend support. It also deprived them of a national program that could provide a radical political direction and context to their local work. The anticommunist purges of the 1940s and 1950s had effectively destroyed communist, socialist, and anarchist efforts, and the new left rejected the organizational and ideological remnants of what remained. SDS and SNCC were student organizations, doing community organizing for the first time, and often working with constituents of a different class and race; and they did so without guidance, without a program, and with almost no historical ties to radical predecessors. Being students with generally little political experience, they were ill-prepared to be *the* left. Almost everything they did was developed from scratch, as if they were the first activists ever to do community organizing. They had to develop strategy, programs, ideology, and structures at the same time that they were deeply involved in the all-consuming, day-to-day tasks of community organizing. It was impossible for them to be *both* the left and the student vanguard.

Except for a few specific SNCC projects like the Mississippi Freedom Democratic Party, new left activity at the local level lacked a national focus. SNCC and SDS saw problems inherent in localism. While staffers were committed to decentralization and community organization, they also understood that the problems poor people faced were not limited to a neighborhood or rural community and that a national movement was the ultimate objective of their work.[24] But SNCC and SDS were too busy fighting for immediate and local issues and demands to be able at the same time to integrate their work into a larger national framework that could break the political provincialism inherent in local work and effectively deal with national problems like class and race divisions. Given the immense burden of their task, however, most SNCC people simply assumed that such problems would be handled successfully once blacks won freedom and equality.

But without a means of linking everyday problems and struggles to an analysis of national power, without a national program and critique that put local activities in perspective as steps to larger and more fundamental changes, successful reform efforts at the local level, such as registering voters or securing welfare benefits, created the incorrect impression that the system was responsive and democratic, and that only reform, not radical change, was necessary. Kim Moody, an ERAP staffer, was right when he complained that "nothing in such [reformist] issues breaks through the localism of the poor. . . . What is there in the block programs that leads to 'revolutionary social change?' "[25] By 1964 and 1965 experienced SNCC staffers were fearing that if the reforms supported by SNCC succeeded, all that would be won was that black middle-class people, too, would have the right to worry about crab grass on their front lawn.[26] The new left knew that without radical change, the needs of the poor, especially the black poor, would not be met. They knew that reforms would only palliate the problems, ameliorate the most pressing and gross instances of poverty, as the later "Great Society" programs would demonstrate, but not attack the causes of poverty or racism and not give poor people the power they needed to alter their situation. But the new left lacked the national organization and direction which could help transform local reform efforts into a nationwide radical program.

Second, and this is more an internal than external problem, there was a critical contradiction within the theory of participatory democracy about the role of the organizer. How do you create a "leaderless" movement of "organizers?" How could you be an organization that organized community people but was fundamentally antagonistic to leadership and structure? Lerone Bennett, Jr., a prominent black intellectual, found SNCC "an organization in revolt against organization, a formless form." SNCC staffers at an ERAP meeting in 1965 pictured the ideal organizer as one "who never organized, who by his [sic] simple presence was the mystical medium for the spontaneous expression of "the people."[27] The most extreme example of this antileadership, antiorganizational ethic was the ERAP Hoboken "nonproject" in which the strategy was to simply find working-class jobs in this industrial New Jersey city, and let the tides take the organizing project where it would.

It is critical in community organizing to provide leadership, to do organization building, and to teach leadership and rudimentary organizational skills, but most new lefters thought this ran counter to the idea of letting the people decide. Clearly, letting the people decide made sense. It was especially applicable in SNCC where local people often *had* to decide because they were the ones who knew how to survive. If local people did not become involved and exert leadership, the SNCC project would not only fail but the organizer and anyone associated with him or her would be in serious physical danger. Nevertheless, a tendency in the new left to romanticize the power and impact of participatory democracy often led local projects to become absorbed with issues of democratic process and individual freedom, rather than skill development, political education, or collective goals. The results often ended up disappointing almost everyone. A JOIN organizer lamented that most people who came to the Chicago office "are revolted by the word 'socialism' and claim to be strong supporters of free enterprise; many conceive of their jobless state as due to their own shortcomings . . . their perception of the 'enemy' is fuzzy or worse."[28]

In creating a theory of community organizing in poor neighborhoods that denied the possibility of nonmanipulative leadership, organizers were led to pretend (sometimes even to themselves) that community people often "were deciding issues that only the organizers knew about, let alone understood."[29] Equally important, they developed an impractical theory which did not correspond with the needs and realities of their daily organizing. This problem was more endemic in ERAP organizing, where staffers tended to be more theoretically oriented and less a part of the communities where they worked. In SNCC longtime staffers with a good deal of field experience were often very pragmatic (they had to be to survive) and tended by 1964–65 to openly argue for a SNCC which was better organized to win collective power and argue against the romantic and counterproductive notion of a "nondirected," structureless organization.

A third, and more obvious, factor was the sheer physical and emotional drain of organizing. This was more the case in SNCC, but was true in ERAP as well. Neither group had the staff or resources equal to the task. Of course, most organizing efforts never do. But most organizers are usually trained and experienced. SNCC and ERAP staffers were often neither, and they certainly did not have the confidence and knowledge to reject or modify the furious pace of organizing. Many left SNCC and to a lesser extent ERAP out of exhaustion as much as anything else, the exhaustion that comes not only from fear but of always pushing to one's physical and mental limits. SNCC especially was hurt by its inability as an organization to help its organizers repair. They had no place to go to relax, to get out of the frontline, to replenish themselves. This meant that temporary "burnouts" were never recovered. People just left and did not return.[30]

Recognition of the flaws and limits of SNCC and ERAP community organizing projects should not lead us to underestimate their importance in the history of community organizing. Coming on the heels of nearly two decades in which progressive and left-wing activities had been destroyed by repression, capitulation to the Cold War consensus, and internal errors, the community organizing efforts of students in the new left, in both SNCC and SDS, were important breakthroughs. They were often brave and always innovative experiments with what democracy meant and what a democratic society should be like. They were significant challenges to the racial and class barriers which since the 1950s separated most radicals from the poor and minorities. Moreover, participation in these activities created the nucleus of a new generation of radical activists who had learned important lessons about community organizing, political power, and what it was like to be poor in America. After 1965 they continued to do community organizing and radical political work—in the antiwar movement, black power organizations, communities, training institutes, college campuses, social welfare programs, unions, and factories. The widespread belief in participatory democracy that bloomed in the late 1960s, prospered in the 1970s, and continues today owes a good deal, directly and indirectly, to the community organizing efforts of student radicals in the years 1961–65.

Equally notable for our purposes, the new left projects reflected a shift of focus by leftists to the local and communal level. Classical radical theory, from Marx onward, had always slighted or ignored community-based organizing, choosing to focus instead on large-scale factory organizing as the proper locus of class struggle. As noted earlier, even in radical community organizing efforts such as that of the Unemployed Councils in the 1930s, the Communist party's priority was organizing laborers at the industrial workplace. There are, of course, good reasons for this decision, most notably that the workplace united working-class people in a clearly focused and common struggle against the owners of capital. A number of factors coalesced by the early 1960s, however, to cause a rethinking of this basic radical premise. Perhaps primary, the civil rights movement, the basis of all sixties organizing, focused on community organizing because its demands for racial equality and human brotherhood were not limited to the workplace and because much of its constituency in the South were not employed in industrial jobs. In addition, important changes had been occurring in the United States' economy since World War II, among them the declining importance of industrial labor and the fact that white industrial workers and their union leaders no longer were the progressive force they had been during the thirties and forties. It was not surprising then that new left activists, who came from nonworking-class backgrounds and the Southern civil rights movement, looked to communities as the natural locus of their operations. The new left was not opposed to workplace organizing. It saw, as noted earlier, the inherent provincialism in community organizing. But for them, community and "issue" organizing at the grassroots level seemed most appropriate to the conditions of the early 1960s. Partly as a result of the factors that turned the new left to community organizing and partly as a result of the new left's efforts themselves, it is no accident that the major social change movements since that time—the antiwar, women's, environmental, and the antinuclear movements—all have had as their locus grassroots, community organizing, not factory or labor organizing.

The Great Society Organizing Projects: Community Action Agencies

It [the Economic Opportunity Act] must be a total effort to bring about broad community change. And this cannot be done by the Federal Government. We can only help by stimulating local action. It must be done by local people and local agencies working closely together.

Robert F. Kennedy, Attorney General

Few undertakings in our time have generated as much hope, produced as many immediate and beneficial results, or excited as much controversy as the anti-poverty program.

Lyndon Baines Johnson, President

Student radicals were not the first or only ones to notice the widespread poverty and social disorder in the "affluent society." On the heels of the recession of 1956–58, which hit black workers in the North and Midwest the hardest, social workers, philanthropic agencies, and the federal government implemented programs to curb youth crime and delinquency. Efforts began in 1958 with a grant by the National Institute for Mental Health (NIMH) to fund an experimental, comprehensive, and systematic juvenile delinquency program—Mobilization for Youth—on the Lower East Side of New York City. The Ford Foundation followed in 1961 with a similar endeavor in Oakland, California, the Richmond Youth Project. That same year President Kennedy initiated the President's Committee on Juvenile Delinquency and Youth Crime under the direction of attorney general Robert Kennedy. The following year, 1962, the president's committee issued planning grants to communities addressing youth problems in nontraditional ways and the Ford Foundation established four new "grey areas" projects. All of these projects shared much common ground. They were planned as "comprehensive" programs to be operated by new community organizations, controlled by the local community, and funded by a national source. They focused on inner-city black ghettos. The emphasis was on using recent social science innovations, disregarding traditional social welfare approaches, and encouraging citizen action and participation. "Experiments in working with the black community," one participant called them.[31]

They were not, of course, the first neighborhood-based projects to attract either national or federal funding. Most notable in the post-1945 era, the President's Advisory Committee on Government and Housing Policies in 1953 supported the development of "a broadly representative private organization . . . with congressional and/or Presidential sponsorship to mobilize public opinion in support of vigorous and responsible action by communities in urban renewal activities."[32] Likewise the NIMH, Ford, and federal projects were certainly not the first to emphasize the value of local control and citizen partic- ipation in social welfare efforts. What ultimately made them unique, however, was that the foundations and the federal government began willingly to initiate social change experiments that rejected traditional methods and encouraged grassroots citizen action, even protests against local public agencies.

The NIMH, Ford, and initial Kennedy programs were too small, however, to have much impact on youth problems or the rising tide of social disorder in cities. As these problems intensified, as SDS, SNCC, and Alinsky organizers continued to give political expression to some of the disaffected poor, and as influential, militant minority leaders such as Malcolm X advised black people to resist white racism "by any means necessary," the federal government re- sponded with a massive antipoverty program. By the fall of 1963, Kennedy's staff had begun working on a comprehensive program, modeled on the inno- vative NIMH and Ford projects, to deal with problems of poverty and discrim- ination. First Walter Heller and then Sargent Shriver, advisers to Kennedy, provided direction, but with Kennedy's death in late November, Lyndon John- son quickly assumed leadership of the project. The following spring Johnson described the outlines of his "War on Poverty" to Congress. Five months later the Economic Opportunity Act sailed through both the House and Senate, and the president signed it into law.[33]

The most innovative and central feature of the legislation and the one that most emphasized the ideals of "maximum feasible participation" and local control was the Community Action Program (CAP). The program established Community Action Agencies (CAAs) to sponsor neighborhood self-help proj- ects, promote social action, mobilize local resources, and coordinate local pro- grams. These CAAs would address concerns heretofore left to city, state, and nationwide organizations, and would be directly supported by public funds, 90 percent of which would come from the federal government. If the city or town refused to put up the 10 percent seed money or in–kind payment, then private groups could do so. Equally significant, the CAA was to be a broadly based program which superceded traditional channels by receiving direct funding and authority from the federal government. As Richard W. Boone, one of the program's activists, explained:

It was an attempt to move administrative authority closer to people directly affected by federal legislation. Not only did it allow a bypass of states, it endorsed new administrative instruments at the local level, thus offering the opportunity to bypass traditional instruments of local government. . . . Concern over neglect of the poor by public and private programs, their oppression by political design and the insensitivity of service systems were reasons for permitting, even encouraging, new conglomerate arrangements for policy and program.[34]

Why? Why would the federal government fund new programs designed to supercede local agencies? Why was the federal government so interested in community organizing and the "maximum feasible participation" of the poor in community-based programs? Urban renewal officials in the 1950s had viewed grassroots organizations with a good deal of trepidation. Why did the federal government establish new programs to address the issues of urban poverty rather than go through established mechanisms like public housing, the Social Security administration, and urban renewal? Why were John Kennedy, Robert Kennedy, Walter Heller, Sargent Shriver, and Lyndon Johnson, not to mention the host of "professional reformers" who designed the programs, so interested in involving the urban, black poor in planning and implementing programs, in "giving them a real voice in their institutions?"[35]

Most significantly, NIMH, the Ford Foundation, and the President's Committee on Juvenile Delinquency designed their early efforts at community organizing to promote social harmony and ameliorate urban social disorder. Persistent unemployment had undermined traditional forms of social control such as religious, family, educational, and community institutions, and had caused an alarming spread of gang delinquency, vandalism, drug addiction, and serious crimes against people and property. The Civil Rights movement and its black clergy leaders ignited this disorder, most often unintentionally, by politicizing the poor and especially the young in nonwhite urban ghettos. Fueled by exacerbating ghetto conditions and the leadership of radicals like Malcolm X, urban disorder was transformed by 1963–64 from individual acts of violence to massive urban rebellions. Urban ghetto residents looted stores, burned property to the ground, and killed police with sniper fire from the rooftops of ghetto tenements. Something had to be done. This collective disorder was creating havoc in the nation's key economic and political centers.[36]

The Great Society, however, was more than a traditional liberal reform program to palliate and coopt mass insurgency. It sought not only to defuse protest from below but to reincorporate blacks into the political process and thereby solidify the support of black voters for the Democratic party. It sought in essence to create new black political organizations in the inner cities and the rural South which would strengthen black political involvement and electoral participation.

Changing electoral patterns were a crucial concern of presidents Kennedy and Johnson. In the early days of the New Deal the Democratic party had been able to forge an enduring North-South coalition. By the late 1940s, as blacks pressed their demand for equality and as the Democratic and Republican parties, responding to the pressures of the Cold War, became more liberal on issues of race and civil rights, the white Southern segment of the Democratic coalition became less dependable and increasingly unstable, moving toward third party "Dixiecrat" candidates or Republicans whose position on domestic questions, especially race, were more in line with their segregationist sentiments. In the extraordinarily close election of 1960, John Kennedy received overwhelming support in the black ghettos of strategic Northern cities. At the same time the States Rights party won in Mississippi and Alabama, while Florida, Tennessee, Kentucky, and Virginia all voted Republican. To counter the loss of Southern strength, the new administration began to seek methods of strengthening its base of support among minority groups. They had especially high hopes for the black vote, but while blacks continued to vote heavily Democratic, local impediments to their active participation in party politics jeopardized the extent of their total voting power and thus the value of their support.[37]

Kennedy and Johnson initiated a wide array of social reform legislation in the years 1961 to 1968 with the intent of using the managerial powers of the president and the allocation of federal dollars to deal not only with social disorder but the more partisan political problem of party realignment. The "War on Poverty" was fundamentally designed for urban nonwhites, especially blacks, not for poor people. While many CAAs, especially those programs in non-Southern rural areas, included few blacks, black predominance is most obvious when the CAP is seen from a national perspective. Only 25 percent of the funds, for example, went to rural areas, and more than two thirds of that was spent in the "black belt" area of the South. In many areas, people of other minority groups and the white working class played active and important roles, but in essence CAP was seen as an extension of the Civil Rights movement, as a "black program."[38]

Of course not all of those who designed the program, from the officials in the White House to the professional reformers, shared a single motive. Few of the professional reformers shared the electoral concerns of the political officials. The more liberal reformers claimed that the CAP was not intended to forestall social protest, but rather to give direction and organization to it. Many others believed that the primary objective was to address urban problems with the latest innovations in social welfare theory. That the architects of the program shared differing methods and objectives is apparent in their still continuing debate over what the program was all about. Nevertheless, the objective of the White House from 1961 to 1968, especially after 1963, and the fundamental animus behind the program was the response to disorder and the realignment of political coalitions in the nation.

Like the Wagner Act, which sought not only to defuse protest but bring industrial workers firmly into the ranks of the Democratic party, CAP became a double-edged sword of social reform. As the Wagner Act was a piece of class-oriented legislation to galvanize the white working class, so CAP was racial legislation intended to develop new local organizations which could assist and empower primarily blacks and other minorities. And as labor activists used the Wagner Act as a mobilizing tool to carry the union movement far beyond what FDR intended, so too did black and other activists see CAP as a grassroots organizing device which could be used to organize and advance the poor, especially the black poor, far beyond what the federal government planned.

The program spread like a prairie fire. Within eighteen months of the passage of the OEO legislation there were over 1,000 funded CAAs in the United States. While CAAs differed dramatically depending on the local political environment, the fights for citizen participation and for neighborhood organizing dominated the first years of most locals. In few instances did citizen participation come without struggle. Initially, OEO did not spell out any specific guidelines regulating the selection and composition of the boards of directors that governed local CAAs. So in the first Community Action Agencies a coalition of public officials, welfare agency leaders, and representatives from groups involved in liberal social causes dominated the boards. For example, when asked why there were no representatives of the poor on the local board, the mayor of Nashville, Tennessee, who made the appointments, asserted "you can't have unqualified people running good programs." In Atlanta, the initial CAA Board had no poor people and only one representative of the poor, Martin Luther King, Sr.[39] In San Francisco, Mayor Shelley made all thirty nine initial appointments, as did the mayor in Oakland, no elections were held in "target area" neighborhoods, and no means created by which poor people could ensure their "maximum feasible participation." Predictably, local leaders had no intention of helping local citizens supercede or oppose local agencies and authorities.

Struggles with community people over citizen involvement ensued. In San Francisco, one year after Mayor Shelley's initial appointments, local activists raised enough protest and exerted sufficient pressure to get the board changed from the mayor's initial thirty nine appointments to a more representative board of forty seven people. Of the forty seven, twenty three were mayoral appointees and twenty four were elected neighborhood representatives, six from each of the four target areas. This happened in CAAs throughout the nation, not just in progressive centers like the Northeast and West coasts. But in the highly politicized CAAs, most commonly found in cities with large black populations, every issue—whether model cities, welfare, CAA funding and personnel, public housing, or service delivery—became an area of contention between neighborhood people and the local "establishment." Local politicians could no longer work behind the scenes, for neighborhood people now demanded a voice in what happened in their city and their neighborhood. Local officials, of course, were not used to this. Shelley complained in 1967 that the struggle over maximum feasible participation in the local CAA "expanded the social revolution in San Francisco into a chain reaction of unrest and distrust that has left its mark on every major civic improvement project attempted here in recent years."[40]

The level of conflict varied from city to city. In cities like Oakland, Newark, New York, and Syracuse, where political conflict between established authorities and citizen action groups was not uncommon, where there was a heritage of civil rights insurgency, and where there was generally a well-organized, militant black community, CAAs were often confrontational, dynamic, and militant. In such places, demands for citizen participation were aggressive and the CAA focused on neighborhood advocacy and organizing, not service delivery. Where the political environment was more conservative, in cities such as Chattanooga and Phoenix, where blacks were fewer and radicals in the poor and minority community were less well-organized, or in cities where the political environment was more constrained, such as Chicago where the political machine tightly controlled the urban bureaucracy, CAAs tended to be less participatory and less confrontational. In these places, CAAs performed essentially service delivery and "watchdog" functions. In all CAAs, however, poor people and activists used the agencies to advance the level of politics in their cities and neighborhoods and increase the flow of benefits to the poor.[41]

The expanded participation of the black poor and their representatives pushed the more politicized CAAs beyond an emphasis on child and social welfare programs to neighborhoood advocacy, organizing, and development. A large number of relatively autonomous neighborhood service centers, commanding 15 percent of the total CAA budget, were formed in target areas in 1965–66 by local CAA boards of directors. In the early years local CAA officials fought with neighborhood people and their board representatives over the content of neighborhood center programs. Chartered to perform "outreach" and "referral" services, neighborhood centers in the more politicized CAAs were often led by experienced community organizers who sought to go beyond the designated service functions. They did advocacy work, primarily defending the rights and advocating the needs of welfare recipients. They did community development work by setting up well-baby clinics and developing school lunch and rodent extermination programs to foster a greater sense of community solidarity and power. They engaged in social action work, for example, pressuring the public housing and public welfare bureaucracies and promoting rent control legislation. The advocacy and social action projects proved most threatening to local officials and accordingly received the lion's share of the program's publicity.[42]

The furor between local officials and neighborhood representatives in the more politicized CAAs in the nation between 1964 and 1967 obscured a widespread inability of the CAP to organize poverty neighborhoods effectively. CAP programs had so many built in bureaucratic restraints, most notably a hierarchical and bureaucratic structure with seemingly endless responsibilities, paper work, and regulations, all outlined in OEO guidelines, that it was impossible for community people to use the agencies as effective vehicles for representing minority-group interests. Exhaustive comparative and case study research of CAAs throughout the nation has concluded that, except in a few cases, local community action agencies served more as traditional service delivery systems to the poor than as social change organizations, and that "no radical redistributions of influence, power, service rewards and other benefits" occurred as a result of the community action program.[43] Because of the intensity of the struggles in the early years of the more radical CAAs, both sides often exaggerated the extent of actual power gained and institutions changed by neighborhood activists.

At the peak of protest activity in the years between 1966 and 1968, national and local officials allied to defuse CAP. From the outset, local officials and agency representatives had been wary of a social reform program that skirted their political control. Such CAA actions as welfare protests and court suits initiated by Legal Aid lawyers mobilized the poor but further fanned the flames of distrust and political reaction. The conservative backlash that occurred in 1967, however, was not unprecedented. Since 1964 local officials in New York had attacked the community action projects of Mobilization for Youth. While MFY was not very successful in addressing problems of poverty, it did engage in some well-publicized confrontations with powerful groups in New York City—the Board of Education, the police, and local landlords. When MFY's talk about the "powerlessness of the poor" and "tenants rights" made opponents even more uneasy, the "redbaiting" began. An editorial of August 1964 in the widely read *New York Daily News,* for example, accused MFY of being "infested with Commies and Commie sympathizers."

Soon MFY's director was forced to resign and all MFY business was ordered to go through city departments.[44]

CAP followed a similar path. From early in 1965, when the federal government made clear that participation of the poor was a condition for receipt of funds, local politicians worked to undercut the legislation. Hubert Humphrey pressured Sargent Shriver, then head of OEO, to ease up on the citizen participation demand. In 1965 the League of Cities and the Conference of Mayors both sought to limit the involvement of the poor in the running of local CAAs. At the mayors' conference, Shelley of San Francisco and Yorty of Los Angeles accused OEO of "fostering class struggle." The federal government, performing a difficult balancing act, moved to appease local officials while allowing the local CAAs to continue their activities. Shriver declared in 1966 that "We have no intention, of course, of letting any one group, even the poor themselves, 'run the jobs' or 'run the programs.' That's not *community* action . . . [which is] maximum feasible participation by *all* segments of the community. . . ."[45] OEO followed the rhetoric with action. It agreed to make private arrangements with mayors in fifteen cities to clear all CAP grants in their areas through city hall. It passed regulations prohibiting partisan political activity and the employment of those in "subversive organizations" and not "of good character." By late 1966 the trend was clear. CAP was tightening the reins on local CAA activities, checking local militancy, and shifting to what Saul Alinsky criticized as a "zoo-keeper mentality."[46]

The so-called Green Amendment passed by Congress in 1967 tightened the screws on community action. Like all federal agencies, OEO had to secure new appropriations each year. By 1967 OEO was in serious political trouble, especially among Republicans and Southern Democrats. Representative Edith Green of Oregon, an advocate of the antipoverty program but a constant critic of OEO, offered an amendment to undercut the power of poor people in local CAAs. First, the amendment required that all CAAs be designated by state or local governments. This rerouted all grants-in-aid through local officials, instead of directly allocating it to local community organizations. A direct channel could be maintained, however, if local officials chose not to intervene. Curiously, eight months after the passage of the Green Amendment 97 percent of local governments chose to continue existing relations with local CAAs and not move to widen their control. Why? Because many local officials had come to terms with the CAA projects and found it easier to live with existing relations than to stir up a hornet's nest, and because the second provision of the Green Amendment made it unnecessary to implement the first one. This provision limited the size of the board of directors to no more than fifty one people, composed equally of one-third democratically selected representatives of the target areas, one-third public officials, and one-third representatives of business, labor, civic, and charitable groups. While community people in places where CAAs had little citizen involvement benefited from the Green Amendment's institutionalization of at least one-third community representation, CAAs with far greater levels of citizen participation were undermined as the poor no longer had a majority on any of the local boards.[47]

Equally significant, the character of the more democratic and militant CAAs quickly reflected the composition of their new boards. They became increasingly "professional." The impulse to confrontation, to fight the local welfare or rent control office, to demand increased community control or expanded allocations for Manpower programs, for example, became mired and then lost in bureaucratic discussions about budgets, accountability, efficiency, and personnel. Increasingly, concerns of community planning, coordination of resources, and management required greater and greater sophistication and skills from board members. The professionals on the staff and on the board often possessed these skills and felt most comfortable with the new emphasis on organizational maintenance. Community people did not, and were relatively powerless to do much more about it than harrass the "pros" or learn how a public bureaucracy functioned, both of which some activists did exceedingly well.

If the Green Amendment cut the heart out of CAA militancy, budgetary changes sealed the coffin. In 1966 all CAP funds, except Head Start, were discretionary. The local agency could use them any way they wanted. By 1968, 60 percent of all CAA dollars were directed to national emphasis programs like Upward Bound, Legal Services, and Manpower. And a sizable percentage of the remaining 40 percent went to administrative salaries and fixed costs such as building upkeep. From the start CAAs had little funding to wage a "war on poverty." By 1968 they had a lot less at their disposal.[48]

Nixon's election in 1968 heralded the end of CAP, for the Republican party knew its constituency did not reside in the poor inner-cities and rural areas of America. From 1968 to 1972 CAAs became even more absorbed in operating programs, certainly not advancing social change or citizen action. They became, as one historian wrote, "part of the problem, another service agency rather than a mobilizer and coordinator of agencies."[49] In some communities agencies informally continued to support social change efforts by providing meeting space and use of resources such as photocopying and mimeograph machines to radical organizations. When Nixon's "New Federalism" passed through Congress in 1972, however, the "War on Poverty" was laid to rest. The "New Federalism" got the federal government out of the grant-in-aid business and into distributing "block grants" to states and cities. Nixon called this "revenue sharing." This program gave local officials and bureaucrats much more control over social welfare funds. The new program continued the pretext of citizen participation, but the participatory component of revenue sharing or community development block grant funding was always token, ad hoc, and purely advisory.

By the early 1970s meaningful citizen action and citizen participation in federally funded social programs was a thing of the past, a memory of the Civil Rights movement and tumultuous 1960s. CAAs continue today under the Community Service Administration, as advisory social service organizations, directing low priority federal programs like energy conservation and fuel assistance and serving as local administrators for United Way funded programs. Their work is often valuable and progressive, often not, but always a mere shell of what was initially intended by some CAP architects and hoped for by community activists.

Was CAP a success or a failure? For whom? For the Democratic White House in the 1960s it was a limited success. As a strategy for rebuilding the Democratic party it did not duplicate the effect the Wagner Act had on the earlier Democratic coalition, for party realignment and the causes of Democratic party decomposition could not be addressed so simply. Nevertheless, in less than a decade many civil rights activists did become government employees and in many cities poverty programs became new black political organizations. It is no accident that the number of black mayors in the United States rose from almost none in 1968 to 108 in 1974. In Newark, the poverty program provided the organizational structure upon which Kenneth Gibson built a power base for his successful bid for mayor. Moreover, the community action programs provided new opportunities and resources, in the form of better salaries, skills, and job experience, which especially assisted the black middle class in taking advantage of the political opportunities created by the Civil Rights Act of 1964 and the Voting Rights Act of 1965. Great Society projects did not secure political equality for blacks in the United States, but they were not intended to do so. Rather, in a relatively short period of time and with a limited amount of funds, the programs not only coopted many of the most militant activists and groups, but also channeled much of their energy into traditional electoral and bureaucratic structures. To this extent, the Great Society served the purposes of its Democratic designers.

For the tens of thousands of poor and black people who became active in local politics for the first time, CAP was an important educational experience. They learned how the political system functioned, how established agencies sought to coopt dissent, how people who were willing to take risks and stand up for their rights—individually and collectively—had power and could successfully pressure the political system for services, benefits, and jobs. They learned that simply bringing issues to light, bringing the problems of poverty, racism, and inequality to public view, was not sufficient. As David Austin and others have demonstrated in studies of CAAs, and as many CAA people learned, mass resistance, direct action, and protest were critical to effect change.[50]

The CAA experience also demonstrated to many the limits of "participationism." The political and economic system was willing and able to let poor people participate in an advisory and token capacity in social welfare decision making at the local level. It was not willing to give these people power, as limited as that power might have been. The class and race cleavages in the economic and political system, especially at the local level, ran so deep that even the slightest power at the bottom threatened to crack the foundation.

To its credit, the federal government, for whatever motives and intentions, did support and fund a grassroots citizen action program. To their credit, community workers, if only minimally, shook up the system, pressured local bureaucracies, gave people a sense of their latent power, and used this as a formative experience for political work in the 1970s. A number of organizations, the National Welfare Rights Organization, for example, evolved directly out of the experiences of the activists and architects of CAP. Ultimately, however, CAP did not alter appreciably the problem of poverty in the United States. It assisted in the expansion of a professional, black middle class, but it did not affect the factors that kept many whites and most black and brown people impoverished. A more substantial program would have developed a national policy of services and jobs to ensure decent housing, health care, education, and, most importantly, employment as a right to everyone.

Furthermore, the programs of the CAAs and the Great Society in general were based solely in rural and urban ghettos, which guaranteed that more widespread changes need not result from them, that people living in affluent communities need not be affected by them, and that the chief contradictions in society—namely, class and race stratification—would remain so. Without a program promoting fundamental political and economic change from the national level on down to the neighborhood, liberal programs such as the CAP and its predecessors in the Progressive era and the New Deal ultimately served to maintain the class status-quo rather than improve the position of people they were intended, in theory, to assist.

CHAPTER 5

The New Populism of the 1970s

Recessions, Inflation, and the New Corporate Conservatism

We believe in democracy—and average people controlling their lives and the right of every person to fulfill his or her God-given potential as a human being. We are willing to take that dream of a truly democratic America and transform it into flesh and blood organizations of average people, who through their own efforts, can make it into a reality for themselves and their children.

Jean Mayer, President, Illinois Public Action Council

The conservative consensus of the 1950s and the welfare-state liberalism of the 1960s were grounded in the continuous and often substantial growth of the United States economy after World War II. The nation was faced with serious problems abroad and at home during these years, but in general the fruits of being the premier world power kept the economy in impressively good health. As economist Robert Heilbroner notes, in the United States as well as other "advanced" capitalist nations the two and a half decades from 1947 to 1972 "were the longest period of growth that capitalism had ever experienced, almost a quarter of a century of nearly uninterrupted expansion."[1] Much of the international capitalist economy's strength in the post-1947 period rested on the ability of the United States to fuse together industrial capitalist nations and dependent Third World countries into a single economic system under the leadership of United States capital and corporations.

By the early 1970s, however, the sound economic foundation began to crack as the worldwide imperial system of United States capital faltered in the

face of successful Third World insurgency and heightened competition from
Japan and West Germany. The crisis, stimulated by a 400 percent increase in
OPEC oil prices, came in 1973–74, just after United States withdrawal from
Vietnam, and began the most serious economic downturn since the Great
Depression of the thirties. Unemployment between 1973 and 1975 rose 75
percent, but even that figure masks the concentrated impact in minority communities and working-class neighborhoods in Northern cities. The recession
produced "pockets of unemployment" in some black ghetto areas, for example, that ran as high as 90 percent of all black youth. Layoffs, plant shutdowns,
"runaway shops" became commonplace in industrial cities in Ohio, Pennsylvania, New York, Michigan, and Illinois. Moreover, this recession was
unique, and especially difficult to resolve, because it was accompanied for
most of the decade by double-digit inflation.

Walter Hoadley, vice-president of the Bank of America, reported that businessmen reacted to the collapse with "sheer fear." No longer was the chief
concern of the corporate community developing a "people's capitalism" or
redistributing wealth in the affluent society. No longer was the problem how
to live well amid luxury. This was an economic crisis, not a boom period like
that of the previous two decades. How were corporations to deal with the unprecedented twin problem of high inflation and high unemployment? How
could they resolve the problems of declining profits and productivity? How
could widespread domestic and international insurgence be prevented as economic uncertainty and crisis grew? These were the new concerns of corporate
and national leaders.

The beginnings of the new corporate response to the economic crisis of the
1970s emerged, political commentator Harry Boyte suggests, in 1972 with
then Secretary of the Treasury John Connolly's call for a "new level of partnership" between business and government in which government would cur-
tail its restrictions on corporate activities and, at the same time, develop new
means of aiding big business. A more complete corporate program emerged
after Watergate. Corporate leaders and "New Right" theoreticians launched a
concerted ideological attack on the "welfare state" of Keynesian economics.
More specifically, the new corporate agenda called for an "age of limits" characterized by balanced government budgets, fewer public social service programs, lower corporate income taxes, higher corporate tax credits and depre-
ciation allowances, and, in general, an attack on progressive gains of the last
generation—from minority and women's rights to health, consumer, and environmental regulations. The object was to get big government off of the back
and out of the lives of the American people. It is inefficient, it is unwieldy, it
is expensive, and it is the cause of our current dilemma.

Corporate leaders were well aware that it was not going to be an easy job selling the "neo-conservative" program to the public. Surely people were receptive to the antigovernment aspects of the corporate agenda. Watergate, Vietnam, government corruption and scandals, haunting disclosures about CIA and FBI activities, and dehumanizing experiences with public bureaucracies had alienated citizens from official representatives and government agencies. But it was one thing for people to think big government was the problem; it was another to see big business as the solution. The movements of the sixties had changed people's political consciousness. Even those who opposed the movements learned about the value of active participation in realizing and expanding what is possible. A sense of grassroots self-assertiveness was a central legacy of the decade. People were energized and empowered by the events of the decade and not about to forget their dreams or acquiesce responsibility to either government or big business. The neo-conservatives had their hands full. As a *Business Week* editorial put the problem:

Some people will have to do with less—cities and states, the home mortgage market, small businesses and the consumer will all get less than they want. It will be a hard pill for many Americans to swallow—the idea of doing with less so that big business can have more. Nothing that this nation or any other nation has done in modern history compares in difficulty with the selling job that must be done to make people accept the new reality.[2]

The neo-conservative strategy was implemented most easily in cities. Elected national politicians such as presidents Carter and Reagan were unable, given among other things their support of increased defense allocations, to cut the national budget deficit. At the local level, however, the situation differed. Fiscal crises, rising unemployment, welfare cutbacks, attacks on public unions, and declining services became the lot of cities in the 1970s. Much of this urban crisis was the result of the general economic situation. Historically when the national economy falters, cities—the central nodes of the economic structure—suffer badly. But not all cities were affected equally in the early 1970s. Northern cities, from commercial centers like New York, Boston, Cleveland, and San Francisco to single-industry towns like Youngstown, Ohio, suffered severe crises. Cities in the "sunbelt," though not without problems of poverty, insufficient services, racial and class segregation, and pollution, to name but a few, did not experience the economic recession to the extent of their Northern counterparts. Houston, for example, a city with vast social problems, experienced massive growth throughout the 1970s, with an unemployment rate consistently around or below three percent.

As long as the boom of the fifties and sixties remained, the fiscal situation, if not the political and social situation, in Northern cities remained intact. These cities were highly vulnerable in the late 1950s to fiscal crises resulting from residential suburbanization and industrial decentralization, which drew the affluent and the tax base beyond the city's taxing borders. But "pro-growth" coalitions, composed of central-city politicians, liberal bureaucrats, corporate executives, and real estate and construction industry representatives united in city after city to push for federal welfare and urban renewal programs, highway projects to connect the central city to the suburbs, and locally initiated and financed downtown redevelopment. They united, often successfully, to revive these cities by bringing money back in and renewing growth.[3]

But the economic base upon which the pro-growth coalition of the 1950s and 1960s operated was largely the product of the unprecedented economic expansion in the post-1945 decades. As the recession and international economic problems hit in the early 1970s and as growth funds receded, Northern cities became burdened by their declining tax bases, increasing city indebtedness, and deteriorating social services. Many of these cities, New York being the most notable, teetered on the brink of bankruptcy. No longer were the bankers, financial analysts, and corporate investors praising and supporting "pro-growth" projects. Whereas cities like New York were previously applauded for their efforts to reinvigorate the central city and maintain social peace, now financiers and federal officials saw them as mismanaged, overly generous, unwieldy bureaucratic messes which needed to be taught the lessons of fiscal responsibility. The neo-conservative solution gradually took hold at the local level. No money would be forthcoming from banks or the federal government unless cities mended their extravagant and wasteful ways. What this meant was that the corporate sector, especially financial institutions, would play a much larger role in the control and guidance of Northern cities.

Neo-conservative strategies for urban change became commonplace. Using models of "planned shrinkage" or "triage," officials planned to bulldoze or ignore the poorest areas of the city. They hoped the residents of these neighborhoods would be coerced into moving out of the city and beyond the city's burden, preferably to the sunbelt where jobs were said to abound. Roger Starr, the New York City housing and development administrator, went so far as to suggest in 1976 that fire and police stations as well as public schools be closed in slum areas as a method of accelerating population decline. No longer were the poor to be helped. The new corporate strategy saw them as bad investments, economic roadblocks to cutting city costs.

The new urban strategy began during the Nixon administration. In the first two years of the revenue sharing program, which replaced the Johnson administration's Office of Economic Opportunity projects, over half of the funds

were used to lower city taxes and much of the rest went to buttress law enforcement, uses intended to aid and protect business development and make
the city more attractive to the affluent. Only 3 percent was spent on social
service programs for those in need. By mid-decade the conservative strategy
had accelerated. Urban economist George Sternlieb, reflecting the drift to the
right, argued that "you can't support the poor without the rich, and every time
someone rich stays in Manhattan it's a triumph for the poor. . . ."[4] But as
Sternlieb was quick to point out, such an analysis was not an easy one to sell
to poor and working-class people. It was not even an easy one to sell to New
York's political leaders who, despite joining the chorus of "fiscal conservatism," found themselves in a terrible economic mess without any assistance
from either the federal government or the banking industry. New York Mayor
Abe Beame incorrectly saw it in partisan terms, as "a Republican pincer
movement responsible not to the people but to financial institutions." But he
was on the mark in decrying that corporate leaders, especially in the financial
institutions, were "using cash as a weapon in an attempt to direct the social
and economic policies of our city."[5]

Of course the people affected by urban renewal in the 1960s or planned
shrinkage in the 1970s did not sit passively by and let the private and public
sectors implement their programs. Urban rebellions in most large cities challenged the architects of urban renewal in the 1960s. More quietly and often
more effectively, ad hoc neighborhood organizations formed to block urban
renewal or highway development plans, win services, jobs, and other benefits,
and demand greater community control. In 1970 there were four hundred ongoing community struggles in the nation against highway construction plans
alone. In a climate of growth and prosperity, such neighborhood organizations
were not able to completely stop development or fundamentally change the
general plans of urban renewal or highway development. But they did slow
down the process, slightly alter the plans to protect their community, secure
marginal participation, and, most effectively, win benefits from a City Hall
and federal government willing to coopt rather than repress grassroots
resistance.

The neighborhood response to urban problems accelerated with the economic crises of the 1970s. "Media-hype" to the contrary, activism did not end
with the turn of the decade, and not all activists became stock brokers or born-
again Christians, as did Jerry Rubin and Eldridge Cleaver. Most activists held
on to their initial vision of social, political, and economic democracy, and
brought it with them into the neighborhoods where they lived and into the
schools, factories, social welfare and health care agencies, and legal and political offices where they worked. As Gale Cincotta, the leader of National Peo-

ple's Action, a national neighborhood coalition, put it in 1977: "I keep hearing that everything's dead and there's no big cause since civil rights and the Vietnam War. But that's a myth. There's a neighborhood movement that started in the sixties. It's not as dramatic with everyone out in the streets, but it's steadily gaining strength in every city and state. The base was there and people reached the point where they just had to do something."[6] While the media continued to tout the conservative drift of the nation and wondered what happened to the sixties generation, many thousands of neighborhood organizations, single-issue groups, and progressive political action efforts formed in response to the economic crisis and the new corporate strategy.

By the end of the seventies the neo-conservative program had secured repeated victories. A *Fortune* reporter glowed that "suddenly business seems to possess all the primary instruments of power—the leadership, the strategy, the supporting troops, the campaign money—and a new will to use them."[7] While he overstated the corporate strategy's success, as the rest of the media had done so with the "death of the sixties," neither claim was without some basis. People may not have been convinced that corporations were their natural allies, but their powerlessness and the absence of an alternative, left program led them to accept the dominant conservative choices presented. Nevertheless, what did not make the pages of the media was the fact that based on the lessons and experiences of the 1960s, a multifaceted, "new populist" citizen action movement had developed in the 1970s to counteract the alienation that most Americans felt from both the public and private sector.

The Roots of the New Populism

The radicalism of the 1960s has become the common sense of the 1970s.

Tom Hayden, political activist

In response to events of the 1960s and the economic crisis that followed, a widespread interest in neighborhood organizing arose throughout the United States in the 1970s. The *Christian Science Monitor,* in a series of articles in 1977, reported a "groundswell movement of citizens calling for the return of political and economic power to the local level."[8] More than twenty million Americans were active in hundreds of thousands of neighborhood groups throughout the nation. Several thousand block clubs sprang up in New York City alone after 1975. The National Commission on Neighborhoods listed over 8,000 larger community groups throughout the nation. Communities Organized for Public Service (COPS) in San Antonio, one of the largest, single-community organizations in the nation, was able to turn out 6,000 delegates to its 1976 convention, only two years after it began. The Association of Community Organizations for Reform Now (ACORN) claimed in 1980, ten years after it was founded, some 25,000 active dues paying members in ACORN neighborhood organizations in nineteen states. Perhaps even more impressive were the more than a dozen organizer-training centers founded in the 1970s to serve the needs of citizens' groups. As people increasingly turned away from public and corporate leadership, they turned inward to spaces and interests where they could have more control, and nowhere was this more visible than at the neighborhood level.

Many commentators see the groundswell as a new populist movement in the making. Traditional populism, ranging from the writings of Thomas Jefferson to the more radical farmer and labor movements of the late nineteenth century, championed America's democratic mission and supported the struggles of "the people" against the "plutocrats." The new populism is very much within this tradition. As Mike Miller of the Organize Training Center in San Francisco describes it, the basic values of the new populism are the values of democracy. Its fundamental analysis is that "unchecked power has become concentrated in the hands of a very small number of people who are at the helm of the major corporations of the nation." Because government remains unaccountable to most people, it too, along with business, is part of the problem. The solution is for people to organize in democratically controlled and administered community organizations built upon "the democratic values and self-interests of the people."[10] Since the nineteenth century, populism has assumed a middle ground between the elitism of traditional liberalism and the class conflict analysis of socialism. While it is critical of elements of the economic system, it sees bigness and unaccountable power, rather than capitalism, as the fundamental problem.

It is not surprising then that much of the new populism began as a reaction against the revolutionary socialist organizing of the late 1960s. Harry Boyte, a prominent new populist commentator and theoretician, epitomizes this when he writes that "contemporary citizen organizing is more down to earth, more practical, above all more enduring and rooted in the social fabric [than sixties organizing]. It seeks to build ongoing organizations through which people can wield power. It is accompanied by a sense of the rightness, creativity, and vitality in people's traditions, folkways, and culture that sixties radicals were prone to scorn or dismiss."[11] Accordingly, new populist neighborhood organizing rejects the emphasis on anticapitalist political ideology, the focus on "consciousness raising," the sectarianism, the single-minded attention to a particular constituency—whether blacks or students— all of which, new po-

pulists contend, isolated late 1960s organizers from working people and prevented the development of effective grassroots neighborhood organizations.
Instead, the new populism offers a "majoritarian strategy" rooted primarily in
the communities and traditions of white and black, low and moderate income
people. It offers an organizing approach which tones down late 1960s emphasis on ideology and focuses on winning power and building organizations
owned and directed by working-class people. To accomplish such goals, these
organizations often ally with traditional community institutions like churches,
unions, and ethnic associations.

Notwithstanding their rejection of sixties revolutionary politics, the new populism emanates directly from the experiences of young men and women,
black and white, in organizations and movements of that decade. The new
populism, above all, reflects a continuous effort since the early 1960s to find a
successful radical program that presents, as an alternative to corporate capitalism, a vision of a more cooperative, democratic, and decentralized society.
For example, Wade Rathke, the founder of ACORN, got his start doing welfare organizing and working with George Wiley and the National Welfare
Rights Organization. Harry Boyte was active in the southern civil rights movement and a co-founder of the New American Movement (NAM), a new left
socialist organization. Heather Booth, the founder of the Midwest Academy, a
training and resource center for new populist organizers, was a leading figure
in the antiwar, student, and women's movements, a veteran of both SNCC and
SDS. Steve Max and Tom Hayden were both active in the initial ERAP projects of SDS and continue to be important theoreticians and leaders of new
populist campaigns for economic and political democracy. Mike Miller was
also prominent in ERAP, worked with SNCC, Cesar Chavez, and the United
Farm Workers (UFW), organized with Saul Alinsky in Kansas City in the mid-
1960s, became the lead organizer in an Alinsky-style project, the Mission
Community Organization (MCO), in San Francisco, and is now director of the
Organize Training Center in that city. What we have then in the 1980s are new
populist organizers and political activists, living and working in neighborhoods and communities throughout the country, with nearly two decades of
political and organizing experience under their belt. And while the 1970s have
altered their political perspective and tactics, the animating core of their experience rests with the antiimperialist, participatory democracy struggles of the
sixties.

It is no accident that the new populist critique of sixties organizing is remi-
niscent of the salvos launched during that decade against the new left by Saul
Alinsky. At his best, Alinsky criticized sixties organizing for not being
grounded in working-class politics and traditions. At his worst, his criticism

smacked of the traditional populist error of throwing the baby out with the bath water, that is, a tendency to deny an entire radical left heritage rather than simply criticize its errors. The connection between Alinsky and the new populism is fundamental. Heather Booth calls him the Sigmund Freud of modern community organizing. And as Freud and his disciples codified the field of psychoanalysis, so Alinsky and his successors have done with the tactics of populist-style community organizing.

Alinsky organizing experienced hard times from the late forties until the early sixties. The Cold War repression kept Alinsky and fellow organizers defensive and ineffective. Their one success during this period was the Community Service Organization (CSO), an effort initiated by Alinsky-organizer Fred Ross in Chicano communities in California in the late 1940s. Throughout the 1950s Alinsky was pretty much forgotten, both in social welfare and what remained of activist circles, but he and his method were revived, along with many others, with the civil rights and antipoverty movements of the early 1960s. It was not until mid-decade, however, that Alinsky's work in lower-class black and white neighborhoods in Chicago came to popular attention. As other left groups became increasingly militant and revolutionary after 1965, as black ghettos rebelled and burned, and as liberal leaders sought more "reasonable" alternatives, Alinsky, once ostracized as a "Bolshevik organizer," seemed more moderate and therefore more attractive.

Alinsky came to national attention as early as 1964 when *Fortune* editor Charles Silberman, in an influential liberal critique of race relations, *Crisis in Black and White,* touted Alinsky and his IAF (Industrial Areas Foundation) organizer-training center as the answer to America's race problems. For Silberman, the IAF organizing project in the Woodlawn neighborhood of Chicago, a neighborhood just south of the University of Chicago, of some 65,000 people, 86 percent of whom were black, was "the most important and most impressive experiment affecting Negroes anywhere in the United States." In a call for more Alinsky-style efforts, he lamented in the book's afterword that there was only one Alinsky and so many black slum areas. The praise and notoriety received by Alinsky and The Woodlawn Organization (TWO) were not accidental. Amid rebellions in comparable black slum areas throughout the nation, Woodlawn did not have a riot. Alinsky saw this as the result of effective, grassroots political organization; the residents in Woodlawn did not have to resort to spontaneous, undirected rebellion. People in power, however, saw Alinsky's populist organizing as a less threatening alternative, a less dangerous political program than the revolutionary black nationalism developing in organizations like SNCC. It was not surprising to find *Time* magazine shortly thereafter heralding Alinsky as the "The Prophet of Power to the People."[12]

Each of the numerous Alinsky projects of the 1960s was decidedly different. TWO was the first Alinsky effort to focus on a black community. The Organization for a Better Austin (OBA) in Chicago organized among local block clubs, while the Northwest Community Organization (NCO), based in a primarily Polish area of Chicago, organized Catholic church groups. In the mid-1960s, especially the period 1964 to 1967, Alinsky and the IAF ventured beyond Chicago, organizing three projects in black neighborhoods: CUA (Council for United Action) in Kansas City, Missouri; FIGHT (Freedom, Intregration, God, Honor, Trust) in Rochester, New York; and BUILD (Build Unity, Independence, Liberty, and Dignity) in Buffalo, New York. But in each project from TWO to BUILD, irrespective of the differing local conditions, Alinsky organizers addressed immediate community concerns and worked to build "people's organizations" based on what they saw as the most prominent community traditions and sources of cohesion.

And despite important differences, Alinsky organizations in the 1960s generally followed a similar development, one most evident in TWO's history. Until mid-decade Alinsky-initiated organizing projects, most notably in Chicago, espoused and practiced the ideology of equality and the tactics of non-violent confrontation of the Civil Rights movement. From the mid-1960s through the early 1970s, Alinsky organizations shifted from a civil rights orientation to an emphasis on negotiation and community development. NCO continued the pressure group, conflict approach of the early sixties, but TWO, FIGHT, and most others moved from "confrontation to coexistence." This development has wide applicability to new populist organizing today and underlines again some of the weaknesses of the Alinsky model.

For example, TWO, formed in 1961, was initially quite militant and confrontational. It held rent strikes and demonstrated against merchants accused of short weights. It formed a procession of buses filled with more than 2,000 Woodlawn residents and in a style similar to that of the Civil Rights movement went down to City Hall to register to vote. Alinsky described one of the confrontational methods of the early TWO this way:

When TWO has a bunch of housing complaints they don't forward them to the building inspector. They drive forty or fifty of their members—the blackest ones they can find—to the nice suburb where the slumlord lives and they picket his home. Now we know that a picket line isn't going to convert the slumlord. But we also know what happens when his white neighbors get after him and say, "We don't care what you do for a living—all we're telling you is to get those niggers out of here or you get out." That's the kind of jujitsu operation that forces the slumlord to surrender and gets repairs made in the slum.[13]

By the late sixties and early seventies, however, TWO was no longer a confrontational pressure group advocating the needs of low-income people in the Woodlawn area. Increasingly it had become a community development corporation, run by the more middle-class segments of the neighborhood, which tended to promote projects that primarily aided upwardly mobile blacks. TWO was able to survive in its new guise, no small feat for Alinsky-style neighborhood organizations which usually have a life span of six years at most. But it survived in a different form than originally intended. It became the co-sponsor and co-administrator of development programs funded and largely designed by private foundations and public agencies. It became part of the externally initiated antipoverty programs of the late 1960s. For example, TWO co-sponsored a 762 unit, middle-income housing project in Woodlawn which demolished 2,000 units of low-income housing. It administered an Early Childhood Development Center, an OEO-funded Head Start program in the neighborhood, with a $100,000 annual budget. It received funds from the Zenith Corporation and later from the federal government to do job training, which ultimately resulted in TWO developing a Career Vocational Institute supported by state and federal funds. It received other grants to develop experimental schools, training centers for mental health workers, and rehabilitated housing. TWO even became the owner of a neighborhood supermarket, a project begun to raise funds for the organization.

As a community development agency TWO was a success, the shining gem of all Alinsky organizations in the sixties and early seventies. The shift from "confrontation to coexistence" was remarkable in its level of measurable accomplishments. But TWO was now a neighborhood development corporation, not a "people's organization." It was run by a paid, professional staff whose attention was fixed on development and growth, organizational stability and professional competence, not on social change or even serving the needs of *all* the neighborhood people. Predictably, neighborhood resident participation declined as technical expertise grew to paramount importance. TWO became just another business in the community, a non-profit business almost as removed from many of Woodlawn's problems and needs as the profit-oriented enterprises.

Moreover, in the face of powerful economic pressure, TWO was defenseless. In 1971, for example, Chicago newspapers ran articles about how East Woodlawn was being burned to the ground. In 1970 alone there were 1,600 fires in a mile square area. While the city did nothing and TWO was unable to mount effective opposition to these obvious acts of arson, developers waited for the complete destruction of this valuable chunk of land bordered by two parks, a golf course, museums, beaches, and the University of Chicago. There was no longer an opposition organization in the neighborhood, as TWO had been in 1961, to challenge the transformation of this area into a "gentrified" upper-middle class section of the city. Ultimately, TWO was unable to stop not only the gentrification of East Woodlawn but the continuing deterioration and impoverishment of residents in other parts of the community. The story of TWO and the Woodlawn neighborhood is more complex than related here. But the evolution of TWO into a neighborhood development agency which was unable to defend neighborhood interests results in large part from problems inherent in the Alinsky method, specifically its localism and its lack of a clear, long-term program for changing power relations at the city level and beyond.[14]

In essence the trend in Alinsky organizations was to ignore issues of social change or concerns beyond the neighborhood and simply bargain for benefits which could develop and improve the local community and assist its long-term residents, usually those who were "better-off." The cooptive pressures of federal and local programs assisted this development. So did the disorganized state of the left. The late sixties and early seventies offered nonsocialist, predominantly white-led groups, such as Alinsky's, two weak alternatives. "Balkanization," a tendency to divide into small, isolated political units, was adopted by most neighborhood organizing efforts. "Single-issue coalition," on the other hand, such as the antiwar movement, was preferred by more national-oriented projects but had no permanent structure and no staying power beyond the issue. TWO, MCO, OBA, and most other Alinsky organizations chose Balkanization with its interest-group style, parochialism, and antipoverty program support.

In the early 1970s, the limits of Alinsky organizing were not well known or understood. People active in movements of the 1960s felt a deep need, especially after United States withdrawal from Vietnam, to continue moving the nation toward greater democracy, equality, and justice. They were attracted to Alinsky-style strategies primarily based on their perception of what was wrong with the student-based and student-led movements of the previous decade. What they knew of the Alinsky method sounded good, especially the fact that it rejected the revolutionary rhetoric and openly socialist ideology of the late 1960s that isolated students from poor and working people. While many sixties activists thought of themselves as socialists, the seventies seemed to call for a rethinking of traditional left views of how to bring about radical change in the United States. The populist, democratic ideology of Alinskyism seemed to many to be a good, if imperfect, place to begin that rethinking.

Neo-Alinskyism

Some people say what does ACORN want? The answer is simple: We want sufficient power in our cities and states to speak—and be heard—and heeded—for the interests of the majority of citizens. We want to participate in community and civil affairs, not as second class citizens because we don't drive Rolls Royces, but as men and women committed to a better future where our concerns are met with justice and dignity; where wealth, race and religion are insufficient excuses to prevent equal participation and impact in government; where any person can protect his or her family and join with others in community strength; and where, as ACORN's slogan goes, "The People Shall Rule." That is what America is. That is what ACORN wants. Nothing more and nothing less.

Steve McDonald,
ACORN President of Executive Board

Many new populist organizations were directly initiated by Alinsky-trained organizers and their students. Tom Gaudette, for example, once a vice-president for the Admiral Corporation, received his organizer training at the Industrial Areas Foundation and helped organize, among other efforts, the Organization for a Better Austin (OBA) in Chicago and the MidAmerican Institute in the early 1970s. The Institute, in turn, initiated community organizing efforts in Oakland, Baltimore, Seattle, New Orleans, and elsewhere. Most new populist efforts, however, had no formal or direct ties with Alinsky-trained organizers. Whether directly or indirectly related to IAF organizing methods, the more progressive new populist groups reflected a modification of Alinsky methods in the 1970s, the development of a "neo-Alinskyite" organizing strategy.

The essence of neo-Alinskyism is to develop mass political organizations rooted in neighborhoods, grounded in local concerns, and focused on winning concrete gains. The goal is to advance social and economic democracy, empower people, and challenge power relations within and beyond the neighborhood. Many organizations in this new populist trend acknowledge that fundamental social change in this country demands a multi-issue, multiclass, multiracial, national organization that rests on grassroots organizing but goes beyond the neighborhood or community unit. They advocate a "majoritarian strategy" geared primarily to the needs of low- and moderate-income people, which they estimate to be 85 percent of the population. They work hard to hurdle the weaknesses of Alinsky-style neighborhood organizing in the 1960s which defined and limited itself to a neighborhood, race, or ethnic group—often pitting one oppressed group against another—and which suffered a good degree of isolation in relation to other groups and the political system as a whole.[15] All neo-Alinskyite projects employ the ideology of the new populism—decentralization, participatory democracy, self-reliance, mistrust of government and corporate institutions, empowering low- and moderate-income people—and at their best see themselves as grassroots organizations working to connect up with the national political process.[16]

Neo-Alinskyism differs in other respects from its founding father. It breaks away from the highly professional orientation and reliance on large-scale institution and foundation support characteristic of the Industrial Areas Foundation model. It criticizes Alinsky's overemphasis on the "super organizer," an emphasis which makes it difficult for working people, who are not used to public roles, to assume leadership tasks and responsibilities. Moreover, neo-Alinskyite efforts do not require, as do IAF programs, a sizable capital outlay from community groups before organizers agree to enter the neighborhood. TWO, for example, was not begun until the IAF received a $69,000 grant from the Schwartzhaupt Foundation, a $50,000 contribution from the Catholic Archdiocese, and the promise of support from Presbyterian churches. Unlike most new populist organizers, IAF "professional organizers" are well-paid and their organizations well-financed.

Traditional Alinskyism remains most effective in Mexican-American communities in large Southwestern cities where the Catholic church is a primary bond of unity and is often willing to play a social action role. Because of centuries of oppression, language barriers, and cultural factors, the Chicano community in cities like San Antonio has been kept politically isolated and inexperienced, ready for the low-keyed, self-empowerment skills offered by the IAF. Where IAF trained organizers, such as Ernie Cortes, have taken the time to work slowly through existing organizations, especially the churches, to involve what Cortes calls the "central core leadership" into citywide organizations drawn from Mexican-American neighborhoods, Alinskyite organizations like COPS in San Antonio, UNO in Los Angeles, and TMO in Houston have had a considerable impact.[17] But even in these cases the traditional IAF model has been altered. Like all neo-Alinskyite organizations, these community efforts, while often localist and based among a single cultural nationality, seek as well to build "majoritarian" organizations which are allied with other low- and moderate-income groups and at least citywide in perspective.

One of the earliest and most successful examples of neo-Alinskyite organizing is the Association of Community Organizations for Reform Now (ACORN). Begun in 1970 in Little Rock as Arkansas Community Organizations for Reform Now, ACORN has direct roots in the organizing strategies of Fred Ross, who studied under Alinsky, and the National Welfare Rights Organization (NWRO), perhaps the most effective, single-issue community organization of the late sixties. Wade Rathke, ACORN's founder and director, received his community organizing training and experience, as well as support for the Arkansas project, from George Wiley and the National Welfare Rights Organization. Officially formed in 1967, the NWRO modeled much of its practice on the work of Fred Ross, not Alinsky. The Alinsky model emphasized organizing the leaders of existing neighborhood institutions, especially churches, to serve as the natural foundation for grassroots projects. In his work with the Community Services Organization (CSO) in the barrios of California, Ross saw the value of such institutional-based support, but found greater success organizing house-to-house on specific issues of concern to community members. And whereas Ross saw the need for a statewide organization which could more effectively advance the interests of neighborhood people, Alinsky feared the "fascist" potential of large organizations. The NWRO, and later ACORN, employed the door-to-door, issue-organizing approach of Ross.

ACORN, however, modified the NWRO strategy to include the development of a mass organization of low- and moderate-income people, the majority of people in the United States, which could pressure the political system from the neighborhood up to the national level. For ACORN the neighborhood was a "training ground" or "staging area" from which to mount larger campaigns for democracy, equity, and justice. The single-issue and single-constituency (primarily poor blacks) approach of organizations like NWRO came to be seen by George Wiley, Wade Rathke, and others as too limiting. Rathke, commenting on his organizing problems while working with NWRO in Massachusetts, put it this way: "The next-door neighbor to the welfare recipient was just as antagonistic to the recipient as anyone else. . . . With the welfare issue you're always dealing with a minority. We all knew that we had to break out of the single-issue campaign. I wanted to build on a majority constituency rather than on a minority, where the next-door neighbors are in it together, not fighting each other."[18] ACORN, then, was designed to be a novel effort at employing the new, "majoritarian" strategy in a mass-based, multi-issue, Rossian-style of community organizing.

Since 1970 ACORN has attracted hundreds of primarily white, college students into community organizing. ACORN job advertisements in 1982 promised "A job you can believe in. ACORN needs organizers to work with low and moderate income families in 26 states for political and economic justice. . . . Tangible results. Long hours and low pay. Training provided." Most of the trainees, now taught at the Institute in New Orleans, are novices, never having done much political work or community organizing. The Rossian method, as it is taught by ACORN, is similar in many respects to the early efforts of SNCC and ERAP. The following general model of door-to-door organizing has been taught by ACORN, depending on local conditions, for over a decade.

(1) *You, the organizer, are sent to a community.* You do not enter a neighborhood with an issue, but neither do you go in just for the sake of getting people organized, as Alinsky-trained organizers often seem to do. Your goal is to help bring about economic and social justice for low- and moderate-income people. Be guided by ACORN's slogan, "The People Shall Rule." The selected area, of some 300 to 1,000 households, should have the constituency you seek and natural geographic boundaries. First see if there are any "external contacts" who can put you in touch with community people or give you a better sense of the neighborhood and its concerns?

(2) *Develop internal contacts.* Get people's names and talk with them in their homes. Begin to sell people on the idea that they too can be organizers and that all people should be organized. You could say, "Doctors are organized, so why shouldn't we be?" Find someone willing to hold the first house meeting. All this time, you should be developing lists of people you talk with and those you need to see, and lists of community concerns. The more lists, the more information you have, the greater your knowledge of and concern with the community. All of the above should take between six and nine weeks.

(3) *Organize the first house meeting.* At the first house meeting you organize make sure that you get a good representation of the community, but keep it under a dozen people. Take time here to get adequate representation. This initial organizing committee is a critical building block of the neighborhood organization. At this first meeting begin to identify issues. Perhaps you can even draft a letter at this meeting, declaring the group's concern about a winnable neighborhood issue. Direct the letter to the community and use it later as an organizing tool when you go door to door. This first meeting will often digress into people's personal and sometimes parochial concerns. It is important to let this happen; people do not often have the opportunity to do this in a collective way. Listen well. You learn from listening, not from talking. If you have organized effectively before the meeting, you will have a good sense of what issues will come up. Nevertheless, meetings are critical for developing

group solidarity and leadership skills, instilling confidence, and heightening people's spirit and willingness to struggle.

(4) ***Promote the organization.*** During the next month go around town, door-to-door, with members of the organizing committee talking to as many people as you can. This "door knocking" is perhaps the most important activity you will engage in. By talking directly with people in the informal, intimate atmosphere of their homes you can reach them in a personal way. Remember, people will get involved not only based on the issue, but also because they like you, or trust you, or are looking for something meaningful to do. They are often frustrated, angry, and tired with local problems which they feel powerless to correct. The door-to-door approach enables you, as no other method does, to engage and draw out people, to learn about them as they learn about you, and to give people a better sense of their collective power.

(5) ***Honor the organizing process.*** During the organizing process, people will surprise you. Do not make assumptions for them or about them. Remain open. Develop a useful index file on each person you meet—you will never remember important things about their interests and their skills otherwise. The door-to-door process is especially valuable in discovering potential leaders. Invite them to join the organizing committee group. One of the chief strengths of door-to-door organizing, as difficult as it is sometimes, is that it finds people who never were or never thought of themselves before as leaders, people who were never before even asked their opinion. Hold more house meetings. Some people will quit; only a few will do work. Remain flexible and open.

(6) ***Identify an issue.*** After talking with nearly everyone in the community the organizer has an incredible knowledge of community people and problems. It is likely that issues that concerned you and the organizing committee initially are no longer dominant. Identify the issue that your work thus far indicates is the best one, the one that will galvanize community people and show them they can win if they organize and work together. Remember, however, not to push people into an issue. It is not important what the first issue is. What is most important is to get people involved. The organizers should be presenting options, tactics, alternative ways of looking at things, information gathered from their full time efforts. But let the people make the decisions.

(7) ***Hold a neighborhood-wide meeting.*** Hold a major second organizing committee meeting. Follow this with telephone calls, flyers, press releases about an upcoming neighborhood-wide meeting to discuss the identified issue. Make this as important an event in the neighborhood as you can. This is the meeting at which the organization will be born. Perhaps the night before it, get together again with the organizing committee and agree upon who will lead

tomorrow's meeting. Get people to nominate each other for the election of
temporary officers. You need only one nominee for each office. Make sure
that everyone who attends the founding meeting gets a chance to speak. People
came to have their say. Make a list of their comments. Hold an election at this
meeting for temporary officers, which will provide an ongoing structure for
the organization. Get people at the meeting to become dues-paying members
($1 a month, $10 a year in the early 1970s). This will provide some funding
but more importantly people relate differently to an organization that they
own. This founding meeting should result in a community-wide action, which
was planned roughly by the organizing committee before hand.[19]

When ACORN first began in Arkansas in 1970, it focused on six neighbor-
hoods of low-income residents in Little Rock. Using their NWRO experience,
Rathke and others found a sentence in the welfare manuals which said that
poor people had a right to get furniture. Before long ACORN had negotiated
with then-Governor Winthrop Rockefeller for a "furniture warehouse."
ACORN caught on quickly after that victory. The Centennial Neighborhood
Association, the Woodrow to Pine Neighborhood Association, and the Nine-
Seventeen Community Organization, as well as others, "seemed to grow overnight." They focused on securing school lunch programs, demanding welfare
rights, and improving public housing conditions.

Two years later ACORN expanded beyond its neighborhood bases, launch-
ing a grassroots "Save the City" campaign. The citywide effort respected
neighborhood interests and at the same time cut across class and racial lines. It
opposed blockbusting in white neighborhoods, demanded more parks in predominantly black neighborhoods, and worked on traditional community concerns like traffic, sewerage, and stray dogs. ACORN organizers stayed away
from issues like racism that might jeopardize a victory. Opposition to blockbusting, for example, was carefully directed by organizers as pro-neighbor-
hood, pro-working people, not anti-black. The thinking, very much like that
of Alinsky's, was to avoid issues which undermined unity and which clouded
focus on the "real enemy." It was the job of ACORN organizers to isolate and
expose any individual or group trying to turn the blockbusting issue into one
of white versus black neighborhoods.[20]

In his assessment of ACORN's first efforts commentator Andrew Kopkind
noted that "winning is what is important in organizing, and it's almost an ob-
session with ACORN." Winning built an organization, and build ACORN it
did. In 1975 they became an interstate organization, branching out into Texas
and other states. By 1980 they had more than 25,000 dues-paying members in
nineteen states. Two years later their federated organization claimed 50,000
members with roots in neighborhoods in twenty six states. When ACORN

came to Houston in 1980, for example, it entered with a reputation. One of the city's two daily newspapers carried front page stories on consecutive days warning about this organization that wanted power for low- and moderate-income people, that believed "The People Shall Rule." The two white ACORN organizers sent to Houston, recent graduates of the University of Texas at Austin, had little firsthand knowledge of the city, and found the organizing difficult. People in the black community, where ACORN often focuses its efforts, were little interested in the new organization. Nevertheless, ACORN's reputation for militant direct action, its successes in Arkansas, Dallas, and elsewhere, and its growing power worried Houston's conservative establishment.

As ACORN grew into a nationwide organization it became increasingly involved in electoral politics. This shift from pressure politics to pressure *and* electoral politics is increasingly apparent in many new populist organizations frustrated with the steady but minimal gains of grassroots, pressure-group tactics. In areas where ACORN is new and a less significant force, such as in Boston, where Mass Fair Share is the dominant new populist group, or as in Philadelphia where the Consumer party and others are well entrenched and strong, ACORN emphasized militant direct action tactics, like house squatting, particularly in poor black neighborhoods which are often ignored by "majoritarian" organizations. In areas where ACORN is more entrenched or where repressive conditions make direct action less productive, electoral political activity is emphasized. The move to electoral politics is consistent with the neo-Alinskyite objective of having low- and moderate-income people win power, rather than simply pressure those in power, and it is consistent with the goal of connecting grassroots organizing with the national political process.

More traditional Alinsky groups, like National People's Action, still adhere to the pressure group model, convinced that electoral participation will undermine the effectiveness and grassroots nature of community organization. ACORN, however, disagrees, emphasizing that real power cannot be won solely by pressuring or exposing those with power. Real power is when low- and moderate-income people, or their true representatives, can make the actual decisions. The strategy used by ACORN in the 1980 presidential elections, for example, was to ask the two major national parties to incorporate into their party platform the issues in ACORN's people's platform. Similar statewide organizations, like the 75,000 family Mass Fair Share and the community, senior citizen, and labor-based Ohio Public Interest Group (OPIG) have also recently rethought their distrust of electoral politics, and are plunging "head first" into the political arena, throwing their weight for and against issues and candidates much like populist political action committees. The assumption is that by organizing people and supporting candidates around programs that emphasize economic democracy and justice, a genuine, not doctrinal or isolated, democratic people's movement will arise and ultimately win power.[21]

A central problem with neo-Alinskyism is that any movement which rests on a reform-oriented populist ideology tends to be dominated by its organizers and highly vulnerable to cooptation by business-backed or conservative union-backed reform movements. Neo-Alinskyite groups seek to build a majoritarian left out of the traditions, hopes, and dreams of working-class and middle-class people. Consequently, with such a diverse constituency they deemphasize political education, especially the anticapitalist vision of many of their organizers, for fear that "red baiting" will divide support at a time when divisiveness might not be survived. This leads to a strong tendency in ACORN and related efforts to remain staff intensive, to see the organizer as an "expert" who practices a method, almost a "science," of organizing. In some projects grassroots participation tends to appear only at selected and critical times—at mass meetings, direct actions, elections; ACORN staff, for example, handle the day-to-day business and direction of the organization. Thus, the depth of political participation and real organizational democracy often remains shallow.

In communities were ACORN has developed a strong presence, they do "a damn good job" of identifying and training local people to be organizers. In many other neo-Alinskyite programs neighborhood people who never before were involved in political activity developed sophisticated organizing and leadership skills. For most neo-Alinskyite organizers, developing indigenous, working-class leaders is what organizing is all about. Ernie Cortes reflected this commitment when he noted that "No organizer should be so arrogant as to pretend he's going to organize an organization. I didn't organize COPS. The leadership organized them. I challenged them and I worked with them on a one-to-one basis. But they did the organizing."[22]

But even in the numerous instances where indigenous leaders are developed, the extent of political education is limited and the training tends to focus on organization building skills—how an organizer can get people to join and build a neighborhood program. The political education of both staff, indigenous leaders, and organization members, critical to any long-term, fundamental political change, is deemphasized. Part of the reason is new populist pragmatism, which encourages winning victories and avoiding potentially divisive positions. Moving from one victory to another in rapid succession is easier than going slowly, giving people political education, and having to deal with some very sticky problems. Victories guarantee that the organization will survive, and a strong argument can be made that people learn best from firsthand experiences. But given the deemphasis on political education and ideology, it is not always clear whose traditions, whose hopes and dreams, whose community the new populism supports. Whose traditions are supported, for example, when new populist organizations refuse to take a stand on busing for school integration or on abortion?

To elaborate the point further, block and neighborhood associations organized around racial exclusion are as apparent in the 1970s as are those organized against redlining. ROAR (Restore Our Alienated Rights) in Boston demonstrated the right-wing possibilities of neighborhood organizations using the rhetoric of the new populism. In the Boston-based ROAR the ideology of participatory democracy is shrewdly manipulated by middle-class business leaders and politicians into an aggressive and militant, reactionary "a, b, c" program—antiabortion, antibusing, and anticommunism. "Let the people decide" and "community control" become the basis for actions against women and nonwhite minorities. In ROAR and in other reactionary, neighborhood-based organizations the multiclass call for "neighborhood power" loosely masks racist alliances between the white working-class and middle-class businessmen and politicians. These alliances are often initiated by middle-class leaders who stand to profit financially and politically by preserving the segregated status quo. In the white, working-class area of South Boston, ROAR supporters saw the organization as a last ditch effort in a period of economic hard times to defend their meager but relative advantage over blacks and to prevent the expansion of slum housing and problems into "Southie." These supporters, however, were mobilized and encouraged by "ward" political leaders who own substantial property and have ties to local real estate and banking interests.[23]

ROAR is exceptional in its size and strength. It is well organized, with a staff in 1976 of 150 volunteers, 400 active members, and 200 paramilitary "marshalls" who do the organization's more "aggressive" work. But it is not unique. Linda Gordon and Allen Hunter, in an article on the new right, recently made clear that democratic grassroots organizing, based on the folkways of church, family, and male authority, often led to conservative and right-wing advocates of the new populism. What political path neighborhood organizations take depends to no small degree on its organizers, founding principles, and on how its victories and defeats are interpreted. In poor and working-class neighborhoods, people get involved to defend their neighborhood, and participation usually produces increased frustration and anger. But what becomes the object of the group's anger depends on its politics, ideology, and the extent of political education around issues of class, race, and gender.[24]

Most neo-Alinskyites see organizations like ROAR as aberrations or as completely unrelated to the new populism. Accordingly, they avoid politically divisive issues related to class, racism, sexism, and nativism, and see a program of conscious political education around an anticapitalist vision as more of a hindrance than a help. This may be very shortsighted. A political critique of the nation's economic, political, and social system which advances specific programs and positions could unify and strengthen such organizations, not to mention prevent conservative tendencies from taking hold.

The New Community Development

In the Bronx and on Manhattan's Lower East Side, in the barrios of East Los Angeles and ethnic neighborhoods of Chicago, across the country in communities once considered "garbage dumps" by city administrators— redlined by banks for years and starved of traditional social services—stirrings of a new spirit have become visible.

Harry Boyte, political commentator and activist

While there is a tendency to see almost any inner-city neighborhood organization as part of the new populist movement of the 1970s, it is not clear exactly how much unity and common ground is shared among the organizations. There appear to be significant differences in origins, goals, strategies and structure among the multitude of groups currently speaking seriously on behalf of neighborhood organizing. While the neo-Alinskyism of groups like ACORN represents the most politically active and consciously left-oriented wing of the new populism, there is another important trend in the new populism, best exemplified by a community development orientation, which is more localist and more conservative than neo-Alinskyite organizations.

Development-oriented organizations share with neo-Alinskyite groups a "let the people decide" ideology, a willingness to use conflict tactics, and a deep frustration with the policies of elected representatives, corporate executives, and bureaucrats. They share an opposition to social forces and public and corporate policies which are hostile to their neighborhood's survival. Like most of the neo-Alinskyite neighborhood movement of the 1970s, they are generally found in blue-collar, white "ethnic" neighborhoods where little left-oriented or civil rights political activity took place in the 1960s, but they appear as well in black, Hispanic, and white working-class neighborhoods with long histories of struggle. These are the neighborhoods in large cities that experienced serious deterioration and displacement by the mid-1970s due to redlining, absentee homeownership, blockbusting, urban renewal, gentrification, insufficient social services, and nonexistent municipal capital improvements.

While neo-Alinskyite and community development groups overlap in many other ways, they differ substantially in what they see as the problems, solutions, and future for neighborhood organizing. Simply stated, neo-Alinskyism seeks to solve the problems of inequality, injustice, and autocracy facing working people by building a locally based, national movement to pressure and change the system, perhaps even to develop a populist political party which could wrest power from the current, corporate-dominated ones. The other trend, as one author describes it, includes the host of localist neighborhood organizations that limit their focus to community development in a single, low- and moderate-income neighborhood and look skeptically on projects "to build new institutions or amass power for 'external' uses." For them the emphasis is on maintaining and strengthening neighborhood networks and organizations, not creating social change or a new political movement.[25] They see neighborhood decline, especially physical deterioration, fostered by working-class powerlessness, as the problem. And they seek to gain maximum benefits for the physical and economic restoration of the neighborhood by working in, maximizing benefits from, and even accepting the restraints of the existing political and economic system. Leaders in development-oriented, new populist organizations are most often the petit-bourgeoisie of the neighborhood, the owners of small homes and businesses, who are concerned that economic pressures are going to wipe out the value of their one major investment. Where such organizations lack a class analysis, where they identify themselves solely as members of a racial, religious, or ethnic group, where they reject alliances with other low- and moderate-income people outside their neighborhood and cultural group, then they, like ROAR, can take on a consciously reactionary cast. More often, however, they adopt a conservative politics as did the Back of the Yards Neighborhood Council and TWO, where goals of neighborhood development and protection became paramount.

The Southeast Baltimore Community Organization (SECO) is a good example of the more localist, neighborhood development trend in the new populism. SECO began in 1966 with City Council plans to put a six lane highway through, and demolish hundreds of homes in, certain southeast neighborhoods of Baltimore.[26] A few people got upset enough to try and stop the road's destruction of the neighborhood. Southeast Baltimore is a white, working-class area of the city. Its approximately 95,000 residents are mostly second and third generation, Eastern European immigrants—Poles, Ukrainians, Greeks, Italians, Germans, and Czechs. Southeast Baltimore is not a slum. People who live there like it, and have liked it for generations, which is why the residents who got together to stop neighborhood deterioration ultimately found so much community support. What got it all started was the formation of a "coalition," called SCAR (Southeast Council Against the Road), to oppose the building of a six lane highway through the neighborhood. SCAR was able to stop the development of Interstate 83 by shrewdly getting the Fell's Point neighborhood named to the national Register of Historic Places, and therefore off-limits to bulldozers. To this day, community people note with pride, this six lane expressway "stops in downtown Baltimore as abruptly as the end of a diving board."[27]

But as in hundreds of other neighborhood organizations which formed to fight "renewal" and highway projects in the late sixties and early seventies, the struggle in southeast Baltimore against Interstate 83 revealed that the highway was only one aspect of a much larger plan to alter the neighborhood. SCAR activists unearthed "development" plans which many people had suspected or had heard about, but about which most people felt little could be done. City planners wanted to rezone one area of the community for industry. Another section was slated for demolition and "renewal." Social services were declining throughout the area and some were in jeopardy of being eliminated entirely. For example, no new school had been built in southeast Baltimore for over a generation. As the city government had boycotted the neighborhood for decades, contributing to the neighborhood's deterioration, so banks had "redlined" it. Redlining is the practice whereby banks withhold mortgage or home improvement loans to "high risk" areas. Through this practice banks encourage a so-called "neighborhood cycle" of slow deterioration, demolition, and renewal. As the causes of southeast Baltimore's problems were brought to light, groups working independently to keep a library open, to stop a rezoning plan, and to set up a recycling center joined with SCAR to establish a community "umbrella" organization to oversee and unite all grassroots efforts.

On a rainy evening in April 1971 more than a thousand people, representing over ninety organizations, came to what was to be the founding meeting of SECO. At its essence, SECO is a coalition of neighborhood groups—block clubs, church groups, union locals, ethnic fraternal organizations—begun, in the Alinsky mold, by uniting leaders from local organizations and institutions and thereby grounding the community organization in the traditional structures of the people who live there. And, like Alinsky organizations, SECO initially used direct action, confrontation tactics to achieve its goals. Mothers with baby carriages blocked and diverted truck traffic to keep trucks off of residential streets. A wheelchair protest march helped keep open the community's only public nursing home. An ongoing battle with city officials secured lower density zoning and thereby discouraged further subdivision of homes into rental units. SECO stopped the library from being shut down; it demanded and secured improved services from the city, including two new schools. It organized housing inspection teams, a neighborhood-based health cooperative, a public school reform program, and a Youth Diversion Project, which is said to have successfully reduced neighborhood juvenile delinquency recidivism rates.

SECO members, working closely with city officials, also got the local Department of Housing and Community Development to formally investigate the practice of redlining by local savings and loan associations. The commissioner's report confirmed SECO's claims, concluding that most of the city's lending businesses were practicing redlining. Neighborhood residents, especially homeowners, united to fight against the banks, whom they now knew to be major contributors to the neighborhood's decline. In a compromise with SECO, the banks agreed to stop redlining Baltimore's poorer neighborhoods if southeast neighborhood people supported lifting the 8 percent usury ceiling imposed by the state legislature. This compromise seems to have marked the end of SECO's "confrontational" phase and the beginning of its neighborhood development approach. The change is one quite similar to that which occurred in other Alinsky organizations, the BYNC and TWO most notably.

Organizers and activists in SECO were never completely agreed on what the organization stood for and what goals it ultimately sought to accomplish, other than defending the neighborhood and advancing neighborhood interests. Even in its confrontational phase it was always willing to work with, even depend on, city officials, like the commissioner of housing and community development. Barbara Mikulski, the "godmother of SECO" who was later elected to the City Council and to the U.S. House of Representatives on a neighborhood-oriented platform, put it this way: "We knew we had to be tough and militant. But the 'issue' was always the enemy. And we knew the very institutions that we challenged were the ones that we would have to work with when peace broke out. So it was never 'the Mayor is our enemy' or 'the City Council is the enemy.' We never attacked people. We attacked issues."[28]

Nevertheless, SECO never spoke on behalf of the need for fundamental political, economic, and social change in Baltimore and the United States in general. Some of the more leftist members, however, believed so privately and argued their position within the organization. What ultimately happened, as was the case in so many other new populist groups in the 1970s, was that SECO split over the direction of the organization. Those more to the left saw SECO becoming just another part of the establishment, another "successful" neighborhood development agency able to improve the quality of some aspects of the neighborhood but unwilling to tackle the broader problem of powerlessness faced by low- and moderate-income people. They argued that only through struggle and confrontation at the neighborhood, city, state, and national level can the political power and economic security of working people be raised sufficiently to give them effective participation in determining the future of their communities, not to mention their own lives.

SECO's first president, Jack Gleason, saw the problem differently. "We knew we could stop the city from doing things through the usual confrontation tactics. But if we were going to achieve the revitalization of southeast Baltimore, there were things *we* had to do, from the positive standpoint—housing, school reform, and so on. That's when we went into the neighborhood economic development stage."[29] Many others, within and without the neighborhood, supported the shift in priorities. Robert Cassidy, discussing the SECO experience in his *Livable Cities,* suggests that the litmus test of a neighborhood organization's maturity is when it effectively uses, as did SECO, both organizing/confrontation tactics *and* development/partnership strategies.

In SECO's case the immediate results seemed to reinforce the revitalization strategy. SECO's tactics were initially confrontational, because it was outside the channels of power. But it learned that effecting modest reforms in an urban environment is not that difficult, at least for predominantly white, multiclass neighborhoods, if conditions are right and neighborhoods are willing, if need be, to collectively and openly challenge the economic and political powers in the city. SECO established a Neighborhood Housing Services as a community corporation with bankers and neighborhood residents on the board of directors. In its first three years the service helped 245 families become homeowners and assisted another 100 with house renovations. SECO formed a partnership with government, business, and other institutions to create Southeast Development, Inc., which creates jobs and business opportunities for neighborhood residents. It also established a community controlled company—Southeast Arts and Crafts—that produces and markets the crafts of elderly and handicapped residents; a primary health-care facility that serves three thousand patients a month; and a Highlandtown Revitalization Corporation that gives technical assistance to merchants. SECO also received a grant from the Ford Foundation to buy attractive properties before real estate speculators did so.

In a six-year period SECO grew from an organization with a single underpaid community organizer working out of a church basement to one with a staff of forty one, a budget of $650,000, and responsibility for another $16,000,000 in neighborhood programs. In a nutshell, southeast Baltimore is no longer the unattractive slum area banks and city officials used to see it as. "SECO has restored entire blocks of new houses. It has restored community pride," one commentator applauded. "In short, southeast Baltimore has become a classic model for reviving the inner city."[30]

Lest we too get carried away with these results, the history of localist, self-help neighborhood organizations in working-class neighborhoods questions SECO's long-term potential and underlines the difficulty of replicating even such a short-term, new populist success. At certain unique times and places, the interests of specific neighborhoods, brought to light and advanced by insurgent and aggressive neighborhood organizations, are not incompatible with the interests of the business community and politicians. The primary concern of the economic and power elite in declining cities in the post–World War II era has been the revitalization of the central business district. In Pittsburgh the revitalization project was called "The Golden Triangle." In Detroit, it was "Renaissance Center." In other cities, like San Antonio, Boston, and Portland, Maine, it is the River, Waterfront, or Old Port District. While the focus is on revitalizing the downtown commercial area to attract business investment and the more affluent back to once declining urban centers, demands from certain neighborhoods whose upgrading could support the city's revitalization, and perhaps even house a new urban "gentry," are not ignored as they normally might be.[31]

Nevertheless, improvement activities that benefit working-class residents are few and far between. As Phillip Clay writes in a study of *Neighborhood Renewal*, "The bootstrap efforts [of the 1970s] are credited with reversing the imminent decay and cynicism that have plagued low- and moderate-income neighborhoods." But such efforts at "incumbent upgrading," Clay suggests, are "manifestly small." Self-help efforts at rehabilitating a rundown neighborhood make for good news copy and "neo-conservative" boosterism, so the media and businessmen's groups exaggerate and romanticize these developments. But the extent and impact of such neighborhood renewal efforts are quickly diminished when compared to the number of families who continue to move to the suburbs, who are pushed out of declining neighborhoods by disinvestment, or who are ultimately forced from upgraded or gentrified neighborhoods by rising rents and tax assessments and by new, white-collar, professional residents.[32] Another commentator suggests that the next step for successful upgrading efforts, like that of SECO, might well be "to mobilize to prevent the improvements it sought from backfiring." It would be ironic though not unusual, Robert Rosenbloom adds, if the people who fought successfully to restore and preserve their communities found themselves powerless to resist the process of neighborhood gentrification.[33]

The strategy of SECO is not to stop "upgrading." Rather the goal is to get as much out of it for the neighborhood's middle- and working-class residents by working with and within the existing system. At the neighborhood level, it is interest-group politics pure and simple. For those with power already, interest-group politics can succeed. For working-class people, like those in southeast Baltimore, the community development strategy may succeed for a time under highly auspicious conditions, but ultimately it only works in proportion to the size, power, activism, and threat of militancy of the neighborhood organization. A single-neighborhood organization is ultimately too small to effect the necessary changes in, and counter the existing pressures against, a low- and moderate-income community. In comparison, while the neo-Alinskyite emphasis on developing statewide and mass-based organizations has its limits, it clearly recognizes the need for a national "people's organization" that could begin to address the underlying causes of community transformation that rest outside and beyond any one neighborhood.

Building Confidence and Developing Working-Class Women Organizers

[Organizing] is building confidence. It is saying, "Hell, if I can do it, you can do it. If I can stand up and have something to say, so can you." It is telling them you are a person, an individual; you've been kicked around along enough, the hell with this noise—they can't do that to you. I like you; let's have at them.

Phyllis Hanson, neighborhood organizer

Serious limitations notwithstanding, there is a power and potential to the new populism, especially neo-Alinskyism, that may well reflect the beginnings of a political realignment in the United States. The great hope of the movement, as Roger Friedland wrote in 1975, is that "by transforming urban daily life into national partisan issues, the large number of poor and working class people who have no meaningful connection or place in the national electoral system could be given choices that make a difference."[34] To their credit, community organizers, leaders, and members were able to develop a nascent national grassroots movement in a decade, the 1970s, when there was no single catalytic issue to do so. Recent new populist victories in Burlington, Vermont, and Santa Monica, California, may well reflect not so much individual successes or unique circumstances as they do the budding of organizing efforts nurtured throughout the nation for over a decade now. They may well represent the first victories of a nationwide populist/socialist agenda still in the making.

One thing is for certain, however: new populist organizing has raised the personal self-respect and political consciousness of tens of thousands of Americans. If it is true as Lawrence Goodwyn suggests in his book *The Populist Moment,* a study of agrarian populism in the nineteenth century, that democratic movements are initiated only by people who have attained a high degree of personal self-respect, then the new populism, as well as its new left predecessor, has made a significant contribution to any future progressive movement that develops in this country. A truly democratic society can not develop without a confident and skilled citizenry capable of self-government. To the extent that people are given dignity, self-respect, political knowledge, and confidence they tend not to be intimidated by highly educated government officials, professionals, and corporate leaders, and they are certainly less willing to accept continued injustices. As organizer Si Kahn expressed it: "The dignity that comes from self-esteem is one of the most important tools the organizer can give to poor people. Belief in one's dignity as a man or a woman is one of the strongest motivating factors; from it comes the refusal to be used or abused, the assertion that 'I been pushed around too long, and I ain't gonna be pushed around no more.' "[35]

People learned a good deal about democracy from their experience in neighborhood organizations in the 1970s. They learned that authority can be challenged, that people generate power in numbers, that there is a long and important history of insurgent, people's movements in the United States. They learned how to work together politically and that "being political" meant more than voting or participating in electoral politics; it meant taking responsibility for and doing something about the decisions that affect your life. In the process people learned about themselves, their neighbors, their community, and, to a lesser extent, the larger political and economic system. Activism opened people's eyes and made them conscious historical actors. "[Public officials] think we're all very stupid and we don't know what's going on. . . . They just automatically assume we're ignorant. . . . Awareness. That's the thing that [the organization] has given us, awareness," was how one working class woman activist in Chicago put it.[36]

Organizers learned too. Alinskyism assumes that people get and stay involved in community organizations out of self-interest. They get involved to put up a traffic light, expand a park, stop a highway, or oppose a slumlord. But neo-Alinskyite organizers came to learn that successful organizations are not built on self-interest alone. Rather, a central element is the vision the organization advances and how it raises people's expectations about themselves, their families, and their communities. If an organization is effective, people come to see themselves and their participation differently after only a few "self-interest" victories. If people stay involved, organizers learned, they do so to develop themselves personally and to accomplish the larger sense of purpose that being involved in the organization has opened to them. As Heather Booth noted recently, people "*stay* involved not simply for self-interest but for broader reasons—the sense of power and of community, of living out their idealism and their vision."[37]

Nowhere has the impact of the new populism on personal and political development been more pronounced than its work with working-class women. As a result of the women's movement of the 1970s, college-educated women began to play increasingly larger roles as both organizers, leaders, and active members in social change efforts. Of course, upper- and middle-class women have always played important roles as organizers in neighborhood organizations. From the settlements to SNCC and SDS, women did much of the day to day organizing while men got most of the credit for it. Women from affluent backgrounds have typically had the time and opportunity necessary to devote to political and social work, if they were so inclined. Settlement houses and most of the social welfare organizing projects of the Progressive era were staffed largely by women, and while men assumed leadership roles in far greater frequency than their total number, women too, like Jane Addams, Mary Simkhovitch, Lillian Wald, and many others, were nationally prominent advocates of the movement. More commonly, women have played fundamental but less visible roles in neighborhood organizing efforts. In the thirties, for example, women played active roles in the CPUSA and the Unemployed Councils, but again men assumed the public leadership positions.

As noted earlier, the upper and middle-class women who joined the SDS community organizing projects in the early sixties faced similar circumstances. Women played key organizing roles in ERAP, but their history was one of male domination. Men and women did the organizing, the going from door-to-door, the endless hours of going to meetings and talking with people. But the men in the organization, up until the late 1960s when the women's movement began to emerge, assumed and held the key leadership and decision-making roles.[38]

Working-class and minority women also have played important roles in neighborhood organizing efforts, though rarely in prominent, leadership positions. From the earliest days of the tenant movement in New York City around the turn of the nineteenth century, for example, working-class women pioneered as protest organizers in their buildings.[39] Many of the organizers in SNCC were black women from working-class and sharecropping backgrounds. These are not isolated examples. Nevertheless, the white, working-class housewife has historically been the least likely person to get involved as an organizer or leader in community political activity. In the new populism, however, these women have begun to follow the paths of traditionally more activist black and college-educated women. As Kathleen McCourt describes in a recent study of women active in neighborhood organizations on Chicago's Southwest Side, "In many of these new assertive community organizations, still struggling for strength and direction, women offer important leadership. Often, too, women are the most active and most numerous rank-and-file members. All along women have been supplying the bodies for demonstrations; they are now beginning to make decisions, speak publicly, and assume more responsible positions in the organizations."[40]

Getting actively involved in a neighborhood organization, struggling on a daily basis with important political and social questions, is an exciting and empowering experience for most people, and it is especially so for those, like working-class housewives, who have tended to shy away from public, political, and leadership roles. Involvement often brings with it dramatic personal and political changes. Participation gives activists a better sense of their power as individuals, as workers, and as women. It is not uncommon for working-class women to begin to see themselves relatively quickly as natural community organizers. "I think it's the women on these [community] issues who have to take the stand. We need men, but they can only give so much of their time," was how one participant put it. "We have the contact in the community. . . . my husband doesn't know the number of people in the community that I know just by virtue of involvement in the school." Another said, "For my husband to be involved in the community, it's jeopardizing a little bit of that security he has. . . . I don't think they can take the chance that a woman can take."[41]

Activism in new populist neighborhood organizations leads many working-class women to become more cynical about and angry with public officials and corporate leaders, but this does not lead them to political defeatism or despair. On the contrary, their organizing experience generally empowers them. It gives them a better sense of self-esteem, a confidence in their ability to convince others to fight back and join the organization, a confidence in their abilities vis-à-vis traditional power brokers. This is often a dramatic political breakthrough. As one woman describes: "I always thought [politicians and corporate officials] were probably very shrewd, very wise, had minds like computers—and they don't. And that came to me as a kind of a shock and it helped my ego and I wasn't afraid to fight them. They're just ordinary human beings. They're not very bright at all. . . . You don't have to fear them at all as far as your mind being able to cope with their mind, not at all. And that helps you."[42]

Participation also affects women's home life and attitudes to the community, the former being stretched, often times both being strengthened. In many working-class households the participation of women in public roles and in organizations where cross-sex friendships are developed often causes strains with their husbands. What usually happens, as one woman put it, is "now he had to adjust to a new reality." Sometimes the new reality threatens marriages; more often it creates new roles and forges new bonds. In both cases, however, the role of the women is strengthened. Regarding the community, activist women tend to develop greater emotional attachments to the community than nonactivists. Their lives become filled with an excitement and challenge rarely experienced before. Community organizing is a challenge and growth experience for anyone. It is not uncommon to hear organizers in ACORN or other neo-Alinskyite efforts say that their skills were tested more strenuously and they learned more from a year of community work than from their entire four years at college. For working-class women, the new role is equally demanding and energizing.

Without doubt the new populism, and especially the neo-Alinskyite trend, has been most successful in introducing working-class women to neighborhood organizing. The legacy of the 1970s may be in its development of working-class leaders—both men and women—who are politically involved and who know how to build organizations, pressure City Hall, write leaflets, build coalitions, and organize demonstrations. A vast number of people in communities now have experience with neighborhood organizing and have the necessary skills to build insurgent community organizations. What they tend to lack is a knowledge of political and economic systems and an alternative vision. Without such knowledge and vision there is the possibility that the nature and direction of the organizations people learned to build may perpetuate rather than solve their needs. The task of the 1980s is therefore to consolidate the people who received training and experience in the 1970s around a clearer, left political vision and agenda than has been offered thus far by the new populism.

CHAPTER 6
Conclusion: The Nature and Potential of Neighborhood Organizing

> We have built clinics in our communities, rebuilt neighborhoods in inner cities, challenged politicians throughout the country, blocked the strip miners and the redliners, won stop signs and bus lines, we have even stopped a war. We need to recognize not only what we are doing wrong and what we still need to do but how much we are doing right.
>
> *Si Kahn, organizer and musician*

It would be presumptuous to conclude this work with a general theory of neighborhood organizing, since the field is still in its infancy and just beginning to develop a body of case studies and theoretical materials. One commentator has specifically warned that "any global assumptions about the results of neighborhood organizing programs across all types of communities is inappropriate."[1] The problem is made more difficult by the inclusion in this work of the three dominant approaches to neighborhood organizing: social work, political activist, and neighborhood maintenance. Almost every study of the subject limits itself to a single type of neighborhood organizing. While the three approaches share much, they are sufficiently different so as to make comparisons, let alone general theories, difficult to construct.[2]

The social work approach views the community essentially as a social organism; it focuses on social issues such as building a sense of community, gathering together social service organizations, or lobbying for and delivering social resources. It assumes that the community's problem is basically social disorganization. The organized group is generally working and lower class.

153

The organizer functions either as an "enabler" to help the community gather itself together or as an "advocate" to secure additional services for the community. The strategy is gradualist and consensual, which means that organizers assume a common interest between dominant groups and the neighborhood and a willingness of at least some in power to meet community needs. The structure of organizations in this tradition tends to be more formalized and led by professionals trained in schools of social work. Organizations in this tradition vary in their extent of indigenous participation and grassroots leadership, but the professional community worker is almost always the core of the program. She or he provides at least the initial stimulus for the program, and, quite often, the focus and personality of the organization. The social work approach to community organization sees itself as a social enterprise and operates within the general orientation of the social work profession.

Moreover, the social welfare approach reflects its liberal origins in charity work and social engineering. At their best social welfare projects coordinate and deliver needed social services to the poor and working class. At their worst they are elitist and manipulative, seeking to maintain existing class arrangements by palliating social problems and coopting social disorder. In both instances social welfare neighborhood organizing projects serve at the pleasure of liberally oriented officials and foundations. Community workers may seek to do more in the way of neighborhood organizing; they may seek to gain some power for working people and even challenge the causes of poverty and powerlessness that plague their clients. But in general the reformist vision, liberal objectives, consensus strategies, scanty resources and power, and professional-orientation characteristic of the social welfare approach militate against developing democratic grassroots projects which, by altering class and power arrangements in their favor, could truly serve the interests and needs of neighborhood residents.

The political activist approach regards the community as a political entity and/or potential power base. It focuses on obtaining, maintaining, or restructuring power. Or, if it does not seek to empower community residents, it is political in that its goal is to develop alternative institutions. The community's problem, as defined by organizers, is the absence of power needed to defend the neighborhood and/or give people more control over their lives. The organized group is generally working and lower class. The organizer's role is first to help the community understand its problem and its potential power and then to mobilize it around this understanding. The strategy of the political activist ranges from consensual to confrontational, but in all cases it is rooted in the presumption of a conflict of interest between the community and those in power. The organization usually has a less professional and less formal structure than groups in the social work tradition, and leaders if not organizers come more often from the neighborhood. Where the organizers focus solely on their own goals of building the organization rather than on meeting community needs and developing meaningful democratic participation, the political activist approach, like its social work counterpart, can take on an externally led and autocratic posture. Where the political activist approach differs most significantly from the social work model is in its class perspective. The social work approach seeks a class rapprochement based on a "partnership" between upper-class supporters, social welfare professionals, and working- and lower-class neighborhood residents. The political activist type, on the other hand, seeks to promote, and sometimes resist, social change by challenging those in power, most often at the local level but not infrequently at the national level, too.

As Paul Wellstone noted of his experience with an Alinsky-style organization, the Organization for a Better Rice County, "If I had to pick out the most significant thing that has happened since OBRC's inception, it would be the dramatic change in the political consciousness among the poor."[3] The raised political consciousness to which Wellstone refers does not develop in social welfare and neighborhood maintenance efforts which seek consensus with the powers that be and which seek to limit and manage conflict. People in neighborhood organizing efforts benefit personally and politically from conflict, though in the short run such conflict may be painful and disharmonious. Kathleen McCourt emphasizes in her study of working-class women organizers that participation in assertive, conflict-oriented, community organizations was a politicizing experience in and of itself, regardless of the issues addressed by the women. Participation in such organizations helped members see the implications of their concerns and armed them with new information, greater self-confidence, and pride. In short, conflict empowers people, for even a defeat against what most of the women saw as an "all powerful" power structure was often a psychic victory which led to continued efforts and greater involvement.[4]

But conflict develops more than individual potential. It prevents a neighborhood organization from becoming a static formal organization and can encourage it into being a dynamic training ground of democracy and political education which, by challenging assumptions about power and poverty in poor communities, has the potential for altering class balance, or providing the breeding ground for such change. In conflict people are forced to examine and confront the political system and to experiment with strategies of resistance and democratic insurgency. Only those adversarial neighborhood organizing efforts that pursue progressive goals, engage in conflict with existing powers, and do not fear principled struggles within their organizations, however, are true training grounds for democracy and its potential for change.

A third tradition, less commonly thought of as neighborhood organizing, focuses on neighborhood maintenance. Here the community is defined as a residential area. The problem is maintaining and improving the neighborhood while opposing external and internal threats to its permanence and commercial value. The organized group is generally upper- and middle-class. The organizer comes from within the neighborhood and serves as an elected representative and civic leader of the association; the neighborhod residents serve primarily as dues-paying members of the organization. The strategy is generally one of consensus, wherein the association first applies neighborhood peer pressure to resolve problems and, then, if necessary, resorts to political and legal channels. Unlike the political activist approach, which will publicly confront local officials, neighborhood maintenance associations function as traditional interest groups, most often working quietly behind the scenes in cooperation with local officials. The goal is to promote the neighborhood status quo, focusing essentially on maintaining, if not improving, property values. Unlike the social work and political activist approach, the neighborhood maintenance tradition is most often found in outer-city neighborhoods and suburbs where residents own single-family homes and where they have a vested property interest in protecting their neighborhood. A study of 197 neighborhood homeowner associations in Indianapolis, for example, did not find a single one in "lower socio-economic" areas of the city.[5] Such neighborhoods have fewer problems obtaining public services or convincing local power brokers of their needs than those neighborhoods where organizers in the social work and political activist traditions are most active. The neighborhood maintenance association, in fact, is usually free of major problems or pressing concerns, except when threatened by forces of commercial development or social change. Whereas the social welfare approach seeks class rapprochement and the political activist type challenges the class in power, the neighborhood maintenance tradition seeks to defend its class interests and maintain the status quo.

Neighborhood improvement associations in affluent communities tend to act as neighborhood interest groups more than as community-oriented organizations. They have limited citizen participation, are led by the more established residents in the neighborhood, pursue political and economic interests by going through established official channels, and in general do little to create or sustain real community life. They may give the neighborhood a stronger voice at City Hall and they may supply or coordinate the delivery of certain services deemed necessary to maintain or improve the neighborhood. But because the primary objective is improving property values, neighborhood improvement associations tend to bind people together only around a limited and material self-interest. To the extent that the fundamental goal is not the maintenance of property values but the promotion of community life or protection of the community against commercial or urban renewal forces, neighborhood improvement associations tend to become more participatory and better grounded in neighborhood life. (See Table 1, pp. xx–xxi, for a sketch of these three approaches.)

It is an error, however, to paint these traditions into completely exclusive corners. Studying them together is difficult, but not like comparing apples and oranges. In the decade preceding World War I, partly because of the still weak professionalization of social work, the social work and political activist traditions occasionally overlapped in the more progressive settlements. Settlement workers pioneered the social work tradition of community organization, but they also sought at times to mobilize neighborhood residents in political struggle against local political bosses and industrial sweatshops. As Mary Follett, a settlement worker and activist in the community center movement, proclaimed in 1918: "Politics can no longer be an extra-activity of the American people, it must be a means of satisfying our wants. . . . Our proposal is that the people should organize themselves into neighborhood groups to express their daily life, to bring to the surface the needs, desires, and aspirations of that life, that these needs should become the substance of politics, and that neighborhood groups should become the recognized political unit."[6]

In the 1960s the two approaches overlapped again as the decade's political ferment forced them together. Activist organizers and the organizations they were involved with—SNCC, SDS, and a host of other programs spawned by the black struggle and new left protest, for instance—forced those in the social work tradition to reexamine their consensual and social service approach to community organizing. At the same time, the Great Society coopted many activists into a form of community organizing which straddled both traditions but, as exemplified by the Community Action Program, was rooted in the social work approach.[7]

Less frequent are connections between the politically conservative, neighborhood maintenance tradition and the other two. Nevertheless, many aspects of Alinskyism and the new populism, especially the neighborhood development approach that appeared in Back of the Yards, The Woodlawn Organization, and the Southeast Community Organization (SECO) in Baltimore, share much in common with improvement association efforts in more affluent neighborhoods. They are fundamentally localist in outlook, consensual, and interested in improving and protecting their neighborhood and securing additional services.

So, despite different class, racial, and political objectives and different origins and methods, all three dominant approaches to neighborhood organizing belong in a history of the subject. And while a general theory of neighborhood organizing is complicated by the inclusion of the three approaches and by a literature which is still in its infancy, this study suggests a number of conclusions which are worth highlighting and embellishing.

Neighborhood Organizing Cuts Across the Political Spectrum.   While neighborhood organizing is a political act, it is neither inherently reactionary, conservative, liberal, or radical, nor is it inherently democratic and inclusive or authoritarian and parochial. It is above all a political method, an approach used widely by various segments of the population to achieve specific goals, serve certain interests, and advance clear or ill-defined political perspectives. Organizations can be creative efforts open to innovation and supportive of progressive struggles as well as defensive responses to external pressures.

In some ways traditional political labels are not entirely satisfactory in a discussion of neighborhood organizing movements, especially since such labels are relative and people's politics are fluid and not neatly categorized. For example, because an organization seeks to defend traditional values and its neighborhood does not make it reactionary or even conservative. Craig Jackson Calhoun, in an important theoretical study of populist insurgency, writes that

traditional cultural values and immediate communal relations are crucial to many radical movements, (a) because these commitments provide populations with the extent of internal social organization necessary to concerted, radical collective action, and (b) because the largely defensive goals of these movements must be radically incompatible with the introduction of modern capitalist-dominated social formations.[8]

Or, put another way, radical organization can develop out of "conservative" communities when these communities confront social changes which threaten communal relations and attachments to family, friends, and customary ways of life, and which leaves them nothing to lose. Most traditional communities tend to develop conservative neighborhood organizations. But given certain historical conditions, such locales do become radical to defend what they have. Similarly, successful "radical" organizations—TWO comes to mind first—may become more conservative when they achieve or seek to achieve greater success. As the process of democracy is not static, neither is the politics of a neighborhood organizing project.

Neighborhood Organizing Movements Develop in an Historical Context that Includes but Transcends Local Community Borders. Conditions at the local level directly spawn and nurture neighborhood organizing projects. The organizers, residents, local conditions, and many other factors at the grassroots combine to forge consistently unique neighborhood organizing experiences. But while neighborhood organizing projects do have a significant origin, nature, and existence of their own at the local level, they are also the products of national and even international political and economic developments. To no small degree, the larger political-economic context often determines the general tenor and success of local efforts.

The national political economy affects neighborhood organizing in surprising ways. Many incorrectly assume, for example, that radical organizing occurs and thrives only during periods of national economic depression, or that conservative neighborhood maintenance groups form and succeed only in periods of national affluence. While such a theory appears accurate for the 1930s and 1950s, it is not appropriate for the early twentieth century or for the 1960s. In the 1960s, for example, a period of national economic prosperity produced profound radical challenges to the contradictions and hypocrisy of an "affluent society."

Nevertheless, specific conditions at the national and local level determine opportunities available to groups to press for their own class interests. That neighborhood improvement associations have been continuously active since the 1890s testifies to the ability of those people with wealth and power to defend and enhance their position in all eras. Improvement associations, however, are more prominent, more powerful, when during national prosperity there is a national, conservative political sentiment against social change, as there was in the 1920s and 1950s, the two heydays of improvement association activity.

Likewise, the efforts of working-class and poor people's organizations develop best in periods of profound social dislocation when (1) the regulatory power of social institutions break down and (2) sharp economic change occurs producing depressed *or* improved conditions, the former encouraging people to defend themselves, the latter raising their expectations. It is not so much prosperity or depression at the national and local level that leads to radical neighborhood organizing, but rather external pressures on traditional communities and a breakdown of the routines of daily life that make people more receptive to activism and alternative organizations. Disturbances in the larger political economy, however, are necessary to create the conditions in which the powerless move to mass political insurgency.[9]

There is a Critical Interaction between Neighborhood Organizing Efforts, National Politics, and Nationwide Social Movements. The response at the national level to grassroots movements either encourages or represses them. The conservative atmosphere and policies of the 1920s and 1950s supported the creation of suburban protective associations. The liberal leadership of the first decades of the twentieth century and the 1960s encouraged the expansion of social welfare neighborhood organizing projects. Sometimes liberal attempts at cooption led to heightened, rather than defused, radical activity. Where liberal leaders failed to coopt insurgency, however, as in the late 1940s and late 1960s, the government ultimately resorted to repression.[10] This is not to suggest that the national government is an all-powerful arm of the ruling groups in the United States. While it functions mainly in the service of the upper-class, the government also serves as a battleground, an arena of conflict, where grassroots groups can pressure the ruling groups for change. The national government is not as formidable, well-directed, or monolithic as it once appeared from the grassroots to be.

A critical interaction also occurs between neighborhood organizing projects and nationwide social movements. Generally, neighborhood organizing and other forms of grassroots activity serve as the building blocks of larger social movements. They provide the spaces, organizational skills, and grassroots heritage which can renew itself in political struggle.[11] At the same time, national movements, once established, provide direction and support to local efforts. This was true in the Progressive era, with national movement leaders coming out of local reform campaigns and then, once in power, assisting directly and indirectly liberal efforts at the local level. It was also the case in the civil rights movement, as the movement developed first at the local level, grew to national proportions, and spawned, often unintentionally, the efforts of SNCC, SDS, and the antiwar and Black Power movements. On occasion, national movements which are detached from local institutions and are organized largely at the national or state level, as was the antiwar movement of the 1960s and 1970s, distract and detract from community organizing efforts. But generally community and national movements of similar political persuasions reinforce each other, and the destruction of one often signals the imminent decline of the other.

Problems Besetting Neighborhoods Demand Political Organization Beyond the Neighborhood Level. Small may be beautiful, more manageable, and more feasible for democratic participation, but commonly the neighborhood is neither the site of the causes of its problems nor the site of the power needed to address them. The limited effectiveness of neighborhood organizing since the 1890s demonstrates the existence of powerful forces beyond the local level which are antagonistic to the neighborhood. Sidney Dillick, the author of the only other monograph on the history of neighborhood organizing, pointed out over a generation ago "the danger of focusing attention upon neighborhood needs to the neglect of the underlying social forces not necessarily originating in the neighborhood. . . ."[12]

Relatedly, what neighborhood organizing movements need, as the experiences of the new left and many other projects since have demonstrated, are ongoing, national political organizations which can provide continuity, direction, and motivation for local efforts and which, in turn, can be guided and reinvigorated by struggles in communities and workplaces at the local level. Without the continuity provided by a federated national organization, neighborhood organizing projects usually start their work anew, in a vacuum, without benefit of historical experience or perspective, and generally must survive on their own, against very powerful forces and odds, and without experience and support.

Neighborhood Organizing Must Be Built on More Than Material Rewards and Incentives.   Most neighborhood organizing projects emphasize the importance of delivering rewards and incentives in order to keep member interest high and the organization progressing. Alinskyism is based on the assumption that people organize solely for their own economic self-interest. Similarly, neighborhood improvement associations are rooted in maintaining property values, and liberal social welfare programs are geared to offering rewards and incentives in the form of social services. Such material incentives are important, but they are not the glue that keeps neighborhood organizing efforts together. Victories are critical; people see themselves and their power differently after initial successes. But effective neighborhood organizing efforts, especially in lower income areas where the neighborhood organization does not have the resources to deliver rewards for very long, demands more than a reliance on incentives. In order to sustain an organization, especially of the political activist type, and promote long-range objectives, neighborhood organizing must be built around issues of personal development and an ideology that articulates a sense of purpose extending beyond individual advantage.[13] It must be committed to developing the knowledge, dignity, and self-confidence of community residents. And these people must come to see themselves as part of a larger cause. While traditional interest-group studies on neighborhood organizing emphasized that indigenous people prefer organizations that deliver services and immediate rewards rather than those which are engaged in social change or revolutionary objectives, those political activist organizations which have been most successful over time, whether the Unemployed Councils in the 1930s or SNCC in the 1960s, were part of larger social movements and incorporated into their work and into their organizing a class- or race-based vision of something worth fighting for which was larger and more important than simply member self-interest.[14]

Neighborhood Organizing Must Create and Sustain a Galvanizing Vision Rooted in People's Lives and Traditions. Most social welfare and neighborhood improvement association projects make no pretense of developing a mobilizing ideology. Populist neighborhood organizing efforts in the twentieth century have never been able to articulate a vision of society beyond corporate liberalism and the New Deal. Alinskyism, for example, accepts liberals in power and sees neighborhood organizations as lobbying groups to pressure brokers for increased benefits and power. This model is not very dissimilar from the interest group approach of most neighborhood improvement associations. Marxist and politically radical neighborhood organizing efforts, from the Unemployed Councils to later projects such as those of the Black Panther party, came closest to articulating a broad ideology that addressed the causes of poverty and powerlessness. But a vision of noncapitalist transformation has to be attentive to such traditional American ideals as equality, self-help, local self-reliance, participatory democracy, group solidarity, cultural pluralism, and grassroots insurgency. Of course, putting forward a clear, long-term vision does not guarantee success. The Populist farmers movement of the late nineteenth century, the CIO organizing drives of the 1930s, and the Black Power movement of the late 1960s all articulated, to greater or lesser degree, a radical, participatory vision, but were destroyed by external pressures and government repression activated by that vision. Lower-class and working-class neighborhood organizing must develop long-range goals which address imbalances in a class society, an alternative vision of what people are fighting for, and a context for all activity, whether pressuring for a stop sign or an eviction blockage. Otherwise, as has repeatedly happened, victories that win services or rewards will *undermine* the organization by "proving" that the existing system is responsive to poor and working people and, therefore, in no need of fundamental change.

Neighborhood Organizing Requires a Gentle Balance Between Organizing, Leading, and Education. The best organizer is not so much a leader as a catalyst. "Grassroots organizations must have organizers," Michael Ansara of Mass Fair Share has written, "just as they eventually must be led and controlled by the local people."[15] To the extent that the organizer assumes a controlling leadership role, he or she reinforces ideas and insecurities among neighborhood people of how and why they cannot lead themselves. To the extent that organizing perpetuates the mystique of the great, gifted, self-sacrificing, professional organizer, people shy away from tasks and rely on the organizer. The organizer may accomplish many things, but he or she will not develop indigenous leaders, will not be able to educate people in the process of democracy, will perpetuate interest-group styles of neighborhood organizing, and will not organize a project with any long-term staying power. The best organizers are not the ones who are the most skilled, energetic, or forceful, but rather those who have a sense of both a larger vision and what is possible and combine this with the knowledge, ability, and skills of local people.

But organizers do need to provide some leadership. Organizing projects, such as those of Saul Alinsky, which completely deny the leadership role of the organizer and emphasize letting the people decide, are often either dishonest and manipulative, or parochial and undirected. James Forman, a SNCC leader, correctly criticized "an ailment known as local-people-itis . . . [which] carried with it the idea that local people could do no wrong, that no one, especially somebody from outside the community, should initiate any kind of action or assume any form of leadership."[16] Organizers bring an ideology, skills, experience, and perspective to their work; they owe it to neighborhood people to share this with them openly and honestly. Not to do so will in the long run increase suspicion. The craft is to do so in a democratic manner where organizers see themselves not only as catalysts and guides but also as recipients of the knowledge, experience, and strength of local people and their traditions, where there is a true sense of sharing in a dynamic democratic process.

All formal organizations tend toward oligarchic control, toward organizational maintenance objectives superceding other goals, and toward defusing citizen participation by giving the impression that since an organization already exists to carry the struggle, personal sacrifice for the cause is no longer necessary. Nevertheless, creating powerful organizations, even if they exist only for a few years, is critical to advancing the interests of neighborhood people. While there are no sure cures for the maladies of formal organizations, neighborhood organizations can make important gains in counteracting and preventing them by espousing an ideology and engaging in a practice of organizing which is committed to membership education, democratic process, and long-term objectives.

Political Education Must Be an Integral Part of Neighborhood Organizing.   Clearly not all organizers can do political education or do it simultaneously with other tasks. Advocating a clear, long-term vision which addresses class imbalances is often impolitic for those engaged in daily organizing activities, especially for leaders of neighborhood organizing projects. What is necessary is a subtle division of labor among organizers, where possible, so that some are able to focus more on organization-building questions and others are more free to address issues of political education. Political education should help people develop the confidence necessary to rely on themselves, win the personal dignity and self-respect basic to participation, and challenge existing authority when necessary. Nor should political education simply develop organization-building skills; it must also reveal the roots of people's problems in the workings of the economic and political system.

Moreover, education must be ongoing and based on a class perspective. If not, most people in neighborhood organizing projects will continue to believe that once those in power are shown the problem and the errors of their ways, either through conflict or consensus tactics, they will support the necessary remedies. Without this, despite continued class and race conflicts, most people will continue to believe that the system, with all its faults, is inherently good, that inadequacies can be corrected, and that racism, poverty, income inequities, and powerlessness are due to individual mistakes or historical circumstances and are not inherent elements in the social, political, and economic structure. The role of political education, which is an analysis that grows out of people's political experience, not a paternalistic classroom exercise, is to broaden people's perspective and to give them more information upon which they can make more reasoned assessments of the conditions, problems, and alternative solutions they face.[17]

Success Must Be Measured in Tangible and Intangible Results. Except when conditions are appropriate, it is difficult for neighborhood organizing efforts to achieve their objectives. External conditions, more than internal efforts, affect success. This is, of course, more the the case for radical and confrontational groups than for social welfare and neighborhood maintenance efforts, since the forces of opposition to radical neighborhood organizations are much greater. But the generalization is appropriate for the other approaches as well. Remember, for example, the difficulty social welfare organizers had securing support during the 1950s or the problems neighborhood improvement associations faced trying to keep together in the first years of the Great Depression. For radical groups, especially anticapitalist ones, the hurdles are much higher and the opposition much more intense. Curiously, even when challenging groups succeed for a time, their victories often make their opponents that much wiser and sophisticated. Opponents refuse to continue to cooperate for long in their own demise; after initial defeats they change their tactics and force neighborhood organizing projects to reevaluate and alter once successful approaches. Success is not a static situation, nor is failure.[18]

If success is measured in the number of members and the longevity of the organization, then the neighborhood maintenance approach is the most successful. If it is measured by the percentage of neighborhood people actively and meaningfully engaged, then the most successful neighborhood organizing projects were those in black communities during the Civil Rights movement, when a religious ideology and an especially identifiable enemy united blacks in mass, grassroots insurgence. Success can also be measured in more specific outcomes, such as the number of buildings rehabilitated, jobs found, evictions blocked, and street lights put up.

Clearly, however, any evalution must include intangible as well as tangible results. The development of dignity, hope, self-confidence, and pride, the planting of seeds of organizational experience which may come to fruition years later and perhaps far away from the initial community experience, the raised political consciousness of organization members, can all prove more important than more measurable victories. In general, the lion's share of gains of neighborhood organizing rests not with tangible results but rather in the lives of the people who participated in them. Many activists share the profound experience of a participant in a neighborhood women's project, who recorded that "I would not have had the sense of what it felt like to be an active participant in history, in my life, Cambridge, whatever, if I had not been in Bread and Roses. I felt like I took my first real risks in Bread and Roses."[19] Few who participate in a significant way in a neighborhood organization, to the point of making it an important part of their lives, leave the organization without being deeply affected.

Moreover, these "real risks" must help form a foundation for building a more egalitarian, democratic America. Neighborhood organizing is clearly only one way to approach this goal. Many people do not live in definable, functional neighborhoods and do not unite along geographic lines. The critical social concerns which people face are often ones of class, race, and gender, none of which the neighborhood is inherently best suited to advance. What is needed is a federated national organization or national political coalition, non-capitalist and egalitarian in vision, formed and guided from above and below, and rooted in grassroots activity in communities and workplaces.

Grounding a movement in both community and workplace organizing is, of course, far easier to prescribe than accomplish. People who consciously act according to their class interests at the workplace often forget or deny class or workplace politics in their neighborhoods. As political scientist Ira Katznelson put it, "American urban politics has been governed by boundaries and rules that stress ethnicity, race, and territoriality, rather than class. . . . The center-piece of these rules has been the radical separation in people's consciousness, speech, and activity of the politics of work from the politics of community."[20] The workers' movement of the 1930s, with roots in both factory and community organizing, is one exception that proves the rule. Nevertheless, neighborhood organizing efforts which do not seek to make ties with a larger national movement grounded in workplace organizing will continue to win, when conditions are favorable, only limited reforms and additional services. Such hard-earned victories have kept neighborhood organizing alive since the 1880s, but have been unable, alone, to address the continued incidence of powerlessness, prejudice, and poverty experienced by large numbers of people in the United States.

NOTES AND REFERENCES

Introduction

1. Robert F. Berkhofer, Jr., "Comment on James A. Henretta, 'Social History as Lived and Written,'" *American Historical Review* 84 (December 1979):1328.

2. Dick Simpson, "Neighborhood Legislation: Prospects in the New Administration," *Social Policy* 11 (March–April 1981):31; Janice Perlman, "Neighborhood Research: A Proposed Methodology," *South Atlantic Urban Studies* 4 (1979):43.

3. Stewart Dill McBride, "A Nation of Neighborhoods," *Christian Science Monitor,* September–December 1977.

4. Peter Berger and Richard Neuhaus, *Mediating Institutions,* cited in *Our Way: Family, Parish, and Neighborhood in a Polish-American Community,* by Paul Wrobel, (Notre Dame: University of Notre Dame Press, 1979), p. 142.

5. See Harry Boyte, *The Backyard Revolution. Understanding The New Citizen Movement* (Philadelphia: Temple University Press, 1980); Robert Cassidy, *Livable Cities: A Grass-Roots Guide to Rebuilding Urban America* (New York: Holt, Rinehart, Winston, 1980).

6. Milton Kotler, "The Purpose of Neighborhood Planning," *South Atlantic Urban Studies* 4 (1979):29.

7. Rachelle B. Warren and Donald I. Warren, *The Neighborhood Organizer's Handbook* (Notre Dame: University of Notre Dame Press, 1977), p. 96; Suzanne Keller, *The Urban Neighborhood* (New York: Random House, 1968), p. 128.

8. Sandra Perlman Schoenberg and Patricia L. Rosenbaum, *Neighborhoods That Work: Sources for Viability in the Inner City* (New Brunswick: Rutgers University Press, 1980), p. 2.

9. Scott Green and Ann Lennarson, ed., *The Neighborhood and Ghetto: The Local Area in Large-Scale Society* (New York: Basic Books, 1974), p. 309.

10. Richard Clay Rich, "The Political Economy of Neighborhood Organization" (Ph.D. diss., Indiana University, 1977), p. 9.

Chapter 1

1. For additional information see Douglass Dowd, *The Twisted Dream: Capitalist Development in the United States* (Cambridge: Winthrop Publishers, 1974).

2. James Weinstein, *The Corporate Ideal in the Liberal State: 1900–1918* (Boston: Beacon Press, 1968), and Gabriel Kolko, *The Triumph of Conservatism: A Reinterpretation of American History, 1900–1916* (New York: Free Press, 1963), were among the first works to advance the corporate liberal thesis about progressivism.

3. Anthony M. Platt, *The Child Savers: The Invention of Delinquency* (Chicago: University of Chicago Press, 1969), p. xxii.

4. Thomas Lee Philpott, *The Slum and the Ghetto: Neighborhood Deterioration and Middle-Class Reform, Chicago, 1880–1930* (New York: Oxford University Press, 1978), is the best critique to date of the settlement movement.

5. Robert A. Woods, *The Neighborhood in Nation-Building* (New York: Arno Press, 1970), pp. 148–49. See also Roy Lubove, *The Professional Altruist: The Emergence of Social Work as a Career, 1880–1930* (New York: Atheneum, 1969).

6. Woods, *Neighborhood,* pp. 112, 287; Jesse Steiner, "An Appraisal of the Community Movement," *Journal of Social Forces* 7 (March 1929):334–35; Allen Davis, *Spearheads for Reform: The Social Settlements and the Progressive Movement, 1890–1914* (New York: Oxford University Press, 1967).

7. Woods, *Neighborhood,* p. 53.

8. Philpott, *Slum and Ghetto,* pp. 76–95.

9. John Daniels, *America Via the Neighborhood* (New York: Harper, 1920), p. 218.

10. Philpott, *Slum and Ghetto,* pp. 80–81.

11. Daniels, *America Via the Neighborhood,* pp. 220–21.

12. Ibid., p. 222.

13. Ibid., p. 223.

14. Because these self-help associations were not fundamentally neighborhood organizations, that is, the residential area was not the primary basis of organization, they are mentioned here only in passing. See bibliography for relevant materials.

15. Philpott, *Slum and Ghetto,* pp. 79, 285.

16. Jeffrey Gurock, *When Harlem Was Jewish, 1870–1930* (New York: Columbia University Press, 1979), pp. 94–98.

17. Clinton Childs, *A Year's Experiment In Social Center Organization* (New York: Social Center Committee, 1912), p. 21.

18. John Collier, "The Dynamics of the Community Movement," *Community Center,* 13 February 1917; John Collier, "Democracy Every Day, III," *Survey* 40 (28 September 1918):710.

19. *New York Times,* 13 October 1918, sec. 4, p. 8.

20. Leroy Bowman, "Community Organization," *American Journal of Sociology* 35 (May 1930):1008. See also Lubove, *The Professional Altruist;* and Jesse Steiner, *Community Organization: A Study of Its Theory and Current Practice* (Chicago: University of Chicago Press, 1930).

21. Wilbur Phillips, *Adventuring for Democracy* (New York: Social Unit Press, 1940), p. 59.

22. Anatole Shaffer, "The Cincinnati Social Unit Experiment: 1917–1919," *Social Service Review* 45 (June 1971):161; Patricia Mooney Melvin, "A Cluster of Interlacing Communities: The Cincinnati Social Unit Plan and Neighborhood Organization, 1900–1920," in *Community Organization for Urban Social Change: A Historical Perspective,* ed. Robert Fisher and Peter Romanofsky (Westport: Greenwood Press, 1981), pp. 58–88.

23. Robert A. Woods and Albert J. Kennedy, *The Zone of Emergence,* cited in "Cluster of Interlacing Communities," by Melvin, pp. 102–3.

24. Melvin, "Cluster of Interlacing Communities," pp. 103–8.

25. Ibid., pp. 105–11.

26. Ibid., pp. 110–15.

27. Phillips, *Adventuring,* pp. 280–307.

28. Shaffer, "Cincinnati Social Unit Experiment," p. 169.

29. Phillips, *Adventuring,* p. 112.

Chapter 2

1. Of course, the more conservative, social welfare approach to neighborhood organizing was alive if not necessarily well in the social settlements and other neighborhood-based social welfare agencies. But the efforts of settlements were more acts of treading water than new and important developments in the history of neighborhood organizing.

2. This overview of the depression and the New Deal relies on many works. Those that come to mind most readily are Frances Fox Piven and Richard Cloward, *Poor People's Movements: Why They Succeed, How They Fail* (New York: Vintage, 1979), especially pp. 44–48, 107–20; Barton Bernstein, "The New Deal: The Conservative Achievements of Liberal Reform," in *Towards a New Past: Dissenting Essays in American History,* ed. Barton Bernstein (New York: Random House, 1967), pp. 263–88; and William Leuchtenberg, *Franklin D. Roosevelt and the New Deal* (New York: Harper Torchbook, 1963).

3. Piven and Cloward, *Poor People's Movements,* pp. 48–49.

4. For more information on the Socialist party's "traditional" and "unimaginative" community organizing see Roy Rosenzweig, "Organizing the Unemployed: The Early Years of the Great Depression, 1929–1933," *Radical America* 10 (July–August 1976):38–39.

5. Ibid., p. 39.

6. Piven and Cloward, *Poor People's Movements,* p. 51.

7. Charles Trout, *Boston, The Great Depression, and the New Deal* (New York: Oxford University Press, 1977), pp. 55–57.

8. Rosenzweig, "Organizing the Unemployed," p. 41.

9. Steve Nelson, James Barrett, and Rob Ruck, *Steve Nelson, American Radical* (Pittsburgh: University of Pittsburgh Press, 1981), pp. 77–78, 176, 414.

10. See Mark Naison, "Harlem Communists and the Politics of Black Protest," in *Community Organization,* ed. Fisher and Romanofsky, pp. 89–126, for an impressive, brief discussion of Party organizing in the black community of Harlem.

11. Ibid., pp. 114–16; Mark Naison to author, 8 April 1982.

12. Mark Naison, "The Communist Party in Harlem, 1928–1936" (Ph.D. diss., Columbia University, 1976), p. 137. This thesis has since been published under the title *Communists in Harlem During the Depression* (Urbana: University of Illinois Press, 1983).

13. St. Clair Drake and Horace R. Cayton, *Black Metropolis* (1945; reprint ed., New York: Harper, 1962), p. 735.

14. Naison, "Harlem Communists," pp. 88–98.

15. Naison, "The Communist Party in Harlem," p. 383.

16. Naison, "Harlem Communists," p. 112; Piven and Cloward, *Poor People's Movements,* pp. 76–79.

17. Rosenzweig, "Organizing the Unemployed," p. 46.

18. Naison, "Harlem Communists," pp. 109–12.

19. Paul Wellstone, "Notes on Community Organizing," *Journal of Ethnic Studies* 4 (1976):78; Marion K. Sanders, "The Professional Radical: Conversations with Saul Alinsky," *Harper's Magazine* 230 (June 1965):45 especially; and Boyte, *The Backyard Revolution,* pp. 49–54.

20. *Playboy* March 1972, p. 72, quoted in Charles F. Levine, "Understanding Alinsky," *American Behavioral Scientist* 17 (November–December, 1973):280; Harry C. Boyte, "Community Organizing in the 1970s: Seeds of Democratic Revolt," in *Community Organization,* ed. Fisher and Romanofsky, pp. 217–38.

21. Sanders, "Professional Radical, 1965," p. 45; Saul Alinsky interviewed in Studs Terkel, *Hard Times,* (New York: Avon, 1970), pp. 358–61; Gurney Breckenfield, "Chicago: Back of the Yards," in *The Human Side of Urban Renewal: A Study of the Attitude Changes Produced by Neighborhood Revitalization,* ed. Martin Millspaugh, Gurney Breckenfield, and Miles Colean (New York: Ives Washburn, 1960), pp. 182–84.

22. Sanders, "Professional Radical, 1965," p. 45. Alinsky exaggerated fascist strength in Back of the Yards in order to overemphasize the success of his work. On another occasion he noted, for example, that a Benedictine priest who was leading the Coughlinite movement in the neighborhood was frustrated because no one "paid him any attention." Alinsky boasted that he later made the priest the chairman of the neighborhood antifascist committee.

23. Michael P. Connolly, "An Historical Study of Change in Saul D. Alinsky's Community Organization Practice and Theory, 1939–1972" (Ph.D. diss., University of Minnesota, 1976), pp. 91–92.

24. Saul Alinsky, *Reveille for Radicals* (Chicago: University of Chicago Press, 1946), pp. 132–33.

25. Breckenfield, "Chicago: Back of the Yards," p. 7.

26. Alinsky quoted in Terkel, *Hard Times,* p. 360.

27. Ibid.

28. Breckenfield, "Chicago: Back of the Yards," p. 186.

29. Connolly, "A Historical Study," pp. 114–24.

30. Alinsky, *Reveille,* pp. 138–46.

31. Connolly, "A Historical Study," p. 122.

32. Breckenfield, "Chicago: Back of the Yards," p. 210.

33. For this quote and additional materials critical of the "system-confirming" aspects of Alinskyism, see Joan E. Lancourt, *Confront or Concede: The Alinsky Citizen Action Organizations* (Lexington: Lexington Books, 1979).

34. Stanley Aronowitz, "Poverty, Politics, and Community Organization," *Studies on the Left* 4 (Summer 1964):104; Wellstone, "Notes on Community Organizing," p. 78.

Chapter 3

1. Gabriel Kolko, *Main Currents in Modern American History* (New York: Harper and Row, 1976), p. 318.

2. Rosenstein quoted in the *New York Times,* 31 January 1953.

3. Stuart Queen, Alfred Carpenter, and David Bailey, *The American City* (Westport: Greenwood Press, 1953), p. 168.

4. See Elmore B. McKee, *The People Act: Stories of How Americans Are Coming Together to Deal With Their Community Problems* (New York: Harper, 1955).

5. American Council for the Community MSS, Social Welfare History Archive, Minneapolis, Minnesota.

6. Phillip Ryan, "Social Welfare in a Changing World," address to New Hampshire Social Welfare Council, 11 September 1953 (National Social Welfare Assembly MSS, Social Welfare History Archive).

7. The agencies included the American Hygiene Association, Child Welfare League of America, Committee on Careers in Nursing, Family Service Association of America, National Board of the YWCA, National Catholic Community Service, National Committee on Social Work in Defense Mobilization, National Federation of Settlements and Neighborhood Centers, National League for Nursing, National Probation and Parole Association, National Recreation Association, National Traveler's Aid Association, National Urban League, and the American Federation of Labor and Congress of Industrial Organizations' Community Services committees.

8. Louis B. Seltzer, *The Nation's Strength* (United Community Defense Services pamphlet, 1953?). For more detailed information on UCDS and "critical defense areas" see Marvin A. Palacek, *Battle of the Bureaucracies* (New York: Vantage Press, 1972), and Reginald Robinson, *Serving the Small Community: The Story of United Community Defense Services* (New York: Association Press, 1959).

9. National Association for Social Welfare MSS, Social Welfare History Archive.

10. United Community Defense Services Minutes, Meeting on Paducah, Kentucky, 31 October 1951 (American Social Health Association MSS, Social Welfare History Archive).

11. Elizabeth Wickenden, "Military Defense and Social Welfare," August 1955 (National Association of Social Welfare MSS, Social Welfare History Archive).

12. Elizabeth Wickenden, "The Social Factor of National Defense," September 1954, p. 38 (National Federation of Settlements MSS, Social Welfare History Archive).

13. American Social Health Association MSS, Social Welfare History Archive.

14. Ibid.

15. For a good introduction to the history of neighborhood improvement associations see Joseph Arnold, "The Neighborhood and City Hall: The Origin of Neighborhood Associations in Baltimore, 1880–1911," *Journal of Urban History* 6 (November 1979):3–30.

16. Zane Miller, "The Role and Concept of Neighborhood in American Cities," in *Community Organization,* ed. Fisher and Romanofsky, pp. 8–10.

17. Roderick D. McKenzie, *The Neighborhood: A Study of Local Life in Columbus, Ohio* (Chicago: University of Chicago Press, 1923), pp. 361–62.

18. Amalie Hofer, *Neighborhood Improvement In and About Chicago, 1909* (Chicago: Newell E. Stiles, 1909), p. 20.

19. Woodland Heights promotion brochure, 1909, Houston Metropolitan Research Center, Subdivision File.

20. Philpott, *Slum and Ghetto,* p. 148.

21. Drake and Cayton, *Black Metropolis,* pp. 70, 178–79.

22. Philpott, *Slum and Ghetto,* pp. 181–200; Drake and Cayton, *Black Metropolis,* pp. 178–87.

23. Truman speech appointing Committee on Civil Rights, 1946, quoted in Howard Zinn, *A People's History of the United States* (New York: Harper and Row, 1980), p. 440.

24. Clement E. Vose, *Caucasians Only: The Supreme Court, the NAACP, and the Restrictive Covenant Cases* (Berkeley: University of California Press, 1959), p. 251.

25. Gunther cited in Don Carleton, "McCarthyism in Houston: The George Ebey Affair," *Southwestern Historical Quarterly* 80 (October 1976):167.

26. In 1965 the City of Houston was given authorization by the Texas legislature to enforce deed restrictions. The funds of the city legal department, however, are insufficient to handle the task, and thus almost all restriction enforcement remains a "private" matter.

27. Woodland Heights promotional brochure, 1909, Houston Metropolitan Research Center, Subdivision file.

28. Southwest Civic Club MSS, Houston Metropolitan Research Center. I also made use of the papers on the Southwest Civic Club written by Kathy Sexton, Cindy Herbert, and others in my urban history course, spring 1981.

29. Bailey, *Radicals in Urban Politics: The Alinsky Approach* (Chicago: University of Chicago Press, 1972), p. 30, says parapolitical "refers to formal voluntary associations which are not mobilized primarily for political purposes but which may become political when matters of interest to them are being considered by decision-makers."

30. Houston *Chronicle,* 18 April 1971, sec. 4, p. 1; Jack E. Dodson, "Minority Group Housing in Texas," in *Studies in Housing and Minority Groups: Special Research Reports to the Commission on Race and Housing,* ed. Nathan Glazer and Davis McEntire (Berkeley: University of California Press, 1960), p. 106. An invaluable study of the transformation of the Riverside area is Barry J. Kaplan, "Race, Income, and Ethnicity: Residential Change in a Houston Community, 1920–1970," *Houston Review* 3 (Winter 1981):178–203.

31. Bertram Mann, a past president of the Allied Civic Club, was kind enough to speak with me about and share some of his materials on the history of the ACC.

32. President, Southwest Civic Club, letter, 1970, Southwest Civic Club MSS, Houston Metropolitan Research Center.

Chapter 4

1. By quasi-anarchist I mean that while these organizations did not reject in principle government or laws, their major thrust as left-wing efforts was to reject organizational forms which they felt perpetuated the status quo and kept the poor powerless.

2. See Seymour Melman, *The Permanent War Economy: American Capitalism in Decline* (New York: Touchstone, 1974).

3. See Dowd, *The Twisted Dream,* especially p. 123 for *Business Week* quote.

4. Michael Harrington, *The Other America: Poverty in the United States* (Baltimore: Penguin, 1963), p. 9.

5. Piven and Cloward, *Poor People's Movements,* pp 190–94; Frances Fox Piven and Richard Cloward, *Regulating the Poor: The Functions of Public Welfare* (New York: Vintage, 1971), pp. 200–205.

6. Bayrd Still, *Urban America* (Boston: Little Brown, 1974), pp. 406–7.

7. Ben B. Seligman, *Permanent Poverty: An American Syndrome* (Chicago: Quadrangle 1968), pp. 41–61.

8. Richard Dalfiume, *Desegregation and the Armed Forces: Fighting on Two Fronts, 1939–53* (Columbia: University of Missouri Press, 1969), p. 138.

9. Clayborne Carson, Jr., "Toward Freedom and Community: The Evolution of Ideas in the Student Nonviolent Coordinating Committee, 1960–66" (Ph.D. diss., University of California at Los Angeles, 1975), p. 140, and Winifred Breines, "Community and Organization: The New Left as a Social Movement, 1962–1968" (Ph.D. diss., Brandeis University, 1979), p. 35. Both of these impressive doctoral dissertations have since been published; see bibliography for citations. Projects affiliated with ERAP were located in Cleveland, New Haven, Appalachia, Baltimore, Oakland (California), Boston, Cairo (Illinois), Hazard (Kentucky), Newark, and Chicago.

10. Davis quoted in Breines, "Community and Organization," p. 51.

11. Bruce Payne, "SNCC: An Overview Two Years Later," in *The New Student Left: An Anthology,* ed. Mitchell Cohen and Dennis Hale (Boston: Beacon, 1966), p. 87.

12. For more information see the excellent anthology by Massimo Teodori, *The New Left: A Documentary History* (New York: Bobbs-Merrill, 1969); and Carson, "Toward Freedom," pp. 302–3.

13. Kenniston quoted in Breines, "Community and Organization," pp. 159–60.

14. Garrett quoted in Carson, "Toward Freedom," p. 320; ERAP staffer quoted in Sara Evans, *Personal Politics: The Roots of Women's Liberation in the Civil Rights Movement and the New Left* (New York: Vintage, 1980), p. 136.

15. Breines, "Community and Organization," p. 66.

16. Richard Rothstein, "A Short History of ERAP," quoted in Breines, "Community and Organization," p. 54.

17. Garrett quoted in Carson, "Toward Freedom," p. 320.

18. Charles McLaurin, "Notes on Organizing," in Arthur Dunham MSS, Social Welfare History Archive.

19. Charles McLaurin, "To Overcome Fear," in Arthur Dunham MSS, Social Welfare History Archive.

20. Davis quoted in Breines, "Community and Organization," p. 55.

21. Teodori, *The New Left,* pp. 130–31.

22. Weinstein, *Ambiguous Legacy: The Left in American Politics* (New York:New Viewpoints, 1975), especially p. 132, is harshly critical of the ERAP projects. So are Milton Kotler, *Neighborhood Government: The Local Foundations of Political Life* (New York: Bobbs-Merrill, 1969); and Paul Bullock, "Morality and Tactics in Community Organizing," in *Poverty: Views from the Left,* ed. Jeremy Larner and Irving Howe (New York: William Morrow, 1968), pp. 137–48.

23. Clayborne Carson, Jr., *In Struggle: SNCC and the Black Awakening of the 1960s* (Cambridge: Harvard University Press, 1982), p. 154.

24. Carl Wittman and Tom Hayden, two of the strongest proponents of this position in SDS, stated it thusly: "The territorial basis of organization should be carefully considered. Not only are economic conditions varying on the regional, state, and municipal level, but political organization may be appropriate on these levels and on the ward and neighborhood level as well. It is clear that solutions to the problems of these areas

are only at the national level, however, and it continually must be kept in mind that such organization is strictly a means to exert pressure nationally and to gain strength for the movement, not an end in itself." See Carl Wittman and Tom Hayden, "An Interracial Movement of the Poor," in *The New Student Left,* ed. Cohen and Hale, p. 201.

25. Moody quoted in Breines, "Community and Organization," p. 68.

26. Bruce Palmer to author, August 1982.

27. Bennett quoted in Carson, *In Struggle,* p. 182; Evans, *Personal Politics,* p. 137.

28. Richard Flacks, "Organizing the Unemployed: The Chicago Project," in *The New Student Left,* ed. Cohen and Hale, p. 144. Flacks's article provides an excellent overview of the Chicago JOIN project.

29. Rothstein quoted in Breines, "Community and Organization," p. 67.

30. Anne Moody, *Coming of Age in Mississippi: An Autobiography* (New York: Dell, 1968). is a most readable and exciting account of her childhood, movement activity, and subsequent "burnout."

31. Ann Neel, "Experimenting with the Black Community: A Case Study in the Sociology of Applied Knowledge" (Ph.D. diss., University of California at Berkeley, 1978), p. 162.

32. David Austin, "Organizing for Neighborhood Improvement or Social Change? A Descriptive Study of the Action Methods and Action Issues of Black Residents" (Ph.D. diss., Brandeis University, 1969), pp. 48–53; Miller, "Role and Concept of Neighborhood," in *Community Organization,* ed. Fisher and Romanofsky, p.22.

33. The act created a number of programs—the Office of Economic Opportunity, Job Corps, Head Start, Volunteers in Service to America (VISTA), and Legal Aid. Each addressed a different aspect of the poverty condition from a different angle, but all kept to the grassroots, citizen action formula of the NIMH and Ford Foundation.

34. Boone quoted in Piven and Cloward, *Regulating the Poor,* p. 270; Economic Opportunity Act, 1964, Title II-A, Section 202 (a); Austin, "Organizing," pp. 48–60. The legislation declared that CAAs were to be "developed, conducted, and administered with the maximum feasible participation of residents of the areas and members of the groups served."

35. The following analysis is heavily influenced by my personal experience as a neighborhood representative from 1973 to 1976 on the Cambridge, Massachusetts, Economic Opportunity Committee; informal discussions with CAP administrators, neighborhood representatives, and community organizers; and, equally important, the work of Frances Fox Piven and Richard Cloward, most notably *Regulating the Poor,* pp. 248–84.

36. Piven and Cloward, *Regulating the Poor,* pp. 236–39.

37. Ibid., pp. 250–56.

38. Paul E. Peterson and J. David Greenstone, "The Mobilization of Low-Income Communities Through Community Action," in *A Decade of Federal Antipoverty Programs: Achievements, Failures, and Lessons,* ed. Robert H. Haveman (New York: Academic Press, 1977), p. 262.

39. Sar Levitan, *The Great Society's Poor Law* (Baltimore: Johns Hopkins University Press, 1969), p. 113.

40. Shelley quoted in Ralph M. Kramer, *Participation of the Poor: Comparative*

Community Case Studies in the War on Poverty (Englewood Cliffs, N.J.: Prentice-Hall, 1969), p. 25.

41. Austin, "Organizing," pp. 222–223.

42. Kramer, *Participation of the Poor*, pp. 215–38.

43. Peterson and Greenstone, "The Mobilization of Low-Income Communities," emphasizes the program's objective of black incorporation in the political system. See pp. 264–65 for quoted material.

44. On the history of Mobilization for Youth, good introductions are Piven and Cloward, *Regulating the Poor*, pp. 290–95, and Daniel Moynihan, *Maximum Feasible Misunderstanding: Community Action in the War on Poverty* (New York: Free Press, 1969), pp.38–60.

45. Shriver quoted in Kramer, *Participation of the Poor*, p. 10.

46. Levitan, *Great Society Poor Law*, p. 115.

47. For information on the Green Amendment begin with Levitan, *Great Society's Poor Law*, especially pp. 66–67, 103–4; and Piven and Cloward, *Regulating the Poor*, p. 268.

48. Levitan, *Great Society's Poor Law*, p. 124.

49. James Leiby, *The History of Social Welfare and Social Work in the United States* (New York: Columbia University Press, 1978), p. 338.

50. Austin, "Organizing," p. 237.

Chapter 5

1. Robert L. Heilbroner, *Beyond Boom and Crash* (New York: Norton,1978), p. 12; Matthew Edel, "The New York Crisis as Economic History," in *The Fiscal Crisis of American Cities: Essays on the Political Economy of Urban America with Special Reference to New York* ed. Roger E. Alcaly and David Mermelstein (New York: Vintage Books, 1977), p. 231.

2. Editorial, *Business Week,* 12 October 1974, cited in Boyte, *Backyard Revolution*, p. 15.

3. Mollenkopf, "Postwar Politics of Urban Development," in *Marxism and the Metropolis,* ed. William K. Tabb and Larry Sawers (New York: Oxford University Press, 1978), p. 123.

4. Manuel Castells, *The Urban Question: A Marxist Approach* (London: Edward Arnold, 1977), p. 422; and William Tabb, "The New York City Fiscal Crisis," in *Marxism and the Metropolis,* ed. Tabb and Sawers, p. 261.

5. Beame quoted in John Mollenkopf, "The Crisis of the Public Sector in America's Cities," in *Fiscal Crisis of American Cities,* ed. Alcaly and Mermelstein, p. 113.

6. Cincotta quoted in Boyte, *Backyard Revolution*, p. 33.

7. Walter Guzzardi, Jr., "To Win in Washington," *Fortune,* 27 March 1978, quoted in Boyte, *Backyard Revolution*, p. 17.

8. McBride, "A Nation of Neighborhoods."

9. One of the first and certainly one of the strongest proponents of the new populism is Harry Boyte, the author of numerous articles and a book, *Backyard Revolution,* on citizen action in the 1970s. For a helpful taxonomy of sixty new populist organizations see Janice Perlman, "Grassrooting the System," *Social Policy,* September–October 1976, p. 4–20.

10. Mike Miller, "The 'Ideology' of the Community Organization Movement" (1979), pp.22–23; working-paper distributed by the Organize Training Center.

11. Boyte, *Backyard Revolution,* p. xii.

12. Charles Silberman, *Crisis in Black and White* (New York: Random House, 1964), pp. 318, 346–47, 356.

13. Alinsky quoted in Sanders, "Professional Radical, 1970," p. 38.

14. See John Hall Fish, *Black Power/White Control: The Struggle of The Woodlawn Organization in Chicago* (Princeton: Princeton University Press, 1973).

15. Best examples are community-based, statewide organizations, such as Massachusetts Fair Share and the Ohio Public Interest Campaign; nationally federated, statewide community organizations, such as Association of Community Organizations for Reform Now (ACORN); coalitions of statewide programs, such as Citizen Action; and loosely organized national coalitions of neighborhood groups, such as National People's Action and the National Association of Neighborhoods.

16. Castells, *Urban Question,* pp. 421–27.

17. Meg Campbell, North Country Institute, Community Organizing Workshop, February 1982; Boyte, *Backyard Revolution,* p. 64.

18. Rathke quoted in Andrew Kopkind, "ACORN Calling," *Working Papers for a New Society* 3 (Summer 1975):14.

19. North Country Institute Workshop, "Models of Organizing" discussion. While this is only a generalized model of ACORN's approach, it is one used and taught by organizers who prefer the methods of Ross to those of Alinsky.

20. Kopkind, "ACORN Calling," p. 15.

21. John Judis, "Playing for Keeps," *In These Times,* 16–29 June 1982, pp. 12–13.

22. Cortes quoted in Boyte, *Backyard Revolution,* p. 63.

23. Jim Green and Allen Hunter, "Racism and Busing in Boston," *Radical America* 8 (November–December 1974):1–32.

24. Linda Gordon and Allen Hunter, "Sex, Family, and the New Right: Antifeminism as a Political Force," *Radical America* 11 (November 1977–February 1978):9–26. For other criticisms of the new populism which question its left orientation, see Frank Ackerman, "The Melting Snowball: Limits of the 'New Populism' in Practice," *Socialist Revolution* 35 (September–October, 1977):113–28, and Mike Davis, "Socialist Renaissance or Populist Mirage? A Reply to Harry Boyte," *Socialist Review* 40–41 (1978):53–63.

25. Paul Levy, "Unloading the Neighborhood Bandwagon," manuscript in author's possession, p. 6. Another version was published in *Social Policy* 10 (September 1979):28–32. Levy's article divides the neighborhood "movement" of the 1970s into three wings: those who see the neighborhood as a power base, a social community, and a political community.

26. Three good sources on SECO's history are Bob Kuttner, "Ethnic Renewal," *New York Times,* 1976, reprinted in *Neighborhoods in Urban America,* ed. Ronald Bayor (Port Washington: Kennikat Press, 1982), pp. 209–19; Cassidy, *Livable Cities,* pp. 15–20, 98–99; and McBride, "A Nation of Neighborhoods," pp. 3–5.

27. McBride, "A Nation of Neighborhoods," p. 3.

28. Ibid.

29. Gleason quoted in Cassidy, *Livable Cities,* p. 98.

30. McBride, "A Nation of Neighborhoods," pp. 3–5; Cassidy, *Livable Cities*, pp. 15–20.

31. For more information on the Pittsburgh experience, see Roy Lubove, *Twentieth Century Pittsburgh* (New York: Wiley, 1969), which discusses the interrelation between corporate, city, and neighborhood revitalization.

32. Philip L. Clay, *Neighborhood Renewal: Middle-Class Settlement and Incumbent Upgrading in American Neighborhoods* (Lexington: Lexington Books, 1979) is a good, if limited, introduction to the subject of gentrification.

33. Robert Rosenbloom, "The Politics of the Neighborhood Movement," *South Atlantic Urban Studies* 4 (1979):116.

34. Friedland quoted in Castells, *Urban Question*, p. 425.

35. Si Kahn, *How People Get Power: Organizing Oppressed Communities for Action* (New York: McGraw-Hill, 1970), p. 59, and Lawrence Goodwyn, *The Populist Moment: A Short History of Agrarian Revolt in America* (New York: Oxford University Press, 1978), p. xix.

36. Quoted in Kathleen McCourt, *Working-Class Women and Grass-Roots Politics* (Bloomington: University of Indiana Press, 1977), p. 182.

37. Heather Booth interviewed in *Social Policy,* May–June 1981, p. 31.

38. See Evans, *Personal Politics.*

39. Ronald Lawson and Stephen G. Barton, "'Women in the Tenants Movement: A Case History in New York City," *Shelterforce* 7 (1982):13.

40. McCourt, *Working-Class Women,* p. 17.

41. Quoted in ibid., p. 135.

42. Ibid., p. 183.

Chapter 6

1. Austin, "Organizing," p. 320.

2. An earlier version of the following typology appeared first in Robert Fisher, "Community Organizing in Historical Perspective: A Typology," *Houston Review* 4 (Summer 1982):75–89. For another typology see Jack Rothman, "Three Models of Community Organization Practice," in *Strategies of Community Organization: A Book of Readings,* ed. Fred Cox et al. (Itasca: F. E. Peacock, 1979), pp. 25–45.

3. Paul Wellstone, *How The Rural Poor Got Power* (Amherst: University of Massachusetts Press, 1978), p. 204.

4. McCourt, *Working-Class Women,* p. 100.

5. Rich, "Political Economy of Neighborhood Organization."

6. Mary P. Follett, *The New State: Group Organization the Solution of Popular Government* (New York: Longmans, Green and Company, 1918), pp. 189–92.

7. Charles Grosser, *New Directions in Community Organization: From Enabling to Advocacy* (New York: Praeger, 1972) and Jeffrey Galper, *The Politics of Social Services* (Englewood Cliffs, N.J.: Prentice-Hall, 1975) reflect changes in the social work profession during the late 1960s and early 1970s.

8. Craig Jackson Calhoun, "The Radicalism of Tradition: Community Strength or Venerable Disguise and Borrowed Language?" *American Journal of Sociology* 88 (March 1983):886–914.

9. Piven and Cloward, *Poor People's Movements,* p. 7.

10. Carson, *In Struggle,* carefully details how the government harassed and repressed the black power movement after 1965.

11. Wellstone, *How the Rural Poor Got Power,* p. 218.

12. Sidney Dillick, *Community Organization for Neighborhood Development: Past and Present* (New York: William Morrow, 1953), p. 69.

13. Wellstone, *How the Rural Poor Got Power,* pp. 200–215.

14. Arthur Hillman and Frank Seever, "Elements of Neighborhood Organization," in *Strategies,* ed. Cox et al., p. 284.

15. Michael Ansara, "The People's First: An Organizer's Notebook," *Working Papers for a New Society* 2 (Winter 1975):36.

16. Forman quoted in Carson, *In Struggle,* p. 156.

17. See Chafe, *Civilities and Civil Order,* p. 350, for a description of how this consciousness developed and was challenged in the Civil Rights movement in Greensboro, North Carolina.

18. William A. Gamson, *The Strategy of Social Protest* (Homewood, Ill.: Dorsey Press, 1975), pp. 49–50.

19. Ann Popkin, "The Personal is Political," in *They Should Have Served That Cup of Coffee,* ed. Cluster, p. 195.

20. Ira Katznelson, *City Trenches: Urban Politics and the Patterning of Class in the United States* (New York: Pantheon Books, 1981), p. 6. For current information on labor/community coalition building, see *Social Policy* 13 (Spring, 1983), an issue devoted to this subject.

BIBLIOGRAPHICAL ESSAY

What follows is a selected list of what I have found to be the most useful readings in the history of neighborhood organizing. The bibliography is intentionally brief, and includes, for the most part, only the most accessible published materials. For references to primary materials on neighborhood organizing or secondary materials on the national political economy and urban history used in this study, please consult the footnotes.

Historical Overviews of Neighborhood Organizing

Most of the materials with a historical perspective of neighborhood organizing are written by social work academics. The only book-length surveys of the history of neighborhood organization are Sidney Dillick, *Community Organization for Neighborhood Development: Past and Present* (New York: William Morrow, 1953), which traces the history of community organization for social welfare from the late nineteenth century through the early 1950s; and *Community Organization for Urban Social Change: A Historical Perspective,* ed. Robert Fisher and Peter Romanofsky (Westport: Greenwood Press, 1981). Monna Heath and Arthur Dunham, *Trends in Community Organization: A Study of Papers on Community Organization Published by the National Conference on Social Welfare, 1874–1960* (Chicago: University of Chicago Social Service Monographs, 1963), is an excellent overview and analysis of articles written by community workers and academics. On community organization theory since the early twentieth century, see Meyer Schwartz, "Community Organization," in *Encyclopedia of Social Work* (New York: National Association of Social Workers, 1965), pp. 179–89. Howard W. Hallman, "The Neighborhood as an Organizational Unit: A Historical Perspective," in *Neighborhood Control in the 1970s,* ed. George Frederickson (New York: Chandler

179

Publishing Co., 1973), pp. 7–16; Fred Cox and Charles Garvin, "Community Organization Practice: 1865–1973," in *Strategies of Community Organization,* ed. Fred Cox et al. (Itasca, Ill.: F. E. Peacock, 1974), pp. 39–58; and Arthur Dunham, *The New Community Organization* (New York: Thomas Y. Crowell, 1970), chap. 4, all provide good, brief surveys of the history of community organization. Robert Fisher, "Community Organizing in Historical Perspective: A Typology," *Houston Review* 4 (Summer 1982):75–88, elaborates on the typology presented in the conclusion of this book. Milton Kotler, *Neighborhood Government: The Local Foundations of Political Life* (New York: Bobbs-Merrill, 1969), provides some materials on the historical origins of neighborhoods and on different approaches to neighborhood organizing. Jeffrey H. Galper, *The Politics of Social Services* (Englewood Cliffs, N.J.: Prentice-Hall, 1975), is a leftist critique that includes some interesting criticisms about community organization as practiced by members of the social work profession. Surprisingly little has been written on community organization by historians interested in the history of social welfare. Even the overviews of social welfare history, most recently James Leiby, *The History of Social Welfare and Social Work in the United States* (New York: Columbia University Press, 1978), devote but a few pages to the subject.

General studies of neighborhood organizing that approach the subject from different perspectives are David J. O'Brien, *Neighborhood Organization and Interest-Group Processes* (Princeton: Princeton University Press, 1975); Rachelle B. Warren and Donald I. Warren, *Neighborhood Organizers Handbook* (Notre Dame: University of Notre Dame Press, 1977); Steve Burghardt, *The Other Side of Organizing* (Cambridge: Schenkman, 1982); and Jeffrey R. Henig, *Neighborhood Mobilization: Redevelopment and Response* (New Brunswick: Rutgers, 1982).

Social Welfare Neighborhood Organizing Before 1929

The liberal reformers of the years 1890–1920 were as prolific as they were optimistic. The first account in the genre was Stanton Coit, *Neighborhood Guilds: An Instrument of Social Reform* (London: Sonnenshein, 1891). Other excellent examples include Jane Addams, *Twenty Years at Hull House with Autobiographical Notes* (New York: Macmillan, 1910); Lillian Wald, *The House on Henry Street* (New York: Henry Holt and Co., 1915); and Robert A. Woods, *The Neighborhood in Nation-Building* (New York: Arno Press, 1970). During and after World War I, some even stronger statements were written on the need for community organizing, the best examples of which are Mary Parker Follett, *The New State: Group Organization the Solution of Pop-*

ular Government (New York: Longmans, Green, 1918); and John Daniels, *America Via the Neighborhood* (New York: Harper and Bros., 1920).

American historians have written widely about the activities of settlement workers, but rarely from the perspective of the reformers as community organizers. The best study is Thomas Lee Philpott, *The Slum and the Ghetto: Neighborhood Deterioration and Middle-Class Reform in Chicago, 1880–1930* (New York: Oxford University Press, 1978). On community centers, begin with Robert Fisher, "Community Organizing and Citizen Participation: The Efforts of the People's Institute, 1910–1920," *Social Service Review* 51 (September 1977):474–90.

The 1920s witnessed the continued advocacy of the neighborhood unit and the professionalization of community organization as a subdiscipline within the field of social work. The first texts on community organization were written by Eduard Lindeman, *The Community* (New York: Association Press, 1921); and Jesse Steiner, *Community Organization: A Study of Its Theory and Current Practice* (Chicago: University of Chicago Press, 1925). One of the best community studies of the period, with a focus on the role of neighborhood organizing efforts, is Harvey W. Zorbaugh, *The Gold Coast and the Slum: A Sociological Study of Chicago's Near North Side* (Chicago: University of Chicago Press, 1929). Wilbur Phillips, *Adventuring for Democracy* (New York: Social Unit Press, 1940), is the autobiography of the founder of the block organizing social unit plan. For secondary sources, see Patricia Mooney Melvin, "A Cluster of Interlacing Communities: The Cincinnati Social Unit Plan and Neighborhood Organization, 1900–1920," in *Community Organization,* ed. Fisher and Romanofsky, pp. 59–88; and Anatole Shaffer, "The Cincinnati Social Unit Experiment, 1917–1919," *Social Service Review* 45 (June 1971):159–72. Roy Lubove, *The Professional Altruist: The Emergence of Social Work as a Career* (New York: Atheneum, 1965) includes some information about the origins and professionalization of the field of community organization. For an analysis of the ideology of community organization in the 1920s and 1930s see Michael J. Austin and Neil Betten, "Intellectual Origins of Community Organization, 1920–1939," *Social Service Review* 51 (March 1977):155–70.

On community life and ethnic associations in working-class neighborhoods which are not specifically neighborhood organizing projects but which serve as important reminders of the alternatives to the settlements and community centers that immigrants used and controlled, see Jeffrey Gurock, *When Harlem Was Jewish* (New York: Columbia University Press, 1979); Emory Tolbert, *The UNIA and Black Los Angeles: Ideology and Community in the American Garvey Movement* (Los Angeles: UCLA Center for Afro-American

Studies, 1980); John Bodnar, *Immigration and Industrialization: Ethnicity in An American Mill Town, 1870–1940* (Pittsburgh: Pittsburgh University Press, 1977); and Josef Barton, *Peasants and Strangers: Italians, Rumanians, and Slovaks in an American City, 1890–1950* (Cambridge: Harvard University Press, 1975).

On the changing conception of neighborhoods in American history and the importance of local history, see Zane Miller, "The Role and Concept of Neighborhood in American Cities," in *Community Organization,* ed. Fisher and Romanofsky; Ronald Bayor, ed., *Neighborhoods in Urban America* (Port Washington: Kennikat Press, 1982); Henry Bedford, *Trouble Downtown: The Local Context of Twentieth Century America* (New York: Harcourt, Brace, 1978); and Thomas Bender, *Community and Social Change in America* (New Brunswick: Rutgers University Press, 1978).

Radical Neighborhood Organizing, 1929–46

Surprisingly little has been written about decentralized, neighborhood organizing efforts during the Great Depression. While the period abounded with organizing efforts on both the right and the left, most organizations, especially after 1933, had a national basis or orientation. Economic problems that the nation and the world faced did not seem to lend themselves to solutions at the neighborhood level.

For information on the Unemployed Council efforts during the 1930s, start with Mark Naison, "Harlem Communists and the Politics of Black Protest," in *Community Organization,* ed. Fisher and Romanofsky; and Mark Naison, *Communists in Harlem During the Depression* (Urbana: University of Illinois Press, 1983). Also of significant help were Steve Nelson, James K. Barrett, and Rob Ruck, *Steve Nelson, American Radical* (Pittsburgh: University of Pittsburgh Press, 1981), an autobiography of a Communist party and Unemployed Council leader; Roy Rosenzweig, "Organizing the Unemployed: The Early Years of the Great Depression, 1929–1933," *Radical America* 10 (July–August 1976):37–60; and Frances Fox Piven and Richard Cloward, *Poor People's Movements: Why They Succeed, How They Fail* (New York: Pantheon, 1977). The Piven and Cloward study was also invaluable for its introductory chapter on social movement literature and for its other essays on the labor movement of the 1930s, the Civil Rights movement, and the National Welfare Rights Organization. While I do not agree with many of their conclusions, Piven and Cloward remain two of the most formidable and important thinkers in the United States on social movement history and theory.

On the early efforts of Saul Alinsky and the Alinsky method, the most helpful works were Saul D. Alinsky, *Reveille for Radicals* (Chicago: University of Chicago Press; 1946); Saul D. Alinsky, *Rules for Radicals* (New York: Random House, 1971); Michael P. Connolly, "An Historical Study of Change in Saul D. Alinsky's Community Organization Practice and Theory, 1939–1972" (Ph.D. diss., University of Minnesota School of Social Work, 1976); and Marion K. Sanders, *The Professional Radical: Conversations with Saul Alinsky* (Evanston, Ill.: Harper and Row, 1965). Robert Bailey, Jr., *Radicals in Urban Politics: The Alinsky Approach* (Chicago: University of Chicago Press, 1974); Paul Wellstone, "Notes on Community Organizing," *Journal of Ethnic Studies* 4 (1976):73–89; Joan E. Lancourt, *Confront or Concede: The Alinsky Citizen-Action Organizations* (Lexington: Lexington Books, 1979); Stanley Aronowitz, "Poverty, Politics, and Community Organization," *Studies on the Left* 4 (Summer 1964):102–5; and Frank Reissman, *Strategies Against Poverty* (New York: Random House, 1969) are good critiques of the Alinsky method. Gurney Breckenfield, "Chicago: Back of the Yards," in Martin Millspaugh, Gurney Breckenfield, and Miles Colean, *The Human Side of Urban Renewal: A Study of the Changes Produced by Neighborhood Rehabilitation* (New York: Ives Washburn, 1960) is the most descriptive study of the Back of the Yards Neighborhood Council.

For related information on the history of the tenant organizing movement, see Joseph Spencer, "Tenant Organization and Housing Reform in New York City: The Citywide Tenants Council, 1936–1943," in *Community Organization,* ed. Fisher and Romanofsky, pp. 127–56; Ronald Lawson and Stephen G. Barton, "Women in the Tenants Movement: A Case History in New York City," *Shelterforce* 7 (1982); and Ronald Lawson, "Tenant Mobilization in New York," *Social Policy* 10 (March–April 1980):30–40.

Conservative Neighborhood Organizing, 1946–60

The years during and directly after World War II witnessed a reemergence of interest in the social work profession in the neighborhood as an organizing unit and in the possibilities of community organizing. A number of now classic monographs on community organizing were published in the decade or so after the war. Most notable are H. Wayne McMillen, *Community Organization for Social Welfare* (Chicago: University of Chicago Press, 1945); Clarence King, *Organizing for Community Action* (New York: Harper, 1948); James Dahir, *The Neighborhood Unit Plan: Its Spread and Acceptance* (New York: Russell Sage Foundation, 1947); Arthur Hillman, *Community Organization and Plan-*

ning (New York: Macmillan, 1950); Murray G. Ross, *Community Organization and Planning* (New York: Harper and Bros., 1955); and Ernest B. Harper and Arthur Dunham, eds., *Community Organization in Action: Basic Literature and Critical Comments* (New York: Associated Press, 1959).

For examples as to how the Cold War affected the practice of community organization, see Elmore McKee, *The People Act: Stories of How Americans Are Coming Together to Deal with Their Community Problems* (New York: Harper and Bros., 1955); Marvin Palacek, *Battle of the Bureaucracies* (New York: Vantage Press, 1972); and Reginald Robinson, *Serving the Small Community: The Story of the United Community Defense Services* (New York: Associated Press, 1954).

On international community development projects, begin with Charles E. Hendry, "Community Development," in *Encyclopedia of Social Work, 1965*, pp. 170–77; Arthur Dunham, *Community Development—Rural and Urban* (New York: International Conference of Social Work, 1962); and Marshall B. Clinard, *Slums and Community Development: Experiments in Self-Help* (New York: Free Press, 1966) which includes material on projects in India.

For information on neighborhood improvement association activity before 1946 this study relied heavily on the following secondary sources: Joseph Arnold, "The Neighborhood and City Hall: The Origins of Neighborhood Associations in Baltimore, 1880–1911," *Journal of Urban History* 6 (November 1979):3–30; Roderick D. McKenzie, *The Neighborhood: A Study of Local Life in Columbus, Ohio* (Chicago: University of Chicago Press, 1923); St. Clair Drake and Horace R. Cayton, *Black Metropolis* (New York: Harper, 1962); and Clement Vose, *Caucasians Only: The Supreme Court, the NAACP, and the Restrictive Covenant Cases* (Berkeley: University of California Press, 1959).

For information on the civic club movement in Houston this study used, almost exclusively, primary sources made available to the author by the Southwest Civic Club, additional materials at the Houston Metropolitan Research Center, and personal interviews. For materials on neighborhood improvement association activity in other cities, a most readable work is Mario Cuomo, *Forest Hills Diary: The Crisis of Low-Income Housing* (New York: Random House, 1974).

The Neighborhood Organizing "Revolution" of the 1960s

The literature on the neighborhood organizing "revolution" is abundant. The best place to start is any of the numerous anthologies which survey recent theory and practice. See, for example, Fred Cox et al., eds., *Strategies of*

Community Organization: A Book of Readings (Itasca, Ill.: F. E. Peacock, 1979); and Ralph Kramer and Harry Specht, eds., *Readings in Community Organization Practice* (Englewood Cliffs, N.J.: Prentice-Hall, 1969). For an invaluable codification of the social science literature related to community organizing and to other areas of social action during the years 1964–70, see Jack Rothman, *Planning and Organizing for Social Change: Action Principles from Social Science Research* (New York: Columbia University Press, 1974). Many of the books on the history of community organizing written in the past two decades are still available in paperback and often contain excellent bibliographies.

On Civil Rights and new left organizing efforts see William Chafe, *Civilities and Civil Rights: Greensboro, North Carolina, and the Black Struggle for Freedom* (New York: Oxford University Press, 1980); Clayborne Carson, Jr., *In Struggle: SNCC and the Black Awakening of the 1960s* (Cambridge: Harvard University Press, 1982), a most impressive study of shifting organizing methodologies and of SNCC in general; Wini Breines, *Community and Organization in the New Left, 1962–1968: The Great Refusal* (New York: Praeger, 1982), which developed from her excellent dissertation cited often in this study; and Sara Evans, *Personal Politics: The Roots of Women's Liberation in the Civil Rights Movement and the New Left* (New York: Random House, 1979), which gives an insider's view of the process of community organizing in the 1960s and 1970s and of the role of women in new left organizing projects. For two good collections of primary sources, see Mitchell Cohen and Dennis Hale, eds., *The New Student Left: An Anthology* (Boston: Beacon Press, 1966); and Massimo Teodori, *The New Left: A Documentary History* (New York: Bobbs-Merrill, 1969).

A voluminous literature exists on the origins and practice of the antipoverty, community action programs of the early 1960s. See Peter Marris and Martin Rein, *Dilemmas of Social Reform: Poverty and Community Action in the United States* (New York: Atherton, 1967); Ralph Kramer, *Participation of the Poor: Comparative Case Studies in the War on Poverty* (Englewood Cliffs, N.J.: Prentice-Hall, 1969); Frances Fox Piven and Richard Cloward, *Regulating the Poor: The Functions of Public Welfare* (New York: Vintage Books, 1971); Sar Levitan, *The Great Society's Poor Law* (Baltimore: Johns Hopkins University Press, 1969); and Paul E. Peterson and David J. Greenstone, "The Mobilization of Low-Income Communities Through Community Action," in *A Decade of Federal Antipoverty Programs: Achievements, Failures, and Lessons,* ed. Robert Haveman (New York: Academic Press, 1977), pp. 241–78.

For criticisms of community organizing during these years, see Katherine Coit, "Local Action, Not Citizen Participation," in *Marxism and the Metropolis: New Perspectives in Urban Political Economy,* ed. William K. Tabb and Larry Sawers (New York: Oxford University Press, 1978), pp. 297–311; John Cowley et al., *Community or Class Struggle* (New York: Stage 1 Publishers, 1977); and Charles F. Grosser, *New Directions in Community Organization: From Enabling to Advocacy* (New York: Praeger, 1972).

For additional materials on the wide variety of neighborhood resistance and community control efforts that flourished in the late 1960s and early 1970s, see Alan Lupo, Frank Colcord, and Edmund Fowler, *Rites of Way: The Politics of Transportation in Boston and the U.S. City* (Boston: Little, Brown, 1971), which chronicles highway resistance efforts; Maurice Berube and Marilyn Gittell, eds., *Confrontation at Ocean-Hill Brownsville* (New York: Praeger, 1969), which details this prominent struggle for community control of schools in New York City; and J. Clarence Davies, *Neighborhood Groups and Urban Renewal* (New York: Columbia University Press, 1966), which describes urban renewal resistance.

The New Populism of the 1970s

For historical and theoretical perspective on pre-twentieth-century populism see Lawrence Goodwyn, *The Populist Moment: A Short History of Agrarian Revolt in America* (New York: Oxford University Press, 1978); Bruce Palmer, *"Man Over Money" The Southern Populist Critique of American Capitalism* (Chapel Hill: University of North Carolina Press, 1980); Craig Jackson Calhoun, *The Question of Class Struggle* (Chicago: University of Chicago Press, 1982) and his "The Radicalism of Tradition: Community Strength or Venerable Disguise and Borrowed Language?," *American Journal of Sociology* 88 (March 1983):886–914. On the Alinsky roots of the new populism, see Harry C. Boyte, *The Backyard Revolution: Understanding the New Citizen Movement* (Philadelphia: Temple University Press, 1980), which is also the best general work to date on the new populism. On Alinsky efforts with The Woodlawn Organization, begin with John Hall Fish, *Black Power/White Control: The Struggle of The Woodlawn Organization in Chicago* (Princeton: Princeton University Press, 1973). Joan Lancourt, *Confront or Concede;* and Janice Perlman, "Grassrooting the System," *Social Policy* 7 (September–October 1976):4–20, are excellent introductions to recent Alinsky and new populist organizing projects respectively.

On neo-Alinsky organizing this study relied heavily on interviews, organizer training workshops, organizational literature, and Boyte's *Backyard Rev-*

olution. Also helpful were Si Kahn, *Organizing: A Guide for Grassroots Leaders* (New York: McGraw-Hill, 1982) and his *How People Get Power: Organizing Oppressed Communities for Action* (New York: McGraw-Hill, 1970); Michael Ansara, "The People's First: An Organizer's Notebook," *Working Papers for a New Society* 2 (Winter 1975):26–38; Robert Rosenbloom, "The Politics of the Neighborhood Movement," *South Atlantic Urban Studies* 4 (1979):103–20; Paul Wellstone, *How the Rural Poor Got Power: Narrative of a Grass-Roots Organizer* (Amherst: University of Massachusetts Press, 1978); and Linda Gordon and Allen Hunter, "Sex, Family, and the New Right: Anti-feminism as a Political Force," *Radical America* 11 (November 1977–February 1978):9–26.

The literature on the new community development is just beginning to develop. See Robert Cassidy, *Livable Cities: A Grass-Roots Guide to Rebuilding Urban America* (New York: Holt, Rinehart, and Winston, 1980); Phillip L. Clay, *Neighborhood Renewal: Middle Class Resettlement and Incumbent Upgrading In American Neighborhoods* (Lexington: Lexington Books, 1979); and Harry Edward Berndt, *New Rulers in the Ghetto: The Community Development Corporation and Urban Poverty* (Westport: Greenwood Press, 1977). On other trends in the new populism of the 1970s, specifically the "neighborhood alternative institutions and technology" perspective, not discussed in this book, see David Morris and Karl Hess, *Neighborhood Power: The New Localism* (Boston: Beacon Press, 1975); and John Case and Rosemary Taylor, eds., *Coops, Communes, and Collectives: Experiments in Social Change in the 1960s and 1970s* (New York: Pantheon, 1979). For materials on the positive impact of the new populism among working-class women, see Kathleen McCourt, *Working-Class Women and Grass-Roots Politics* (Bloomington: Indiana University Press, 1977).

INDEX